AMERICAN KULAK

AMERICAN KULAK
SOCIALIST PROGRESSIVES WILL BRING THE AMERICAN AFFLUENT CLASS TO RUIN

————

MARCUS SAGIRE

Table of Contents

———

During President Trump's third State of the Union Address delivered to the House of Representatives on February 5, 2019, he famously declared that America will never become a socialist country. He has repeated that assertion many times since. While I find this proclamation comforting and appropriate, I have come to doubt that America can avoid the socialist/Marxist utopian allure. The undeniable fact is that in this era of American history, Americans are embracing Marxist based economics to a degree and extent they never have before. For example, a recent Gallup Poll revealed that 40% of all Americans surveyed embraced some form of socialism.[1] This same poll showed 43% of American adults saying that some form of socialism would be "a good thing" for the country.[2] To get an idea of the level of radicalization this represents, when The Roper Center for Public Opinion Research asked the exact same question in a 1942 survey, only 25% of adults answered in the affirmative.[3] In short, the portion of the U.S. adult population formally sympathetic to an economic system based on Marxist principles has nearly doubled since World War II.

Trump may or may not be able to forestall the ostensibly inexorable trend towards some American version of Marxism. He didn't win the popular vote in 2016, having to rely on an Electoral College victory to win the Presidency. He regularly polls in the 42-45% range for his approval rating averages, and his party was decimated in the 2018 Congressional Mid-term elections, losing 40 seats in the House of Representatives. And the now Democratically controlled House has pulled the trigger on threats Democrats have made for years by initiating a formal Impeachment inquiry for the 45th President. It remains to be seen whether there will be 20 Republican Senate votes needed to reach the 67 total that is required in order to convict and remove Trump from office. Still, the impact the entire episode will have on the remainder of his Presidency is very much open for debate. What does seem clear is that if public opinion materially moves away from Mr. Trump, especially amongst his core supporters, it is a safe bet that increasing numbers of Republic Senators may wind-up favoring Impeachment after all. It is an open question whether Trump will win a second term and be in any position to thwart the seemingly relentless march towards Marxism in America.

For these reasons, this book offers a warning. There may well be a massive and "perfect" storm gathering, where multiple forces converge to wreak considerable damage to our way of life. The

---

[1] Mohamed Younis, *Four in 10 Americans Embrace Some Form of Socialism,* (Gallup, May 20, 2019).

[2] Ibid.

[3] Ibid.

America you have come to know and love is in serious jeopardy in the intermediate term. This is no joke and it is no overstatement. The American federal super-state could conceivably not survive the current century in its present form and may become completely unrecognizable. What was once limited to the province of dystopian fiction and Sci Fi may one day prove to be all too real – America could indeed be falling apart politically. If the American republic cannot hold in its current form past mid-century, then one of the great experiments in self-government will have come to a tragic and premature end. By way of contrast, the Roman "republic" survived for 500 years, (even if "imperial" Rome would extend its life for several additional centuries). The American republic may not see even half the life Rome enjoyed in its phase as a republic. There are now massive cracks in American cohesiveness culturally, economically and politically. For the first time since the American Civil War, the U.S. faces a very real possibility of violent civil strife, outright civil war or insurrection. The evidence is all around us and has been for years. The America of the middle and late 20th century is gone, and what is replacing it may not be anything you will want to live in. The examples are numerous enough to form the basis of this book.

For those readers who are skeptical, I challenge them pay even cursory attention to the news, current affairs and events, and notice the proof piling up quickly. Even the Washington D.C. Beltway insiders, the defenders of the corporate faith, know full well that the number of Americans under age 40 telling pollsters that they have a favorable view of socialism and a negative view of capitalism is far higher than for any other generation in American history, and it is rising with each passing year.[4] The bedrock principles of free enterprise that made America an unparalleled global force almost from its inception, are now considered "suspect" by an alarmingly high number of our fellow citizens. Then there are core tenants of Western Civilization that are routinely under assault. The presumption of innocence (remember the Kavanagh confirmation?), free speech (how 'bout those campus speech codes?) equal protection under the law (race and gender based preferential treatment anyone?), are all increasingly treated with contempt by the current crop of progressive intellectuals. In the world of the liberal elite, western civilization is derided as a malignant force for patriarchy, racism, and misogyny. The U.S. Constitution is often chalked up by the American Left (now representing a large plurality of the American electorate) as the progeny of men long dead who have no legitimate standing to act as the "forefathers" of the current American nation. These views are not limited to radical activists, indeed they are widely held among liberal intellectuals who now basically control and run our major universities and large cultural institutions including most of the "free" press.

Even more ominous is that these views amplify the younger the portion of the population one analyzes.[5] The implications of this dynamic for the future are portentous. As the older generation

---

[4] Felix Salmon, *Generation Z Prefers "Socialism" to "Capitalism"* (Axios, January 27, 2019), siting a SurveyMonkey online poll of 2,777 Adults. The poll found that 61% of 18-24 year olds had a positive view of socialism versus 58% with a positive view of capitalism. *See also*, Maxim Lott, *Fox News, Americans Warming to Socialism Over Capitalism Polls Show* (January 4, 2019). Lott cites a recent *Gallup Poll* depicting that, as of August 2018, 51% of Americans age 18-29 years old prefer socialism versus 45% the same age who prefer capitalism. The article points out that the same *Gallup poll* taken in 2010 showed this age group approved of capitalism over socialism by 68% to 51%. By 2019, a small simple majority of young Americans support socialism according to Gallup. The support for socialism has become much stronger than that among the young.

[5] Robby Soave, *Socialism is Back, and the Kids Are Loving It: How Dangerous Is the Democratic Socialist Resurgence?*, (Reason, September 2019 Issue). Mr. Soave notes that as of summer 2019, the average age of a Democratic Socialist of America member is 33, down from 68 as recently as 2013. *See also*, Victims of Communism Memorial Foundation Survey performed by *YouGov®*, released November 2, 2017. This poll depicts that 51% of the largest demographic cohort in America (the "Millennials") would rather live in a socialist or communist country than a capitalist one. Only about 42% of Millennials prefer

passes on, and the Millennial generation (currently ages 24-39) and Generation Z (currently ages 18-23) assumes an increasingly large portion of the electorate,[6] these trends will eventually reach critical mass. A recent article published by Stef W. Knight writing for *Axios*, astutely noted that Millennials and the new younger Generation Z taken together will account for approximately 37% of the electorate in 2020.[7] The election of Alexandria Ocasio-Cortez, and Ilhan Omar to Congress in New York and Minnesota, and the near election of Stacey Abrams and Andrew Gillum as governors in Georgia and Florida respectively, is but a mere foreshadowing of what is to come. Each of these candidates are card carrying and unapologetic socialists in the mold of Vermont Senator Bernie Sanders. Membership in the Democratic Socialists of America (DSA) organization, the largest socialist organization in the U.S., has soared in the aftermath of Bernie Sanders 2016 Presidential Campaign. According to DSA's own website, its membership reached 24,000 members by July 2017.[8] Morgan Gstalter, writing for *The Hill*, put the DSA membership number at 40,000 as of June 2018, with a large spike in membership after the Ocasio Cortez primary victory in 2018.[9]

True to her DSA roots, Ocasio-Cortez campaigned on "Medicare for all", which is often estimated to have a price tag of $33 *Trillion*! – and once elected to the seat, she has since proposed a 70% top marginal tax rate to pay for it.[10] Got that? Not to be out done, newly minted Democratic Representative Ilhan Omar (D-Minn) has called for tax increases as high as a 90% top marginal rate.[11] Additionally, Ocasio – Cortez has proposed a Green New Deal, which will be discussed in greater detail later in the book, with initial cost estimates coming in at an astonishing $93 Trillion within the first decade of enactment.

So that we maintain perspective, it is worth remembering that the entire annual budget of the US for *all expenditures* is a bit over $4 Trillion. So Ocasio-Cortez is proposing something that will dwarf all current spending. Indeed, Senate Majority Leader Mitch McConnell has noted that

---

capitalist countries according the findings of this poll. *See also*, Felix Salmon, *Generation Z Prefers "Socialism" to "Capitalism"* (Axios, January 27, 2019).

[6] Anthony Cilluffo and Richard Fry, *An Early Look at the 2020 Electorate,* (Pew Research Center, January 30, 2019). The authors note that in 2020 those Americans under age 40 are expected to represent 37% of the total electorate, with Millennials at 27% and Generation Z at 10%. Hence, those under age 40 will comprise the largest single voting block in the Electorate when compared to their older Generation X, Baby Boomer and "Silent Generation" counterparts.

[7] Stef W. Knight, *Exclusive Poll: Young Americans Are Embracing Socialism,* (Axios, March 10, 2019).

[8] Joseph M. Schwartz, *A History of Democratic Socialists of America 1971 – 2017:Bringing Socialism From the Margins to the Mainstream.* (DSA National Political Committee 2017). For further details see., https://www.dsausa.org/about-us/history/.

[9] Morgan Gstalter, *Democratic Socialists of America Sees Membership Spike After Ocasio – Cortez Win,* (The Hill, June 28, 2018), referring to AOC's victory over Joe Crowley in a primary race in the 2018 midterm elections.

[10] In a January 2019 interview with Anderson Cooper for the CBS show "60 Minutes," Ms. Ocasio – Cortez proposed a top marginal tax rate of 70% for the "rich" in America. She did not define rich but alluded to incomes exceeding $10 million per year. Given the scope and magnitude of the proposals she makes (e.g., a Green New Deal and Medicare for all, etc. etc.), what qualifies as "rich' will surely be revised downward. It is worth remembering that a 70% top marginal rate was a rate last in effect just prior to Ronald Reagan signing the Kemp-Roth tax reform legislation in 1981, which touched off an economic boom lasting some 96 months. She appears to want to go back to the good old days of stagflation (high unemployment coupled with high inflation) that were the impetus for the 1981 tax relief in the first place.

[11] Rep Omar made this proposal on a weekly half hour weekly news show hosted by Zainab Salbi entitled *Through Her Eyes*, on the Roku channel. These comments were made on January 29, 2019. This episode was viewed via yahoonews.com. During the interview she railed the familiar progressive line that "the rich must pay their fair share. While the current definition of who is to be considered "rich" at the present time includes multi-millionaires and billionaires, given the huge appetite for spending the progressives bring to the table – that threshold is sure to be lowered to just about anyone with an income when all is said and done.

the all federal spending in the entire 240 history of the US would not equal the price tag of her Green New Deal proposal. Andrew Gillum had proposed a 40% increase in the Florida corporate tax rate. Ms. Abrams campaigned on gun confiscation in complete contradiction to our Second Amendment rights. Since then this position has been taken by several Democratic Presidential aspirants, including Beto O'Rourke, Bernie Sanders and others. They say they'd just start with assault rifles, but if you believe they would stop there, then I would like to sell you the Golden Gate Bridge. And as the first year of the new Democratic Congress rolled on through 2019, Ocasio-Cortez and Omar have teamed up with Ayanna Pressley (D-Mass) and Rashida Tlaib (D-Mich.) to collectively become what Speaker of the House Nancy Pelosi (D-CA) has come to refer to (not so affectionately) as "The Squad", (Senator John Kennedy (R-LA) calls them the four horsewomen of the apocalypse). They have become the face of the Democratic party and they collectively and continuously advocate for ideas that are far outside the American political mainstream; they seek the abolition of the Immigration and Customs Enforcement (ICE), they have referred to ICE agents as Nazi's running concentration camps on our southern border and so on. They regularly espouse Marxist economics as solutions to major issues of the day and have an abject disdain for the business community.

While all of these aforementioned politicians are relatively new to the American political scene on a national level, they have been successful at goading established politicians to jump on the socialist high tax bandwagon. For example, Massachusetts Senator Elizabeth Warren proposed a 2% wealth tax on those with a net worth of $50 million dollars or more. [12] Only about 0.055% of the 150 Million US individual tax returns filed each year would involve a net worth this large.[13] For net worth of one billion or more, Ms. Warren would increase the tax to 3%.[14] In Ms. Warren's world, the reward for building a large net worth and achieving the American Dream is that you will get to pay a hefty tax on your investment corpus every year just for the privilege of having it. And if you attempt to renounce US citizenship to avoid the tax, well, Ms. Warren has thought of that too. You would get to pay a punitive "exit tax" of 40% of the value of the net worth (if greater than $50 Million) as of the time of renunciation.[15] Clearly, the 2018 midterm Congressional elections have emboldened liberals to become hard core progressives and hard core progressives to become more traditional socialists on the road to radical Marxism.

The states are not going to miss out on this high tax "soak the rich" party either. A perfect example is already tax-happy New Jersey. As soon as Phil Murphy took the governor's office succeeding Chris Christie, one of his first acts was to enact a large tax increase on individuals earning $5 million or more, taking their New Jersey income tax rate to over 10%.[16] Governor Murphy had attempted to get the state income tax raised to over 10% for anyone earning $1 million or more but that was rejected by the state legislature.[17] Not to be discouraged, Governor Murphy

---

[12] John Cassidy, *The New Yorker,* January 31, 2019. As Mr. Cassidy notes, there are only about 80,000 Americans with a net worth this high, out of a national population of 328,000,000 according the United States Census Bureau population clock. According to the IRS, as of 2016, there are about 150 million individual tax returns filed each year.

[13] Ibid.

[14] Ibid.

[15] Ibid.

[16] Bloomberg Daybreak: America, Amanda Albright interview with Daniel Solender, partner and municipal bond group director at Lord Abbett. March 7, 2019.

[17] Ibid.

has re-introduced his proposal to raise taxes on those making $1 million per year or more to 10.75% (up from 8.97%).[18] The reasoning for the push to increase taxes on top earners in New Jersey is the same for every other hard left state, and for a future Bolshevik progressive federal government – New Jersey is running out of money due to runaway pension liabilities and other spending, and the bond rating agencies are getting antsy.[19] Murphy's budget contains massive proposed increases in spending for health benefits ($2.7 billion), and an equally massive contribution to the pension system ($3.8 billion – the largest payment in state history), and the list goes on.[20] The New Jersey situation is *prima facia* evidence that the spending appetite for a left-wing progressive Democrat is a bottomless well of desires to be funded by those who have achieved economic success. The scariest notion of all is that this may only be the beginning! In line with that notion, one should understand that these proposals, if ever formally adopted, would only be the starting point. The wish list for progressives is long and expensive. Sooner or later, anyone with an income above the HUD median will be paying much higher taxes.

With unabashed Marxism now making its way into the mainstream of American political discourse, especially at the top of the economic cycle with record low unemployment, some important questions arise. What is likely to happen to this leftward trajectory during the all but certain recession we will experience sometime in the next few years. What will say – 7 or 8 percent unemployment do to stoke this leftward lurch? If young people are abandoning capitalism in a time of relative prosperity, what happens when that prosperity inevitably ebbs? This begs a series of additional questions. What if ten years from now, politicians like these are getting elected not as anomalies, but as a norm on the Democratic side of the aisle? What if fully half of the American Electorate supports at least some form of outright socialism or other manifestation of Marxism? What if the radical "progressivism" of today becomes the normative baseline for an organizing principle of American democracy? What if in the not too distant future the hard left has the same political reach as any other political philosophy? What if the hard-left progressivism of today becomes as "mainstream" as Franklin Roosevelt's "New Deal"? What if views espoused by Senator Warren, Vermont Senator Bernie Sanders or the aforementioned "Squad" come to represent the political center as opposed to the radical left? What would it be like to live in such an America? That indeed is what this book aims to explore, and I suspect if you adore America's achievements as a free enterprise driven republic, you will not like it much at all.

In contemplating such questions, history provides many illustrations of what life is like under harsh Marxist rule. You won't hear much from the media or academia on this point, though there is a considerable body of work available for such an exercise; hence the rational for writing this book. The reason you have not likely been exposed to the atrocities of various Marxist regimes over the past century is that it is commonly understood there is an explicit "take over" by the American Left of nearly all major disciplines of what is often referred to as the "humanities" and the social sciences in our colleges and universities. The impact this has had on the kind of information available to the American People is to quash any conventional understanding among the general public, especially young people, of the horrors of Marxist rule. As commentator Arnold Ahlert has noted, the American Right has abjectly surrendered any attempt at influence in

---

[18] Andrew Seidman, <u>NJ Gov Phil Murphy Calls for 'Millionaire's Tax' in Budget Address</u>, (Philadelphia Inquirer, March 5, 2019).

[19] Ibid.

[20] Ibid.

America's higher education system for the last half-century[21], with the effect being that American youth are fully indoctrinated in Marxist based ideology. Tragically, the Western university, especially in America, has become a repository of hard-core leftist progressivism, so in that sense we can at least understand that these institutions would be reluctant to highlight all the modern examples of the grim wasteland of failed Marxist states. We are left with the present condition where American liberals and progressives talk all day about Nazi atrocities, but say comparatively little about the killing fields of the Khmer Rouge, the Soviet Gulags, or the political prison camps of Mao Zedong. It is well documented that each of these aforementioned communist regimes killed literally millions upon millions of innocent people for political expediency. So if the current intellectual class is not likely to alert the American People of the potential death trap they stumble and meander towards, then I will; because Americans are owed, at a minimum, some kind of clarion warning that they are about to land face first into a political buzz saw.

To facilitate understanding the risks of Marxist rule, there is a dour if ultimately effective historical account from the early 20th Century that elucidates the risks Americans take in any flirtation with Marxism. As we have previously noted, there is a discernable trend towards radical progressivism and outright Marxism in the United States today, one that may in fact one day drive America to becoming an outright socialist state, or even a communist one – as unthinkable as that might be at the moment. When and if that day comes, one only need look at how the collectivization efforts were undertaken in the early years of the former Soviet Union, when the Bolsheviks first took over Russia in the early part of the twentieth century. When Tsarist Russia was overthrown and the Bolsheviks took control, one of the first orders of business was to institute the collectivism ordained by their Marxist-Leninist ideology. In so doing, they built an apparatus to systematically destroy any resistance to these policies and actions. There was no better class of people to illustrate the ruthlessness of this effort than those Soviet citizens who were identified as "Kulaks". To be legally deemed a Kulak was a virtual death sentence, often in the most inhumane manner possible. Who – you ask – were the Kulaks? Oh so glad you inquire. They were the most successful, relatively wealthy farmers among the peasantry in Russia and the Ukraine, and they were often disliked by many factions, including other peasants. But no one hated them more than the Soviet Government, including Lenin and Stalin themselves.

One of the reasons you do not often hear the term "Kulak" nearly a century later is that Lenin and more particularly, Stalin, were so effective at literally wiping them from the face of the earth by quite literally any means at their disposal. But when one delves into who the Kulaks actually were, they bear a peculiar resemblance to today's American and European affluent professional and small business owner class. I believe the comparison is eerie because the manner in which the Kulaks met their ultimate demise was nothing short of horrific. The affluent in America today could well meet with a fate that resembles an echo or an overtone to what the Kulaks endured. Sound fantastical? Surreal? Wild Fantasy? I will freely admit that such an outcome might be improbable or unlikely, but it is most certainly possible, after all, how many of the Kulaks understood they were within a generation of extinction in 1910? I am guessing not very many. Yet twenty years later they were staring death right in the face. Then in 1931-33 they were systematically starved, murdered or relocated to Gulags which of itself was very often a death sentence, and a very gruesome one at that.

---

[21] Arnold Ahlert, *2020 Is the Critical Mass Election: Will Leftist Indoctrination In Politics, Business, Media, Hollywood, and Academia Finally Bear Fruit?* (The Patriot Post, July 5, 2019).

I proceed with this analysis with great care and empathy for what the Kulaks endured. I have no intention of cheapening the atrocity of their murder by a casual comparison to modern day American affluent professionals; but the reality is, I see parallels, and feel compelled to discuss them with and disseminate to the widest audience possible, so that we don't meander to this end unwittingly. While the Kulaks were farmers and village lenders, their relative affluence set them apart from the rest of the villagers. One can similarly observe as much with modern day American affluent professionals, who may not be farmers, but their specialized training and relative affluence sets them apart from the average wage earning American, and would make them an easy target for an American Marxist regime.

As you read this book, I submit to you that you will find yourself asking why on earth so many affluent suburbanites are embracing hard left candidates such as Ocasio-Cortez, Gillum, Abrams, Sanders and Warren. This book will show, I believe convincingly, that the affluent suburban professional would be the first ox to be gored – literally. Indeed that process has already begun, and surprisingly with Republican assistance. As part of the Tax Cuts and Jobs Act of 2017[22] signed by President Trump, the deduction for state and local taxes (SALT as it is commonly referred to) was capped at $10,000. For affluent suburbanites who easily pay $15,000 – $20,000 in property taxes each year on their primary residence, AND may well pay a similar amount in state income tax on top of their property tax, a deduction cap of $10,000 will result in literally thousands of dollars per year in additional tax liability. The Republicans made a cynical ploy that most of the impact will fall on well off suburban professionals in blue states such as New York, New Jersey, Massachusetts, Maryland, California and Illinois who don't vote Republican anymore and are in states Republicans don't win anyway.

The impact of this deduction cap was noticeable almost immediately, as within a year of enactment, high income earners in New York for example, have left the state by moving their primary residential legal address to another state.[23] On February 4, 2019, New York Governor Andrew Cuomo announced that he expected state income tax revenue to drop by $2.8 billion, and blamed it on the large number of wealthy earners moving their legal residence out of state.[24] He went on to note that just a few thousand of these taxpayers have a large impact on New York revenues, as the top one percent of New York taxpayers pay nearly 50% of New York's tax bill.[25] The point is that the affluent have already begun to be dismembered economically. Republicans do not see these voters as allies any longer and Democrats never really did. While the Democrats propose far higher taxes on the rich and super rich, they will work their way down to just the "well off" and "comfortable", as their wish list is unsurprisingly very high. We will discuss this "annihilation by taxation" concept at several other points throughout the book.

In light of the foregoing, and the case I make throughout this book, a quick caveat is in order. While I am harshly critical of the progressive left in America, including self-avowed socialists like Senator Sanders and Congresswoman Ocasio-Cortez, as well as uber liberals like Senator Warren, I do not mean to imply that they themselves will orchestrate an authoritarian communist take-over of the United States; but rather, that their stated policies will initiate America fundamentally on a

---

[22] Pub.L 115-97

[23] Michael Gromley, *As Revenue Drops, Concern About the Proposed State Budget Rises,* (Newsday, February 4, 2019).

[24] Ibid.

[25] Ibid.

path towards a form of Marxism in the United States. Policies such as "Medicare for All" which would eviscerate the private health insurance industry, the Green New Deal which would do the same for the oil and gas industries, are de facto nationalizations of industries. As such they remove the means of production out of private hands and under the control of government. That is the essence of Marxism. Once on the Marxist trail – where does it end and how do we get off of it should we later determine we do not like the journey?   History has not been kind regarding this question. Yet few in the upper income suburban areas seem to be troubled by any of this.

Therefore, notwithstanding the duly noted caveat that I do not mean to assert liberals and progressives will necessarily take us to authoritarian communism, I do find it astonishing that today's upper income professional and "well healed" small business-person cannot see the bear trap they may be walking into. I am not a proponent of mass stupidity – these are not stupid people. But they *are* misinformed and ignorant of the past. And this ignorance can easily come back to haunt them. It may be that this danger will not really occur to them until it is too late, until the moment at which they realize they are the bullseye for the newly minted Marxist rulers that could well be in our future. Will these "Bohemian Bourgeoisie", as David Brooks once called them, wake one day to realize they have become instead the "American Kulak" with all the grim reality that may ultimately entail?

CHAPTER I

THE BOLSHEVIKS ARE COMING! THE BOLSHEVIKS ARE COMING!

———

History repeats itself, the first as tragedy, then as farce[26]

As noted in the Preface, this book is written with the supposition that there are strong indicators pointing to an increasingly hard leftward lurch in American politics to the point that a socialist or even communist takeover of the American system can no longer be categorically ruled out. This book will thread together the evidence of these developments and demonstrate that the affluent are indeed playing a significant role. Perhaps the cruelest of ironies will be when the time finally comes that formal collectivism is the order of the day, these affluent voters will find themselves in a similar condition to that of the Kulaks a century ago. Agree to forego all your net worth and the lion's share of your earnings by submitting to ridiculous levels of taxation, and you will live fine within the system. Resist in any way, and the new American Bolsheviks may have you vaporized or extirpated, just like Lenin and Stalin did to the Kulaks 10 decades before. If the 21st Century plays out for America the way I suspect it might, and the American affluent class does in fact wind up as a modern era version of the Kulaks, then history will have literally repeated itself, or at least occurred, to paraphrase Mark Twain, with a discernable "rhyme."

If that is ultimately to be the case, then the Marxian aphorism noted above in the epigraph will have played out with all degree of wretched determination. What happened to the Kulaks was a 20th century tragedy of the highest magnitude. Something similar happening to the American affluent class, especially when they have history as a guide, is nothing short of a pathetic farce. Fool me once, shame on you. Fool me twice, shame on me. The fact that young and affluent voters are actively furthering this possibility by continuing to vote in large numbers for increasingly hard left candidates is grotesque and avoidable recklessness – pure and simple. The trend towards Marxism in America has been well documented, to the point that well established news agencies are writing articles about socialism in America becoming "mainstream".[27] In addition to the polling and other supporting information available as to the membership explosion of the Democratic Socialists of America (DSA), the largest formal socialist organization in the

---

[26] *Karl Marx The Eighteen Brumaire of Louis Napoleon* (1852).

[27] MacKenzie Sigalos, *Here's How Socialism Went Mainstream in American Politics,* (CNBC.com July 31, 2019).

country, the press is also finally beginning to chronicle the transformative political developments in the direction of Marxism in America.

To illustrate, we will summarize some recent examples. First, we take note of an excellent journalistic accounting of the surging movement towards democratic socialism in the state of Iowa, a key initial battleground in U.S. Presidential elections. In an Article published in the *Atlantic* online in early April 2019, Elaine Godfrey surveys a newly created Democratic Socialists of America chapter that was formed during 2016 in the midst of the surging Presidential candidacy of Senator Sanders. What Ms. Godfrey describes is very supportive of the notion that the gravitation towards socialism is especially intense among the millennial generation. Specifically, Godfrey notes that the subject of the story, Caroline Schoonover, the co-chair of the Central Iowa DSA chapter holds the explicit goal of systematically dismantling capitalism, an especially ominous fact given that according to Godfrey, DSA membership has surged to 56,000 as of April 2019.[28] Moreover, almost in passing, Godfrey points out the irony of Iowa being a place where you can find "a budding movement to overthrow the country's political and economic system," in reference to DSA expansion in that state.[29] Perhaps the most frightening aspect of Godfrey's coverage of DSA in Iowa is the detail she covers, pointing out that for the Iowa DSA, Bernie Sanders is not even far left enough for their proclivities, although he is certainly more preferable than any other of the candidates.[30] Ms. Godfrey writes:

> "So it was frustrating for many of them in March when the DSA's governing body formally voted to endorse Sanders for president. Sanders, who identifies as a democratic socialist, helped open Iowans' eyes to the political possibilities of the movement with his 2016 campaign, ***but Schoonover and other members of the Central Iowa chapter still have issues with the senator from Vermont. For example, he hasn't publicly backed any measures for reparations for black Americans, and he doesn't support the boycott, divestment, and sanctions movement, a campaign advocating financial separation between the United States and Israel***.
>
> But more important, they say, working on behalf of a single candidate will only distract from their efforts to organize tenants and build power in their communities. 'We don't talk about Bernie,' Schoonover explained. 'He's not a factor in our organizing at all.' Most of them would certainly prefer Sanders to other Democrats in the 2020 field, and individual members can volunteer for him on their own time, Schoonover said. 'But we're not a Bernie Sanders fan club just waiting for our chance to finally knock doors for him.'"[31] (Emphasis added)."

Remember in the *Preface* of this book where I challenge the reader to imagine a world where Senators Sanders and Warren would be considered moderates? Apparently for Ms. Schoonover,

---

[28] Elaine Godfrey, *Socialism, But in Iowa*, (The Atlantic, April 5, 2019). For the full article, see, https://www.theatlantic.com/politics/archive/2019/04/democratic-socialism-surging-iowa-ahead-2020/586441/.

[29] Ibid.

[30] Ibid.

[31] Ibid.

that is exactly what they are. For the Central Iowa DSA chapter, Sanders is too moderate because he won't back reparations for slavery that ended 155 years ago (a position he has since modified)[32] and won't support sanctions and a boycott on Isreal, a longstanding ally. The purpose of recapitulating key points in Godfrey's article is to drive home the notion that among a rapidly growing portion of American young people, hard left progressive socialism and Marxism are becoming so mainstream that political figures who were once considered radical leftists like Sanders and Warren are now becoming almost ordinary.

These discussion points from Ms. Godfrey's article are completely and expressly corroborated by what is clearly articulated in the Democratic Socialists of America Website, which has the following statement:

> "Democratic socialists believe that both the economy and society should be run democratically—to meet public needs, not to make profits for a few. ***To achieve a more just society, many structures of our government and economy must be radically transformed through greater economic and social democracy so that ordinary Americans can participate in the many decisions that affect our lives.***
>
> Democracy and socialism go hand in hand. All over the world, wherever the idea of democracy has taken root, the vision of socialism has taken root as well—everywhere but in the United States. Because of this, many false ideas about socialism have developed in the US."[33]

The statement advocates a radical transformation of the American economy. While it is replete with the usual disclaimers that all of this radical transformation will be done in the context of the democratic process, which is he typical reassurance socialist often provide – that their mission is not to create a centralized bureaucratic tyranny in the mold of the former Soviet Union. However, in doing so, they pretty much miss the point. The people of Venezuela democratically elected Hugo Chavez, who then used the levers of the Venezuelan democratic republic to go about implementing an agenda that "radically transformed" the Venezuelan economy in accordance with Marxist principles. The result was a Marxist dictatorship and a failing state that to this day is crumbling by the minute.

The DSA website does not go into specifics on what is meant by "radical transformation" as their leadership is too savvy to provide specifics that would let the American people know what their true intentions are. However, their rank and file and mid-level leadership is more honest about what they are attempting to do. In a 2018 interview with all 13 members of the North Central West Virginia Chapter of the DSA, National Public Radio Reporter Danielle Kurtzlebin cited the following interview excerpts from the members:

---

[32] Nolan Hicks, *Bernie Sanders Now Says He'll Back a Bill To Study Reparations for Slavery,* (New York Post, April 5, 2019). The media has treated this as an outright reversal of Sander's former position, but in fairness to the Senator, he has only agreed to take formal steps to study the idea. He has NOT as yet endorsed a position to start writing checks for reparations. It is fair to assume that the pressure on the Senator from his left is immense and it may be only a matter of time before he winds up acquiescing to a position that would start printing money for reparations.

[33] See, https://www.dsausa.org/about-us/what-is-democratic-socialism/.

"Here's how one socialist sums up his beliefs:

'*__I think we just need to realize that the end goal is, ultimately, like social
control of the means of production__*,' said Joe Cernelli, a founding member
of that West Virginia DSA chapter. '*__You know we don't just want to improve
capitalism, we will ultimately want to get rid of it__*.'

That's not just his idea; the DSA views capitalism as an oppressive system —
'We see it as fundamentally undemocratic,' as DSA National Director Maria
Svart put it. Here's how she sums up what the group wants:

'When it comes right down to it, we believe people need to be able to live a
dignified life. I mean, **there are certain things** *__that should not be left up to
the market__*," she said.

*__Removing some parts of the economy from the forces of the free market,
for example. In other words, socialism__*.

In the DSA's ideal economy*__, some sectors — like health care and utilities
— would be government-controlled. Other businesses would be worker-
owned, as Svart explains it.__*'"[34] (Emphasis supplied)

So, from these excerpts, concurrent with the ones provided by Ms. Godfrey in her *Atlantic* article, we can clearly discern the true intentions of the DSA, notwithstanding the innocuous official statements on its website. These articles allow us to clearly see the perspective of the grass roots DSA members. The above quotations prove they are not here to reform capitalism, rather they seek to destroy it and replace it with socialism, which is inherently a Marxist based economic system. They seek to nationalize industries and strip their current owners of control over these assets, and place this ownership under government control. This is Bolshevism pure and simple, a redistribution of the wealth as the Marxist theory goes. For these reasons, we can, as the title of this chapter boldly asserts, confidently exclaim that the Bolsheviks are coming, no matter how hard the DSA leaders try and place a benign facade on their obvious communist intentions. They may not attempt to seize power violently the way the Bolsheviks did, but have no illusions, these socialists are essentially Marxists seeking to dismantle the free enterprise system.

Furthermore, it is not incredulous to assume that one day the Millennial generation along with their younger partners in Generation Z will willingly embrace authoritarian approaches to their quest for Marxist utopian ends. Even *New York Times* Columnist and NeverTrumper Bret Stephens has had to admit today's youth have embraced unfortunate tactics as part of their culture. Stephens describes the most troubling features of their culture as being of coddled minds and a *"censorious manner."*[35] He concluded his op-ed article by saying that while sensible moderates in the center of the American political spectrum want to limit Trump to a single term, they won't if

---

[34] Danielle Kurtzlebin, *What You Need to Know About Democratic Socialists of America* (NPR, July 26, 2018). For the full article see, https://www.npr.org/2018/07/26/630960719/what-you-need-to-know-about-the-democratic-socialists-of-america.

[35] Bret Stephens, *Dear Millennials: The Feeling is Mutual,* (New York Times, Mary 17, 2019).

ousting him means empowering what he refers to as "junior totalitarians of the left."[36] It is quite simply becoming impossible to ignore the increasing fascist undercurrents and overtones of the Millennial political zeitgeist; from demanding Harvard law professors lose their jobs because of who their clients are, to the disgustingly violent behavior towards conservative speakers on college campuses. The up and coming generation under 40 is not at all wedded to long standing liberal principles of freedom of expression and the right to peacefully assemble.

Long time Democrat and civil liberties advocate, Harvard Law Professor Emeritus Alan Dershowitz recently penned an article for the *Gatestone Institute* literally referring to the "woke" hard-left as "dangerous Stalinists."[37] Professor Dershowitz lambasted the intolerance of today's left-wing extremists for their disdain for core liberal tenants of Western Civilization such as free speech, due process and the presumption of innocence. Dershowitz emphatically makes the point that today's "woke" hard-left is more dangerous to civil liberties than the political right as the left regularly uses violence to suppress voices with whom they disagree. The left would take us on the road to tyranny were we to follow their present course.

To further expand on the point being made by Messers Stephens and Dershowitz, our popular cultural icons are echoing these autocratic sentiments. For example, Hollywood Actor and *Westworld Star* Jeffrey Wright published the following Tweet on May 29, 2019: "Message from the GOP: There are no principles – not ethical, moral, religious, spiritual – NONE. ***There is only power, everybody else fucking duck. Lesson for everybody else. Get the power***."[38] Mr. Wright's Twitter-tantrum was in response to the public statement made by Special Counsel Robert Mueller in closing down the Special Counsel's Office to conclude the Russia Collusion Investigation of the 2016 Trump Campaign. He sends a very clear warning, when Democrats return to power, "there is only power, everybody else fucking duck." This kind of near epileptic seizure on the part of the hard left is not atypical. Any policy outcome that they do not agree with, any political development they do not approve of, basically whenever they do not get their way – their response is to invoke violent invective. Episodes like this tell you everything you need to know about how they intend to act when they control the Presidency and the Congress. So any notion that I am exaggerating the situation can easily be countered with facts like this one. American Bolshevism, should it ever come to pass, can easily be expected to be as brutal and blood drenched as any other experiment with Marxist rule.

And their Marxist worldview is becoming mainstream at an astonishingly rapid rate. The fact that the age-old AFL-CIO, one of America's oldest trade unions, is fully on-board with a purist form of Marxism and publicly states as much is case in point. Tim Hains of RealClearPolitics recently posted a re-tweet from the AFL-CIO official Twitter account which itself had re-tweeted a video posting from "Means – TV", which Hains describes as the "world's first post-capitalist streaming platform."[39] The video features Dan Whelan, a self-escribed "Marxist roofer," pitching the notion that there are only two classes of people in the American economy: The "ownership class" controlling the "means of production", which is defined as a factory, farm or office building

---

[36] Ibid.

[37] Alan Dershowitz, *The Dangerous Stalinism of the "Woke" Hard-Left* (Gatestone Institute.org, August 31, 2019).

[38] Jerome Hudson, *Actor Jeffrey Wright: When we Get the Power, Everybody Else Fucking Duck,* (Breitbart, May 29, 2019)

[39] Tim Hains, *AFL-CIO: "We All Need to Seize the Means of Production",* (RealClearPolitics, May 16, 2019). To view the video, see, https://www.realclearpolitics.com/video/2019/05/16/afl-cio_we_all_need_to_seize_the_means_of_production.html.

– things of that nature, and the workers who have only their skills and labor to sell.[40] The video claims only about 10% of the American workforce is part of the "ownership class" and the other 90% are all workers of some form or another.[41] The caption from the AFL-CIO tweet presenting this video reads: "We all need to seize the means of production."[42] Of course the 2 and a half minute video doesn't address the fact that shareholders own the means of production in many cases, and those shareholders comprise millions of small investors who have money in retirement accounts, but then again, a true blue Marxist really isn't into detail that much – they rather prefer the class conflict, as creating wealth isn't there gig – spreading it around is much more fun. Suffice it to say that cramming 159 million work force participants into two classes will be a stretch even for the Marxist geniuses.

These stated intentions of DSA and AFL-CIO members begs the following questions. How exactly do they intend to nationalize entire sectors of the American economy? How do they intend to "seize the means of production"? Do they think that will happen peacefully? Do they think those who own the assets of these industries will just hand them over to Bernie Sanders? Isn't such a redistributionist practice a form of theft? After all, wouldn't the socialists be taking something away from someone else who had lawfully procured it? When Hugo Chavez did exactly this, how well did that work out for Venezuela? Whether the DSA members and their ideological ally's in the media, labors unions and academia know it or not, such actions cannot be condoned in a free society, and to execute on them will be viewed as larceny by those on the other end of the divestiture; and those being forcibly divested will likely resist – just as the Kulak's did. Therefore, it is entirely plausible that an American version of the Kulak experience is exactly where we may indeed be heading in the next two or three decades if the intellectual trend espoused by the DSA continues. American's who have earned their wealth by following the rules in place over a lifetime will not freely hand it all over to the nearest DSA chapter chairperson. It is entirely foreseeable that to nationalize entire industries will result in massive and probably violent resistance.

As I mentioned earlier, in conducting the research for this book, it became increasingly clear that not only can a Bolshevik takeover of the American system occur, there is significant evidence that some degree of wealth confiscation among the affluent has already begun. We will demonstrate in later chapters that this sequestration is occurring via stealth tax increases on ever increasing portions of income that have hitherto not been taxed. In fact, we are well on our way to an as yet non-violent form of "dekulakization" of American Affluence, even without a hard form of socialist or communist system. It turns out that the last three decades of successful professionals and small businessmen leaving the Republican Party has put them in conservative and populist cross-hairs. Just as the early 20th Century Kulak had few allies, the 21st century American Kulak is winding up hated by all sides.

At this juncture, it is worth mentioning that while it might be tempting to attribute these developing circumstances to "poetic justice", or some other form of "Schadenfreude," especially for those of us who think it ridiculous that upper bracket suburbanites would have ever "hitched their wagon" to a socialist buffoon like Bernie Sanders and his ilk. The facts on the ground; however, will not allow for such thinking. It is undeniable, as this book will show, that these

---

[40] Ibid.

[41] Ibid.

[42] Ibid.

upscale voters are some of America's most productive and intelligent citizens. Any political system that purges them will undoubtedly leave our civilization poorer and worse off economically, culturally and politically. Nothing good will come of the demise of the American affluent class. Any kind of persecution by way of a 21st Century version of literal or figurative "dekulakization" will be nothing less than a stain on our collective American History.

If the foregoing sounds outlandish and surreal, or an egregious exaggeration to you, by the end of this book, hopefully you will see what I see; that to an extent the process of a 21st Century "dekulakization" is already well in motion. I will show you that this process has been underway, very subtly for decades, and the process is sure to escalate in the next 20 years, especially if American politics continues its leftward march. What would likely start off with a gradual degradation of purchasing power via increases in taxation and student loan debt, will escalate to an outright impounding of income through crushing personal and business taxes. Today's high income earner, though comfortable but not "wealthy" or "rich" in any sense that they can stop work and live off their asset base for the rest of their lives, will be denigrated to a much lower status in life by operation of the US Tax Code and laws surrounding the accumulation of debts (think of the bankruptcy reform legislation of 2007 which made discharging student debt nearly impossible). Finally, this book will explore other methodologies of "dekulakization" that a 21st Century Bolshevik America may deploy.

Many a reader at this point is likely to be thinking – who cares? Why worry about the upper middle and upper class income earner being busted down to mere "average" in terms of their after tax spending power? I will tell you why, by asking several "why" related questions myself. First, why would anyone go through the rigors of medical school, dental school, law school, get an MBA or any other advance degree – just to have an "average" standard of living? Why would anyone borrower the vast sums of money to get an advanced degree, and carry that debt for literally decades, just to have the same after tax purchasing power as his or her next door neighbor who did none of those things? A doctor or lawyer gives up their 20's in order to gain the skills and education needed to enjoy a much higher income down the road. While their age mates are living the fun and sun of youth, professional school students are spending weekends at the library or laboratory studying hour after hour. And if you take away the pecuniary incentive associated with the large disposable income that is anticipated after all that hard work, what would be the reason to proceed with such a large financial and emotional sacrifice? Pure Altruism?

Sure – that will work for some, but I dare say most successful professionals and business people will want a financial reward. They will want a higher standard of living as payback for the investment of time, money and tears. Similarly, no rational person risks financial ruin to start a small business (and that is exactly what happens all too often when they fail), only to find the reward was the same if one took none of those risks. What would very likely happen is that the most talented people would no longer take such gambles, even though calculated risk taking is the key to the success of the free enterprise system. They would instead look for other occupations where either the tax treatment is more favorable, or they will manage their income right up to the point that the tax burden becomes punitive and stop their efforts. This may not sound all that dire, but ones perspective might change when he wakes up and realizes the only people willing to be a doctor, lawyer or small business person are people who are simply not talented enough for those occupations by present-day standards. When today's day laborer can get into medical school or law school because someone more capable sees the financial dead end of it all, well, you can discern for yourself what you think the quality of your medical care or legal advice would be. As an example, when today's citizen of average intelligence is the only one willing to take on hundreds of thousands in debt to go to medical school or law school only to be treated as a "high income *pariah*" upon graduation and pay absurd levels of taxation, you will surely see a massive degradation in the professional capabilities at the other end. If the idea of today's department store manager as cardiac surgeon does not bother you – then good luck with that triple bypass surgery when the time comes.

This is basic economics. But then again, the tired intellectual badlands of Marxism have very little regard for "rational" economic theory. The hard-core Marxist progressive is driven by wishful thinking more than any formal study of how incentives drive desired behaviors that "create wealth." *Bone fide* socialists and progressive are generally not concerned with wealth creation as it is the re-distribution of already created wealth that is their fancy. But re-distribution works, as Margaret Thatcher once famously said, until you run out of "other people's money" to pass around. Then the collectivist system falls apart. It fell apart in the former Soviet Union, it also fell apart in Mao's China, and so they adopted economic reforms in the late 1970s to become communist politically but otherwise embrace free market economics where possible. The ones that still cling to hard core unrefined communism like North Korea or Venezuela pay a stiff price with very low economic development and atrociously low living standards.

These are the sentiments that will form the basis for discussion throughout the book, and will be supported with ample and publicly available information taken from a variety of sources such as well recognized historical publications, government statistics, news outlets and the law. Stylistically, this book will provide footnote citations to evidence the sources used for substantiating factual assertions. It is also worthy of mention that the approach taken with this book is to treat its theme as a hypothesis, which is that the current trend towards radical progressivism may in fact wind up driving America to becoming an outright socialist state, or even a communist one – as implausible as it may presently seem. When and if that day comes, the Marxist/Leninist experience, as carried out by Stalin provides a horrific example of what collectivist initiatives could ultimately look like. No better example exists than what happened to the Kulaks, a group of people that bear some resemblance to present day American affluent professionals. The fate the latter may well bear a frightening resemblance to the former. Each of the following chapters of this book is a component of an overall argument structure designed to defend the hypothesis.

First things first, in order to make the analogy that the American professional class may wind up being a *de facto* 21st Century Kulak, and could face a similar fate, we need to understand the 20th Century Kulaks and the world in which they lived. To facilitate that purpose, chapter two will describe in detail who the Kulaks were and explain the political and economic backdrop that was concurrent with their demise. This chapter is basically a historical summary of the evolution of the Kulak from serfdom to their status as Kulaks. We will also explore how they were identified and legally defined by the government under Soviet law. To understand the Kulak peasant, one must also understand the Soviet collectivization aspirations and the latent Ukrainian nationalism that underpinned the fate of the Kulaks.

Chapter three will discuss the gory detail of what ultimately came of the Kulaks in the early decades of the Soviet Union. Their plight is one of the great blood drenched stains on the history of the 20th Century. As I noted in the preface, there are alarming similarities between the Kulaks and the modern day American affluent in terms of group identification, and there are also unnerving analytic comparisons in terms of the of the fate of each group in the early stages of a Marxist regime. Understanding the gruesome specifics of the Kulak demise will be useful in avoiding such a fate for the present day American affluent professional or small businessman.

Chapter four will entail an in-depth survey of the current day American professional class and small business owner. Basically doctors, highly paid medical professionals and administrators, lawyers, middle and even some upper level managers of medium and large companies, engineers and accountants would be a typical sample of this class. If you had to get a college degree and even a post graduate or professional degree to do your job, and your job in 2019-2020 pays you $150,000 or more per year, but less than $750,000, you would be smack in the middle of this class of American. Ditto if you run a successful small business. We will explore the income and debt profile of this class in great detail, as well as their tax treatment. Chapter three and four taken together will demonstrate the similarities that can be ascertained between the 20th Century Kulak and the 21st Century American professional or small business owner.

Chapter five is where I demonstrate the case to be made that the American professional and small business owner has already seen some degree of "dekulakization", mainly through the developments associated with the ever-increasing payroll tax among high income earners. As this dynamic continues, it will move from an irritant for a well-off taxpayer to becoming a quite burdensome "ball and chain" for already highly taxed affluent income filers. Then there are the other tax related developments that are sure to have the effect of "goring the ox" for this class. I will compare what was done to the Kulaks and then look at the effect of taxation and compare the two. The conclusion I reach is that the American tax code can and does easily assume the role as formal instrument of ever-increasing degrees of "collectivization". The tax code is how the 21st Century communist will transform America – if they are ever afforded the opportunity, to a radical level of Marxist economics. The IRS would probably be highly militarized to facilitate these collectivist objectives. To this point, there is ample historical context for the IRS using paramilitary tactics, which will be surveyed in detail, as such capabilities and tactics may again be re-authorized and deployed over the next couple of decades. As we have seen with prior periods of a militarized IRS, even seemingly minor tax infractions can have a major financial impact on the offending party. A future hyper aggressive IRS is quite capable of acting politically and has done so in the past, all of which will be documented in this chapter. The degree of the offence is all too often not relevant to the degree or intensity of IRS action. The American affluent may well come face to face with the brutal hand of the state, just like their 20th Century Kulak counterparts.

Chapter six is where I explore the likelihood or probability that political developments like this could actual come to be. I will stipulate that the odds of a "literal" dekulakization of the American upper class might be remote as of the time this manuscript was drafted, but I maintain this risk is not zero and cannot be ruled out. Then there is the prospect that the more benign "dekulakization" through crushing levels of taxation is really quite probable. This chapter explains and discusses the legal and political vectors pointing in this direction. Current political trends point in a very ominous path and they are intensifying. A storm is gathering which could level much devastation on fellow citizens who are affluent. This is the chapter where I provide the basis for this assertion.

Chapter seven, the final chapter of the book, is an attempt to survey what can be done to change the political vectors currently in place and heading towards the perfect storm. This is the Chapter that will explore what the average citizen can and should do to head off this disaster before it is too late. I suspect you "have a dog in this fight" whether or not you are actually part of the well to do. If you are not affluent, the odds are you have family members who are, or you hope your children at least retain a shot at upward mobility to become so. That has been the American Dream for generations, and it will very much be threatened if radial progressivism takes control of our political and economic system and slams that door shut. I will offer what I think it will take to forestall this potentially disastrous future.

CHAPTER II

CHAPTER II

THE KULAKS OF THE USSR AND UKRAINE

The massive task of introducing a planned economy in a country undergoing rapid industrialization and enforced collectivization of agriculture could not have been achieved by democratic means. The population would not willingly have voted to undergo the sacrifices of the 1930s.[43]

Peace under Communism has Killed Far More People than Wars against Communists.
-     Richard M. Nixon[44]

In order to sufficiently argue there is an analogy between the 20th Century Kulaks of the former Soviet Union and the modern day American affluent professional in the event the U.S. government ever falls under Marxist rule, some considerable discussion is warranted regarding who the Kulaks were, and the political and economic backdrop surrounding the events of the early Soviet era through the 1930s. Once the reader is familiar with what defined a peasant as a "Kulak", the comparison to the present-day suburban professional should become more readily understood. Fortunately for this exercise, there is a large body of scholarship on the story of the Kulaks and their ultimate tragic demise. Perhaps the best known account of these events comes from the late British historian Robert Conquest in his seminal work *The Harvest of Sorrow*, published in 1986.[45] Another excellent, albeit more recent exposition has been provided by opinion columnist and history scholar Anne Applebaum in her 2017 book *Red Famine: Stalin's War on Ukraine.*[46] While the purpose of *American Kulak* is not to re-visit the mind-numbing detail of the history of the Soviet peasants summarized in these monolithic and epic works, an at least somewhat detailed recount of these events is necessary to defend the hypothesis for this book in later chapters.

---

[43] Martin McCauley in the Forward to *Memoirs*, by Mikhail Gorbachev, (Doubleday 1995) at p.xi.

[44] Richard M. Nixon, *No More Vietnam's,* (New York: Arbor House, 1985), 159. Former President Nixon expanded on this sentiment by stating that "[t]hose who supported our efforts had argued that ***a Communist peace would be more brutal than an anti-Communist war***," when describing the aftermath of the fall of Saigon and Phnom Penh, where an estimated 2-3 million Vietnamese and Cambodian nationals were murdered by Communist leaders between 1975 and 79. Ibid., 202 – 205. (Emphasis added).

[45] Robert Conquest, *The Harvest of Sorrow: Soviet Collectivization and the Terror-Famine* (Oxford University Press, 1986).

[46] Anne Applebaum, *Red Famine: Stalin's War on Ukraine*, (First Anchor Books Edition, 2018, copywrite 2017).

THE JOURNEY FROM SERF TO PEASANT

The story of the Kulak has its antecedents with the historical evolution of the Feudal Serf to the 20th Century peasant. A serf was a virtual if not literal slave with no ownership interest in the property he farmed, as compared to the peasant, who did have ownership interests in the land he worked, and had property rights in the crops it produced. The Emancipation of the Serfs occurred in Russia under the rule of Tsar Alexander II in 1861.[47] Now a free landowner, the peasant had incentives to raise production as he had a vested right in the fruits of his efforts. Indeed, Mr. Conquest notes that even with "snags" along the road to reform, such as continued high debt levels and residual ownership by the previous landowners in a portion of the property being worked by the newly liberated peasants, yield per acre increased by about a third from 1861 – 1900.[48] The reforms of Tsar Alexander II were clearly needed for the purpose of brining Russian civilization to a par with Europe and as just noted had some definite early successes.

Nevertheless, the initial success proved inadequate to fully close the productivity gap with other economic powers in the West. One glaring weakness was that even after the Emancipation of the serf, the peasant communes remained responsible for various administrative tasks in peasant communities such as the collection of taxes.[49] Moreover, these inefficient communal administrative bodies were coupled with antiquated farming methods such as the "field strip system" and outdated physical farm equipment.[50] The economic pressure on the peasant to produce coupled with inadequate farming methods of the day resulted in social discontent, strikes and other forms of resistance.[51] These events over the course of the latter part of the 19th Century lead to the famed "Stolypin Reforms" of 1906, which sought to break up the 'reparational' land (where the previous landowner still held an interest and peasant paid reparations) into private holdings.[52] These consolidated farms immediately resulted in increased agricultural output, but not enough to "revolutionize" Russian agriculture as compared to the West, and were mostly aborted by the Bolshevik Revolution of 1917.

Even as peasants had earned their freedom in the last half of the 19th Century, and acquired ownership rights in their land, that by no means meant that they had any sort of "high" social status or esteem in Russian society. It is true that some among the Russian intelligentsia viewed them as the "People incarnate, the soul of the country, suffering, patient, the hope of the future;"[53] however, other members of the elite class viewed them as "the 'dark people', backward, mulish, deaf to argument, an oafish impediment to all progress."[54] As Marxism progressed as a movement within Russia in the early 20th Century, it enamored a material portion of radicals who were then provided with an ideological reason for their skepticism that the peasantry would be the hope of

---

[47] Conquest., 15.

[48] Ibid., 16. Conquest notes that the yields increased from 387lbs. in 1861 to 520 lbs. in 1900.

[49] Ibid.

[50] Ibid., 17. Conquest writes: "But even in 1917 only half of the peasant holdings had iron ploughs. Sickles were used for reaping, flails for threshing.

[51] Ibid.

[52] Ibid., 18.

[53] Ibid., 19.

[54] Ibid.

Russia.[55] Moreover, the Bolshevik faction Russian intellectuals held an especially hostile level of vitriol for the peasantry that exceeded even that of the Marxist general theoretical disdain.[56] It was typical for Marxist townsmen to view the peasant as illiterate deadweights, uncivilized, stupid, turgid people who impeded Russian progress towards Westernization and culture.[57] According to Robert Conquest; the founder of Russian Marxism, Georgi Plekhanov viewed the peasantry as "'barbarian tillers of the soil, cruel and merciless, beasts of burden whose life provided no opportunity for the luxury of thought.'"[58] Indeed, Conquest goes on to note that Marx himself had spoken of "the idiocy of rural life," which was a remark that Vladimir Lenin quoted often, and believed the peasant to be "fiercely and meanly individualistic," secluded and savage.[59] Mr. Conquest goes on to write that for Stalin, "peasants were scum."[60]

As the Bolsheviks assumed formal power and control over Russia in 1917, and begun the task of creating the Soviet Union, when Lenin assumes the role of its autocratic leader, his antipathy towards the peasantry ascends to formal policy considerations. In a new civilization that was bent on dismantling the private ownership of property and the "means of production", Soviet Communism was inevitably going to collide with the interest of the peasantry, who had only been given the right to any form of land ownership a mere 56 years previous to the Bolshevik Revolution. Lenin was acutely aware of the inherent threat the peasantry posed to collectivization efforts. More importantly, notwithstanding any previous conflicting views Lenin may have had regarding the peasantry, the one overriding assessment he would always maintain insistently, as would his successors, was that of the "Kulak" as the enemy.[61] In Lenin's view, the Kulak was "a rich exploiting peasant class against whom, after removal of the landlords proper, peasant hatred could be equally directed."[62]

ENTER THE KULAK

According to Conquest, a Kulak, originally meant to refer to a village money lender and mortgagor, and it was only when lending money became a material source of his income was the peasant seen as a "Kulak" by the other villagers.[63] This definition would expand over time and by the late 1920s, Soviet labor codes would provide a specific legal definition of Kulak for the purpose of identifying them in the countryside. We will explore that in much more detail later in the chapter when we focus on the formal steps the Soviet government would ultimately take to literally eradicate the Kulak people. At this point in the discussion, the point is that Mr. Conquest depicts Kulaks as natural village leaders and were economically more prosperous than the other peasants.

---

[55] Ibid., 20.

[56] Ibid. It is noted by the author that this degree of contempt exhibited by the early Bolsheviks cannot be understated in terms of accounting for the genocidal events that would unfold against the peasantry in early Soviet history following the October 1917 Revolution.

[57] Ibid.

[58] Ibid. Author quoting Georgi Plekhanov.

[59] Ibid. Author quoting Marx and Lenin.

[60] Ibid. Author quoting Akita Khrushchev.

[61] Ibid., 23.

[62] Ibid.

[63] Ibid., 23

Ms. Applebaum summarizes the classification of Kulak and the actual use of that term as borne of necessity in order to facilitate Bolshevik desire to requisition grain from Ukraine.[64]   For Applebaum, the term arose by way of a Bolshevik by the name of Alexander Shlikhter, who was appointed Peoples Commissar of Food Collection in Ukraine in the latter part of 1918.[65] According to Applebaum, the only way Mr. Shlikhter could collect the volume of grain expected by his superiors would be through an aggressive and forceful coercion – violence if you will.[66] Specifically, the idea was to manufacture a class system or "pecking order" among peasants and stoke animosity and antagonism between them, with ultimate goal to prod the peasants into giving up their grain without the need to purchase it.[67]   In so doing, Mr. Shlikhter's actions had the consequence of rendering the Kulak a salient scapegoat for the Bolsheviks for any grain shortages, and the other peasant classes became allies for the Soviets where there was previous risk they would align with the Kulak.[68]

To summarize, Applebaum enumerates three basic classifications for peasants, the bednyaki (poor), serednyaki (middle) and Kulak (wealthy).[69]   There was some upward mobility within these castes as Mikhail Gorbachev wrote in his memoirs that his grandfather was able to migrate from bednyaki to serednyaki during his father's early years.[70]   Generally speaking, we can conclude from the works of Conquest and Applebaum and the memoirs of Gorbachev, that the peasant social stratification can be further explained as follows: **bednyaki** = poor peasant household with insufficient resources to sustain life without "hiring out" to other farmers; **serednyaki** = the "middle peasants" who were able to sustain their existence with the resources form their own land; **Kulak** = the "high" or prosperous peasant who could not only sustain his family with his own resources, he could loan money to villagers and often owned livestock, horses and mechanized farm equipment or other machinery. While the Soviets had low regard for the peasantry in general, they did view the poorer peasants as a potential ally where the Kulak as village leader was always going to be much more suspect. And to be identified as a Kulak, an enemy of the state, meant with the certainty of being shunned by the other peasants. For example, Gorbachev would describe life during the famine of 1933 and the purges of 1937, recalling his grandfather's arrest, and the ostracization that came from it as other peasants did not want to be considered "enemies of the state" for maintaining contact with a political foe of the Soviets.[71]

What is worth reiterating at this juncture is the degree of animus that Lenin had for the Kulak in particular, which is nowhere stated better than in his own writings. As an example, in a composition called *Comrade Workers, Forward To The Last, Decisive Fight!*, Lenin referred to

---

[64] Applebaum, 40-41.

[65] Ibid.

[66] Ibid.

[67] Ibid.

[68] Ibid., 42.

[69] Ibid, 41-42.

[70] Mikhail Gorbachev, *Memiors,* (Doubleday, 1995), 27.

[71] Ibid., 24-27.

the Kulaks as spiders, vampires and leaches who sucked the blood of working people.[72] He also openly advocated formal hostilities towards them in this work, which contains a passage that states:

> "Ruthless war on the Kulaks! Death to them! Hatred and contempt for the parties which defend them – the Right Socialist Revolutionaries, the Mensheviks, and today's Left Socialist-Revolutionaries! The workers must crush the revolts of the Kulaks with an iron hand, the Kulaks who are forming an alliance with the foreign capitalists against the working people of their own country."[73]

The ill will Lenin had for the Kulaks essentially speaks for itself. There is not an inkling of subtlety regarding his intentions when these words were first written in 1918.

In August of that year, Lenin issued a formal "hanging order" targeted at the Kulaks which was a telegram sent to commissars in Penza, a few hundred miles south and west of Moscow.[74] The communication is blunt and ruthless, as it admonished the Commissars to make an example of the five Kulak volosts (regions) by suppressing them without mercy.[75] The means of enforcement were to be public hangings of at least a hundred Kulaks, to whom he referred to (as he had in the past), as "bloodsuckers", and who were to have their names published and their grain seized and confiscated.[76] When the Commissars had failed to timely deliver on this directive, Lenin followed up with a second one with ear splitting indignity chastising them for their inactivity, calling it "criminal" and demanding that they telegraph him when they have completed or "fulfilled" the task.[77]

While this is certainly not the formal genocide that would occur a decade and a half later under Stalin, the point is that the harsh treatment of the Kulaks began almost immediately from the outset of Bolshevik rule. These communications offer a glimpse into the mind-set of early Soviet leadership from its inception: No trial, or at best a show trial; no appeal of any lower court verdict if there were a trial; no gathering of evidence subject to cross examination; basically no rights. The directive was clear, go find 100 or so Kulaks and hang them as publicly as possible and with as much humiliation as possible. Make an example out of them for all to see. This is what totalitarian rule looks like. It isn't pretty. The sheer horror of the Kulak bystanders seeing all this unfold is nearly unimaginable for the average American in 2020.

The foregoing makes exceedingly clear there is no serious argument suggesting Lenin did not have a deep antipathy for the peasant – especially the Kulak. The only logical question for Lenin would be how to identify them. As we alluded to in this chapter, Robert Conquest points out that

---

[72] Vladimir Lenin, *Comrade Workers, Forward to the Last, Decisive Fight!*(Lenin's Collected Works, Progress Publishers, Moscow, volume 28, 1965), pp 53-57. The particular version I relied on is the Online Version V.I.Lennin Internet Archive, 2002. This work was written originally in 1918 and then first published in 1925.

[73] Ibid.

[74] A copy of this telegram in English can be found on alphahistory.com, specifically, See, https://alphahistory.com/russianrevolution/lenins-hanging-order-kulaks-1918.

[75] Ibid.

[76] Ibid.

[77] Ibid., Citing from the follow-up telegraph sent approximately one week later.

the initial "proper" definition of a Kulak was a village money lender, but that would significantly evolve and expand over time. We have also seen from the work of Ms. Applebaum and Mr. Conquest that defining the peasants into classes, with Kulaks on top, served the purpose of fostering class warfare amongst the peasants, and the preventing them from forming a unified force. As the most common understanding among the Soviet government was that a Kulak was primarily a peasant who as a bit better off economically than his village peers, a "well off" farmer if you will;[78] the methods identifying which peasants were Kulaks would over time come to focus on their economic status as opposed to religious affiliation or political views.

Of course, what was deemed "well off" or wealthy was a matter of perspective, as Conquest is careful to note that when one thinks of the Kulak as "the richest exploiter on a grand scale", even the most prosperous Kulak had maybe 2-3 cows and a maximum of 10 hectares of "sowing area" supporting an average family of 7 or so.[79]

More importantly, the richest of any peasant group, including Kulaks, received only 50-56% more income on a per capita basis than the lowest earning peasant group.[80] And most important of all is that the Kulaks represented only an estimated 3-5% of peasant households, but produced around 20% of the grain.[81] These last two points are salient in very important ways. First, a small sub-group significantly "out producing" much larger affiliated groups is an easy target for envy. Second, the Bolsheviks and later the Soviets would find stoking this kind of envy most useful in fostering a class war in the countryside that was seen as an essential strategic element in furthering their collectivization efforts. This dynamic will be very relevant when I illustrate the effect of the class war efforts on the American affluent later in the book. In other words, the Soviet use of class war against the Kulaks may well wind up a strategy hard left Marxists one day deploy against American affluent in our own era.

The notion of class war as a means to further a policy goal such as forced collectivization in the early days of the Soviet Union cannot be overstated. We have already covered Ms. Applebaum's commentary on this point. Mr. Conquest similarly summarizes a multiplicity of reasons for the Bolshevik contrived class war amongst the peasantry. First, Conquest notes the idea of Soviet rule from the beginning was one of Oligarchy, and cites remarks by Lenin to the effect that if a few hundred thousand noblemen could rule Russia then he would ensure a few hundred thousand communists could do the same.[82] In order to further this intention, the Soviet strategy would be to forge an alliance with the poorer peasant and 'village proletarian' against the Kulak.[83] The Soviets were well aware that there was no natural class conflict among the peasantry, so one would be created, where two opposing hostile camps would be agitating each other, the "poor against the Kulaks (we noted that Applebaum also touched on this point with remarks in

---

[78] See Conquest, Harvest of Sorrow at P. 73-5. Conquest spends a bit of time surveying the various interpretation of this label and many inconsistencies, but concludes that the notion of a "well-healed" peasant is ultimately what was thought of to associate with the term "Kulak."

[79] Ibid.

[80] Ibid

[81] Ibid

[82] Ibid., 45.

[83] Ibid.

connection with Alexander Shlikhter)."[84] Class warfare had been a strategy for success the Bolsheviks used in seizing the cities, and it would be deployed in the countryside as well.

If the countryside was to be collectivized as Marxist doctrine dictated, then land owning peasants posed a problem. If collectivism ultimately meant the peasant would lose the ownership rights he had gained a mere half century earlier, then the question for the Bolsheviks would be how to accomplish such a policy objective that would not naturally lend itself to the consent of those subject to it. The answer was a class war where all frustration, anger and bitterness would be focused on a class of people perceived to be unjustly enriched from the prior order – the Kulaks.

Mr. Conquest notes one additional reason to demonize the Kulaks, and that had to do with the probability that without a class war, there was the potential that the Kulaks would naturally have assumed a leadership role or at least act as a source of influence among other peasants. Soviet policy would eventually seek to "decapitate" peasant resistance to collectivization and what better way to do that than go after the class of people most likely to arouse and orchestrate resistance within the group targeted for destruction. Getting rid of Kulaks would, in the eyes of both Lenin and Stalin, alleviate a potentially significant threat to collectivization efforts in the villages.

THE FORMAL DEFINITION OF "KULAK" BY THE SOVIET GOVERNMENT

We have spent a considerable amount of time discussing who the Kulaks were as a matter of history, from the evolution of serfdom to peasant, and then the better off class of peasants becoming known as Kulaks in the Russian and Ukrainian countryside. Over time, as the Bolshevik driven class warfare against the Kulaks escalated, the Soviet government, through the Council of Peoples Commissars would finally provide a formal definition of a Kulak farm by way of the Sovnarkom Resolution of May 21, 1929 and enumerate it in the Soviet Labor Code.[85] This was a decree from the Counsel of Peoples Commissars that codified the characteristics that would be the basis for the Soviet government to treat a peasant as a "Kulak", and thus be justified executing formal sanctions against them on that basis.[86] Under this decree, any of the following would be considered attributes of a Kulak: (1) use of hired labor; (2) ownership of a mill, a creamery, other processing equipment, or a complex machine with a mechanical motor; (3) systematic renting out of agricultural equipment or facilities; and, (4) involvement in trade, money lending, commercial brokerage, or other sources of non-labor income.[87]

This government action to formally identify who would be a Kulak was a crucial step in initiating the process of formally extirpating the Kulak peasant from Soviet civilization. The definition was broad enough so that almost any peasant could be prosecuted as a Kulak; moreover,

---

[84] Ibid

[85] Conquest, 100. *See also,* Internet Encyclopedia of Ukraine, *Kulak.* For full reference, see, http://www.encyclopediaofukraine.com/display.asp?linkpath=pages%5CK%5CU%5CKulak.htm.

[86] Ibid.

[87] Ibid. The definition provided in the Internet Encyclopedia of Ukraine notes that the definition also contained a reference to a minimum annual income of 300 Rubles per person or 1,500 Rubles per farm, and further suggests that this income threshold while not especially high for industrial workers, was on the high end for most peasant farmers. However, this parity would become problematic enough for the authorities to modify or relax this particular definitional element.

as Conquest notes, the republican, territorial and provincial authorities had wide latitude to adjust the definitions in the Sovnarkom decree to accommodate local conditions.[88] One has to marvel at the nimbleness of such a rule. There is nothing quite like a "living" legal definition subject to the whim of the local authorities to trample the rights of the average person. It is no co-incidence that it was Lavrentiy Beria (Stalin's longest serving secrete police chief) who coined the phrase, "show me the man and I will show you the crime," served as deputy premier from 1941 to his execution at the hands of Khrushchev in 1953. It appears the weaponization of the law was endemic throughout the entirety of the Stalin era. The Kulaks would get an early taste.

It is worth mentioning here that Anne Applebaum provides further detail on the matter of defining the Kulak farm by noting that in August of 1929, the *Ukrainian* Council of People's Commissars issued a decree identifying what would be termed "symptoms" of a Kulak farm.[89] The definition she summarizes is nearly identical to the one provided in the Sovnarkom Decree issued three months prior, but there are some nuances so I will re-state the definition she provides as follows: (1) A farm that regularly hired labor; (2) a farm that contained a mill, a tannery, a brick factory or other small "industrial" plant, (3) a farm that regularly rented out buildings or agricultural implements; and (4) any farm whose owners or managers involved themselves in trade, usury or any other activity that produced unearned income.[90]

She too acknowledges that this definition was allowed to evolve, and was not static, but she also brings to light the notion that Soviet authorities would employ a rationalization that even poor peasants who were not "technically" Kulaks by operation of these definitions could be viewed and treated as Kulaks.[91] The theory went that if an authority viewed the peasant as a "podkulachniki" or "under-Kulaks" or "Kulak agents", they would get the same treatment whether or not they satisfied any of the formal terms in the labor code.[92] Essentially this line of reasoning would come to be deployed in any instance where any peasant, regardless of status, refused to embrace the collective farm.[93] Suffice it to say that given the extreme numbers of persecuted Kulaks, numbering in the millions, the legal definitions quoted above would have been most a useful tool by operation of their breadth. This coupled with the definitional "adjustments" that were afforded local authorities essentially meant that anyone the government wanted to deem a Kulak would have been snagged in the wide legal net cast to scour the countryside of unwanted peasants.

When it comes time to explain why the 20th Century Kulak may well be analogous to the 21st Century affluent American, who in most cases is not even a farmer, the Sovnarkom decree of May 21, 1929 and the Ukrainian Decree issued in August of that year will be a central analytic focal point. Step aside from the Kulak's chosen occupation for a moment, and attempt to understand the labor code definitions in a more general sense; and we can see that it included anyone who hired another person, owned the means of production regarding some kind of business activity, owned equipment and facilities and earned non-labor income – why such a definition would include literally millions upon millions of Americans now wouldn't it? And if any of said

---

[88] Ibid.

[89] Applebaum, 147.

[90] Ibid.

[91] Ibid.

[92] Ibid.

[93] Ibid.

Americans happened to be "affluent", say, in the top 10% of income earners as defined by the US Census Bureau, well then, we would have the makings of an American Kulak now wouldn't we? There will be much MUCH more said on these points in Chapter 4.

THE ROLE OF UKRAINIAN NATIONALISM

As has been summarized earlier, there were two great threats to Soviet Rule in 1918, the peasantry and Ukrainian nationalism. Here we discuss the latter. Before we get into the specific notion of Ukrainian nationalism, it is useful to survey the writings of Marx and Lenin on the notion of nationalism generally. It is widely understood that Lenin was no fan of the idea that the right of nations to self-determination was superior to the interests of socialism. Nor was Stalin. Both had written with conviction that the right of the working class to consolidate power and embrace Marxist principles was a right higher than any right of a "nation" to govern itself.[94] To the extent the interests of the nation-state posed an obstacle to the preservation of a socialist republic, then the latter must take priority. These views represent a strict interpretation of Marxist doctrine that the proletariat is oppressed universally in all societies where the ownership of property and the means of production is in private, not collective hands. Lenin spoke of merging nations as an aim for socialism.[95]

As the Soviet Union was to be a republic with many other states, the idea of nationalism was not a minor affair for Lenin at the time of the Bolshevik revolution. He was acutely aware of the factious nationalistic movements and sought to approach the matter by bifurcating it. In pre-revolution writings, Lenin wrote that those nationalistic movements that would align with the socialist\Soviet interests would be tolerated; those that would not, would be crushed without mercy.[96]

In the early aftermath the October 1917 revolution, Mr. Conquest points out that the Soviets would learn an astringent lesson in just how entrenched the nationalistic sentiments were, particularly with respect to the Ukraine. He summarizes the long history of Ukrainian cultural and political interconnectedness going back all the way to even before Catherine the Great, but all through this historic intertwine, Ukraine maintained a stark independent streak for a number of reasons.[97] Anne Applebaum's *Red Famine* enumerates many of these reasons beginning with the fact that by the late Middle Ages, a distinct Ukrainian language evolved with Slavic roots in the territories that are now present day Ukraine.[98] They had also by then developed their own cultural identity with "their own food, their own customs and local traditions, their own villains, heroes and legends."[99] Applebaum further notes: "From the end of the Middle Ages onwards, the people of this region shared a sense of who they were, often, though not always, defining themselves in opposition to occupying foreigners, whether Polish or Russian."[100]

---

[94] Conquest, 32, citing the writings of Lenin and Stalin.

[95] Ibid., 31.

[96] Ibid., 32

[97] See Generally, R. Conquest, Chapter 2.

[98] Applebaum, 2-5.

[99] Ibid.

[100] Ibid., 5.

It is also worth mentioning with respect to the Ukraine that in addition to centuries long cultural ties as a Slavic people, the USSR needed Ukraine strategically, as its geographic location provided much needed agricultural output given the richness and fertility of its soil and a longer growing season. Much of Russia is frozen tundra, and another large portion is forest land with soil not especially hospitable to growing crops. It is not unreasonable to assume that the USSR was never going to allow the Ukraine to remain a sovereign state. There was too much shared yet contentious history between Ukraine and Russia, coupled with Ukraine's acute strategic relevance to establishing the USSR as an international socialist power.

Then there was the "fear factor." As noted, Marxist doctrine does not have much of a warm embrace to the idea of nationalism generally, and both Lenin and Stalin had reasons to be especially apprehensive of Ukrainian nationalism. Especially with regard to Stalin, who is dubiously credited with the most vicious forms of dekulakization, Applebaum succinctly articulates this fear when she writes in her Epilogue:

> "Eighty years later, it is possible to hear the echo of Stalin's fear of Ukraine – or rather his fear of unrest spreading from Ukraine to Russia – in the present too. Stalin spoke obsessively about loss of control in Ukraine, and about Polish or other foreign plots to subvert the country. He knew that Ukrainians were suspicious of centralized rule, that collectivization would be unpopular among peasants deeply attached to their land and their traditions, and that Ukrainian Nationalism was a galvanizing force, capable of challenging Bolshevism and even destroying it. ***A sovereign Ukraine could thwart the Soviet project, not only by depriving the USSR of its grain, but also by robbing it of legitimacy.*** Ukraine had been a Russian colony for centuries, Ukrainian and Russian Culture remained closely intertwined, the Russian and Ukrainian languages were closely related. ***If Ukraine rejected both the Soviet system and its ideology, that rejection could cast doubt upon the Soviet project. In 1991, that is precisely what it did***."[101] (Emphasis supplied)

The economic and political backdrop surrounding the plight of the Kulaks as discerned from the historical narrative explained in both *The Harvest of Sorrows,* and *Red Famine*, is one of strong Ukrainian national "feeling" or undercurrent juxtaposed with the intense aim of Soviet collectivization. This meant that a peasant living in the Ukraine found himself with two strikes against him in the eyes of the newly minted Soviet government. First, he was a peasant. Second, as a Ukrainian peasant he was suspected of possessing a nationalistic predisposition that could undermine Soviet objectives, which put him in the crosshairs of suspicion with Soviet officials before uttering a word. As we have noted, the Soviets feared the peasantry because, before 1933, they had not fully collectivized the rural countryside. The Bolsheviks consolidated power in the cities and urban areas relatively quickly. Not so in the countryside. Hence the peasantry was viewed with suspicion, and as noted earlier in this chapter, with outright disdain by the Bolsheviks. Ukrainian nationalism just added fuel to that fire. And in the worst position of all – the Kulak. A peasant – strike one; a Ukrainian peasant – strike 2; and, a Ukrainian Kulak peasant – strike 3, and he was odd man out. In the next chapter, we see that he was also basically a dead man walking.

---

[101] Ibid., 428.

The role of Ukrainian nationalism in fostering the vicious wrath of one of the most evil men to have ever inhabited our world will be a central point of contention in the event a Marxist regime ever comes to control the American institutions of government. The American left routinely derides what it sees as a sort of "corny voice crackling patriotism" of the American masses. It treats any form of American nationalism with disdain, and if the strain of nationalism is associated with people of Anglo, Nordic, Teutonic or Caucasian descent, then it is chalked up to "white nationalism" and quickly placed in the moral company of fascism and Nazi-ism. Any expression regarding "love of country" is viewed as an embrace of America's history of oppression and white supremacy. It is not an unreasonable point of view for a mainstream American, libertarian or conservative to see the present-day left, with its often-stated Marxist based economic message, as being staunchly antagonistic towards the notion of American nationalism.

When and if the day comes that America finds itself ruled under the strictures of Marxist dogma, there will certainly be a clash between the masses who adore America's heritage, warts and all, and those Marxist elites who would be running America who view nationalism as a sort of cancer to be eradicated. This clash may not be at all a peaceful affair. In fact, just the opposite is the more likely. As we will demonstrate later in Chapters five and six, American socialists are increasingly radicalizing around purist Marxist doctrine by asserting that entire industries should be nationalized and that confiscatory levels of taxation should be the order of the day. This is likely to provoke a resistance amongst America's affluent class which holds a considerable amount of assets, but is not "rich", putting them in a political and economic position analogous to that of the Kulak. It simply is not irrational to point out the similar situation a staunchly patriotic small-town business owner with a million or two in assets (again, affluent but not "rich") will ferociously resist collectivism, high taxation and the nationalization of his affiliated industries. It is equally plausible that a furiously determined Marxist elite that regularly shows its disdain for the "deplorables" would be very capable and even inclined to use a militarized federal government to eliminate any resistance.

Just so the left-minded reader, or outright Marxist, reading this understands in the clearest possible terms, those of us who revere the principles of free enterprise, and believe it has brought more good into the world and improved the human condition better than any economic system yet to be devised; for us, collectivism and nationalization are one in the same. They are synonymous. Whatever pithy academic differentiation can be made between the two is irrelevant in every-day life, for their effect is the same. Both result in the loss of private ownership of property and the fruits that can be harvested from that ownership. Therefore, to the extent that Kulaks resisted "collectivization" of farming versus the bourgeoisie industrial owner or manager in a large Soviet city resisting "nationalization" of industry – the distinction is one without a difference. Both the Kulak and the industrialist are two peas in the same pod. Prior to the Bolsheviks, both had an ownership interest in real property or improvements thereon, and both enjoyed the fruits of their work or their investment. Both would have this stripped from them by the Bolsheviks and any resistance was met with severe violence.

The Kulaks resisted collectivization and ultimately paid for it with their lives. Every day Americans will resist any 21st Century version of collectivism and will surely face prosecution from a weaponized IRS in the event of a tax revolt, and resistance to the tax collection could bring in other armed federal agencies. As we will see later in the book, the federal government already has a massive armed infrastructure that can easily be brought to bear on cracking down on unruly and overly nationalistic masses who refuse to "get with the Marxist program". If this seems outlandish, ask yourself whether any citizen of any of the murderous communist regimes ever saw their genocide coming until it was upon them. From Lenin/Stalin to Mau to Pol Pot, how many citizens saw the carnage that was to come until they were in the middle of it? Did an affluent peasant in Russia or Ukraine 1915 have any idea of what would be in store for them in the decades that followed? The next chapter is for the purpose of understanding just how far a Marxist regime will go to adhere to purist Marxist principles such as collectivist farming and the nationalization of industry.

CHAPTER III

FORMAL STATE SPONSORED EXTIRPATION OF THE KULAKS

I dedicate this
to all those who did not live
to tell it.
And may they please forgive me
for not having seen it all
nor remembered it all,
for not having divined all of it.

-Aleksandr Isayevich Solzhenitsyn
Dedication of The Gulag Archipelago 1918-56

One of the greatest Russian literary works in the 20th Century was crafted by a survivor of the Soviet Gulag prison system by the name of Aleksandr Isayevich Solzhenitsyn entitled the Gulag Archipelago, originally published as a three volume set in the early 1970s.[102] This prodigious account of the Soviet Gulag prison system was one of the most widely published works throughout the industrialized world in the last quarter of the century of its' publication. It has sold millions of copies in America alone. Solzhenitsyn's account of Soviet imprisonment is crucial in our understanding of one of the great genocidal massacres in human history, not just because he was a splendid writer, he was all of that, but more importantly he was a literal eyewitness to the horrors of this system having received an 11 year prison sentence. His crime was that he included remarks critical of Soviet policy in letters he wrote to a colleague while serving in the Red Army. These letters were intercepted by Soviet intelligence authorities, and Solzhenitsyn's fate would be sealed for the rest of his life. It is simply no exaggeration to refer to the Gulag Archipelago as an epic body of work. Solzhenitsyn will be relied upon heavily as an authority regarding what life would have been like for Soviet Kulak peasants sentenced to these prisons.

During the first years of Soviet rule, as power was consolidated and entrenched, Lenin nearly immediately began to arrest political dissenters, persons thought to be resisters to the Bolshevik Revolution, officers in the Russian army who served under the Tsars, the religious and essentially

---

[102] Aleksandr Solzhenitsyn, *The Gulag Archipelago 1918 – 56,* (The Harvill Press London, abridged edition 1986). The *Gulag Archipelago* was originally published as a three volume set, but the version cited for this book is the one volume abridgement of the original three volume work. As Solzhenitsyn himself said in the Forward to the abridged version, it is for the purpose of facilitating the reading of the work for those who have limits on their time. As this book provides an eyewitness account of the severe and malicious nature of communist rule, the abridged version of *Gulag* is "must reading" for all informed citizens in a free society.

any other human being thought to pose a threat to Soviet authority.[103] Solzhenitsyn puts the arbitrariness and malevolence of the selection process very succinctly by stating:

> "There is also no little difficulty in deciding whether we should classify among the prison waves or on the balance sheets of the Civil War [Bolshevik Revolution] those tens of thousands of *hostages*, i.e., people not personally accused of anything, those peaceful citizens not even listed by name, who were taken off and destroyed simply to terrorize or wreak vengeance on a military enemy of a rebellious population.
>
> This action was in effect explained openly (Latsis, in the newspaper *Red Terror,* November 1, 1918): 'We are not fighting against single individuals. ***We are exterminating the bourgeoisie as a class. It is not necessary during the interrogation to look for evidence proving that the accused opposes the Soviets by word or action. The first question which you should ask him is what class does he belong to, what is his origin, his education and his profession. These are the questions that will determine the fate of the accused. Such is the sense and essence of Red Terror*. ...'"* (Emphasis Supplied) [104]

The 21st Century American, long accustomed to the rule of law, not of men, and to the due process protections provided in our constitutional governance structure, would surely be appalled at such mean-spirited arbitrariness used in meting out harsh punishments. The idea of formal government policy articulated in the starkest possible terms that an entire class of people should be "exterminated" is an anathema to every long-held value mainstream America has.

We know from a large body of scholarship and academic work brilliantly summarized by Robert Conquest in *The Harvest of Sorrow* cited at length in the last chapter, that staggering numbers of Soviet peasants, including Kulaks met their end in these gulags or from starvation by formally forced famine.[105] We also introduced work from Anne Applebaum entitled *Red Famine* which demonstrated definitively that the famines of 1931-33 where not accidental results of bad policy, but were intentionally administered by Stalin's government. In *Red Famine* she touches on the Gulags as a means for brutally enforcing Soviet rule, but it is her work in *Gulag: A History*, for which she would win the prestigious Pulitzer Prize, that she covers the historical narrative of the Gulag prison system in mind numbing detail.[106]

The purpose of delving deep into what happened to the Kulaks and the various methods used to crack their resistance is to illustrate in the starkest possible terms, the lengths a committed Marxist regime will go towards implementing the core components of Marxism, primarily collectivization and nationalization of industries. Therefore, we will explore later in this Chapter

---

[103] Ibid, 21-23.

[104] Ibid.

[105] Conquest, 127. Mr. Conquest points out at the beginning of Chapter 6, where the fate of the Kulaks is discussed in detail, that "the destruction of the Kulaks was in part designed to decapitate the peasantry in its resistance to the imposition of the new order." Ibid., 117.

[106] Anne Applebaum, *Gulag: A History,* (First Anchor Books Edition, 2004, Copyright 2003).

what kind of literal hell on earth these camps were, and the additional atrocities the Soviet government exacted on the Kulaks and others deemed a threat to the state.

Americans simply *must* understand the gulag experience as academic institutions in our country are and have been derelict in their duty in this regard. Very little is taught of these events, as your author can attest, being a product of the liberal arts department of a large well-regarded west coast university. In the four years I studied Political Science, I cannot recall a single text, reading assignment, or lecture that even mentioned Solzhenitsyn's name. And I went to University in the mid-1980's!!! – about the same time Robert Conquest published the *Harvest of Sorrow*. I only heard of this book and of Solzhenitsyn via a newspaper article in a conservative journal I had read at the time. Nothing about the book, the Kulaks or the gulag was ever mentioned in any of my advanced coursework in those years. Fast forward to today, if Americans are to wander carelessly down the path of Marxism in the name of ending "income inequality" and "fairness", they owe it to their posterity to have considered the known and proven atrocities committed under Marxist rule over the past 100 years. Once started on the primrose path to collectivism, it may be next to impossible to leave, and that path may lead to an absolutely horrid place.

Before plunging into the horrific details, it is useful to explore the progression of harassment that the Soviet government deployed on the Kulaks before it got ever got to the point of actually arresting and deporting, or summarily executing them *en masse,* recognizing that harsh treatment befell the peasantry and in particular, the Kulak very early in the Soviet regime. This progression will be highly relevant to the assertion that a newly minted Marxist American government might treat the affluent similarly to the way the Soviets treated the Kulaks in the event the affluent were to resist official collectivist policy in any way.

THE PHASES OF KULAK DESTRUCTION

Governments rarely start out a genocide by "shooting first" on a mass scale. There is usually some kind of build-up, a phase where the targeted class is defined, demonized and then subjected to increasing levels of hostility. So it was with the Kulaks.

We have already discussed in the last Chapter how the Soviet government formally identified and defined a Kulak for purposes of formal persecution, and we covered some of the ways in which they were formally denigrated and demeaned by government officials up to and including Lenin and Stalin themselves. Once the group or subgroup targeted for persecution is identified and properly vilified, the next logical step is to then initiate formal hostile actions against them with increasing frequency and severity. As is so often typical in the first stages of oppression, one of the main tools the Soviets used in "ratcheting up" such aggression on the peasantry was to increase production quotas and "taxes" on production of the Kulak farmers, and if they fail to meet either one, their land, homes, equipment and agricultural output in their possession were confiscated and sold off.[107] Outright refusal to pay the taxes resulted in being sent off to forced labor on the gulags.[108]

---

[107] Ibid., 135. Here Conquest notes that there are literally hundreds of first-hand accounts of what happened to those unfortunate enough to be considered a Kulak, and then proceeds to chronicle several of them in explicit detail.
[108] Ibid.

The open hostility towards the Kulaks came in phases which are depicted concisely in the Internet Encyclopedia of Ukraine. The phases are noted as follows:

1) <u>Ukrainian-Soviet War, 1917–21</u>:

Soviet Scholars estimate that in 1917 the Kulaks were 12.2% of peasant households throughout the Ukraine representing over a half a million households, but had quickly fallen out of favor with the new Soviet government.[109] During the Ukrainian-Soviet War, over a period of four years, nearly all Kulak farms were annihilated.[110] The initial method used by the Bolsheviks to destroy a Kulak farm would be to seize or confiscate any surplus grain the farmer had in his possession, and his land as well as any farm equipment or livestock.[111] Furthermore, concurrent with the Ukrainian – Soviet War was a period referred to as "War Communism", which involved official governmental decrees by the Soviet regime, making it illegal to employ another worker (by prohibiting the "exploitation" of another man's labor), and formally abolished the leasing of land.[112] It was during this period that the official term and notion of "dekulakization" was introduced.[113]

This period was also the beginning of the formal collectivization efforts by the soviet government where Kulak farms and other private property were impounded outright by the government and the Kulaks literally driven from their villages.[114] As we have noted throughout this book, any resistance to these governmental actions resulted in either being shot on site, deported, or sent to a gulag.

2) <u>New Economic Policy Era</u>:

During this period, the Kulak continued to be regarded as a class enemy, even as the Soviet government eased some of the restrictions on leasing of land and hiring of workers, mainly skilled tradesmen such as a blacksmith or a Sheppard.[115] The Soviet government refused to allow the children of Kulak farmers to enlist in the Red Army or attend post-secondary schools; a Kulak was not allowed to vote, assume any official position in government or even get a bank loan or receive a tax reduction available to others.[116]

It was also in this period that tax policy became a weapon of mass destruction. As we noted earlier in this Chapter, taxes are a universal method of mischief for governments inclined to oppress a targeted class of people. So it was with the Soviets in their increasingly aggressive dekulakization efforts. By the late 1920s and early 1930s it was not uncommon for a "well to do"

---

[109] Internet Encyclopedia Ukraine. See specifically:
http://www.encyclopediaofukraine.com/display.asp?linkpath=pages%5CK%5CU%5CKulak.htm.
[110] Ibid.
[111] Ibid.
[112] Ibid.
[113] Ibid.
[114] Ibid.
[115] Ibid.
[116] Ibid.

peasant to pay upwards of 85% of his gross income in taxes, as opposed to a more reasonable 20% of gross income for an urban worker or functionary – resulting in them having a net after-tax income almost eight times that of the peasant with similar gross income.[117] To add insult to injury, the purchasing power of the ruble in the countryside was a mere 16% of what it was in the more favored urban state sector, so the net effect is that, in the countryside, the ruble purchased a mere $1/6^{th}$ of what it would for a worker in the city.[118]

Ms. Applebaum also touched on the use of heavy-handed taxation of the Kulaks as a method of confiscation in *Red Famine*. The extent of the tax burden and the utter brutality with which it was enforced is succinctly chronicled when she writes:

> "In some instances expropriation took place through the means of heavy, retrospective taxation. One peasant donated his livestock to the collective farm. He worked for a year, but then tried to take his cows back: his children were starving and he needed the milk. He was allowed to do so, but the following day he was asked to pay the heavy taxes required of the "individual" peasant. To do so, he had to sell a cow, two goats, and some clothes. Taxes kept increasing anyway, until the family finally had to sell the house and move into the barn where they slept on the hay. Eventually they escaped, blending into the urban landscape of Leningrad."[119]

She goes on to note instances where the authorities used taxation as a form of dekulakization, describing a situation where a farmer, who had recently had his cow confiscated, was nevertheless imposed with tax quotas for butter, cheese and milk, which they no longer had; and when there was nothing left to give, the authorities began to confiscate all possessions whatever, up to and including the residence.[120] Hence the Soviet tax policy as applied to the Kulak and other well-off peasants was designed to virtually ensure a fetid and inhumane level of poverty.

3) <u>The Era of Forced Famine, Deportation, and the Gulag – All On Steroids:</u>

The third and final era of dekulakization was the most genocidal and horrific. Robert Conquest in his masterful work *The Harvest of Sorrow* refers to the period 1932 – 33 alone as the "Terror Famine".[121] In Chapter 16 of his book, Mr. Conquest in summarizing the available scholarship and official government records, attempts the gruesome task of re-capitulating the death toll from this final phase of dekulakization (1930-37). Specifically, he estimates 11 million "peasant dead", with 3.5 million more arrested in this period and ultimately dying in the gulags, for a staggering grand total of 14.5 million dead.[122] Of this there were an estimated 6.5 million peasants killed as a direct result of formal dekulakization, and a mind boggling 7 million additionally killed in the

---

[117] Ibid.

[118] Ibid.

[119] Applebaum, *Red Famine,* 152.

[120] Ibid., 151 – 152.

[121] Conquest, 4.

[122] Ibid., 306

1932-33 "terror-famine" as he has called it, with five million of those deaths specific to Ukraine.[123] Among academic historical circles world-wide, what Conquest refers to as the "Terror Famine" is commonly termed "Holodomor," which refers to the extermination by way of famine in the Ukraine, (so "Holodomor" = "Terror Famine" of 1932-33).[124] Literally translated, Holodomor means "death inflicted by starvation."[125]

We Americans simply have no historical recollection of such genocide on our soil on such a massive scale. To be sure, American history has its own atrocities with slavery and the treatment of Native American's foremost in our minds; but fourteen and a half million souls systematically and viciously crushed by their own government is of a magnitude rarely matched in human history. Even the five million Ukrainian deaths that occurred in the Terror Famine according to Conquest constituted approximately 13% of the Ukraine's total population at the time. For present day U.S., 13% of 330 million would be a death toll of 42.9 million souls. There is nothing – no event - in the American collective memory that even comes close to killing that many people. We entered WWII because of the attach on Pearl Harbor where naval casualties were a bit less than 3,000 souls. We initiated the War on Terror because of the 9/11 attacks which had a similar casualty count. These are miniscule losses compared to what was exacted on the people of Ukraine by their own government. To be clear, in making this comparison, I do not seek to downplay the atrocities of Pearl Harbor or the 9/11 attacks, I merely seek to demonstrate the stunning magnitude of what befell the good people of Ukraine in the Holodomor. The word that comes to mind from the recitation of the foregoing is – staggering. The death toll itself was staggering. We can add up all civilian and active duty combat related casualties for every war America has been involved in since July 4, 1776 and the number is a bit over one million, occurring over 240+ years. Losses like what was inflicted on the Soviet peasantry, particularly in the Ukraine, was, well - staggering. The individual human suffering and agony was equally astonishing.

When Anne Applebaum published *Red Famine* two decades after Conquest published *The Harvest of Sorrow,* she covered much the same material as did Conquest but she benefited from two decades of access to official Ukrainian and Russian documents and scholarship that became available after the fall of the USSR. On the matter of tabulating the death toll from the Soviet persecution of the peasantry in connection with the manufactured famine of 1932-33, Applebaum's tabulation is pretty much in line with that of Mr. Conquest. She acknowledges that there had previously been a wide range of estimates on this point ranging from 2 million to 10 million.[126] She the proceeds to summarize some relatively recent work from Ukrainian demographers and enhanced statistical measuring methodologies, there is growing consensus around an estimate of 4.5 million "missing Ukrainians" either as a direct result of starvation in the famine of 1932-33, or "lost births", i.e., births that did not occur due to the famine, relative to what would have otherwise been expected.[127] Dr. Conquest had estimated five million Ukrainian peasant deaths from the "Terror Famine." As the tie breaker, we turn to the writings of Oleh Wolowyna, whose published work for the Holodomor Research and Education Consortium at the Canadian Institute

---

[123] Ibid.

[124] Holodomor Research And Education Consortium Website, *Introduction*, (Canadian Institute of Ukrainian Studies, University of Alberta as of 2019).

[125] Ibid.

[126] Applebaum, 333.

[127] Ibid.

of Ukrainian Studies at the University of Alberta arrives at the conclusion the Holodomor death toll at approximately 4 million Ukrainian deaths.[128] Given that these numbers are statistical estimates and the methodologies could well undergo future revision, just as prior methodology has, I see no reason not to go with the original estimate set forth by Dr. Conquest. Therefore, for purposes of the point being made in *American Kulak,* we will consider the all-encompassing 14.5 million figure offered by Dr. Conquest to be the reasonably authoritative grand sum of all murdered peasants as a result of Soviet hostile actions whether by way of treatment in the Gulag, execution, forced relocation to inhospitable territories or by government contrived famine. His 1986 estimates have held up reasonably well over the past 34 years.

The death toll summarized above suggests the barbarity of what the Soviets did in this period cannot be overstated or exaggerated. Every adverse adjective and adverb in the English language could be deployed and it would not be out of proportion to the utter inhumanity that took place for these fourteen and half million human beings. An arachnologist treats his entrapped specimens with more dignity and care than the butchery that was shown these unfortunate people, whose main crime was the "perceived" threat they posed to the Soviet government, one of the most monstrous reigns in human history. Ronald Reagan was in no way using hyperbole when he referred to the Soviet Union as the "Evil Empire", for that is exactly what it was.

In order to fully understand the inhumanity and outright boorish brutality of Soviet Policy towards the Kulaks, there is a useful passage from *The History Place™*. The excerpt below illustrates nicely what it would have been like to live as a Kulak in this period:

> "Declared "enemies of the people," the Kulaks were left homeless and without a single possession as everything was taken from them, even their pots and pans. ***It was also forbidden by law for anyone to aid dispossessed Kulak families.*** Some researchers estimate that ten million persons were thrown out of their homes, put on railroad box cars and deported to "special settlements" in the wilderness of Siberia during this era, with up to a third of them perishing amid the frigid living conditions. Men and older boys, along with childless women and unmarried girls, also became slave-workers in Soviet-run mines and big industrial projects."[129] (Emphasis added)

To be considered a Kulak was a virtual death sentence, if not on the spot for in any way resisting collectivization efforts, then by deportation or imprisonment in the gulag. As the afore cited passage notes, the demonization of the Kulak meant fellow peasants were not able to assist in any legal way. The Kulak was literally thrown to the streets and into the elements with nothing but the clothes on their backs. Another passage from The History Place™ offers additional color on the plight of the Kulak:

> "Mothers in the countryside sometimes tossed their emaciated children onto passing railroad cars traveling toward cities such as Kiev in the hope someone

---

[128] Oleh Wolowyna *Understanding Holodomor Loss Numbers,* (Holodomor Research And Education Consortium, Canadian Institute of Ukrainian Studies, University of Alberta as of 2019).

[129] The History Place, *Genocide in the Twentieth Century.* See, http://www.historyplace.com/worldhistory/genocide/stalin.htm.

there would take pity. But in the cities, children and adults who had already flocked there from the countryside were dropping dead in the streets, with their bodies carted away in horse-drawn wagons to be dumped in mass graves. Occasionally, people lying on the sidewalk who were thought to be dead, but were actually still alive, were also carted away and buried.

While police and Communist Party officials remained quite well fed, desperate Ukrainians ate leaves off bushes and trees, killed dogs, cats, frogs, mice and birds then cooked them. Others, gone mad with hunger, resorted to cannibalism, with parents sometimes even eating their own children."[130]

The one primary emotion that comes to mind upon reading such passages is the revulsion at the pure evil of it all. Nothing about the Soviet treatment of Kulaks and other peasants could even be remotely considered reasonable by any civilized person. The treatment of the Kulak was quite simply one of the most mean-spirited acts of inhumanity as any ever recorded in human history. As hard as this mercilessness is to fathom for those of us living comfortable lives in the peaceful West, more must be said. As we have shown, the scholarship on the Kulak experience points to at least 3.5 million peasants, including Kulaks, meeting their violent end in the Gulags, we must understand what life was like in these camps. If radical Venezuelan socialism or Soviet style communism ever comes to America, as I suspect it could, then the alarm must be sounded and Americans casually flirting with hard left Marxism must be reminded of the fact that in nearly all of the examples of such systems over the last 100 years, there were some form of concentration camp – or gulag.

THE GULAG AS HELL ON EARTH: DEATH BY THE MOST PROTRACTED AND EXCRUCIATING MEANS AVAILABLE

As we started out this chapter with Aleksandr Isayevich Solzhenitsyn, we shall conclude it with him. His prodigious work, *Gulag Archipelago* provides us with a sobering first-hand account of what it would be like to live in these destructive labor camps, as he called them. Rather than explain the entire story of Mr. Solzhenitsyn's experience in these camps, which is not the main thrust of this book, I will draw on selected excerpts from it that provide an apt illustration of the horror these camps entailed. We also have previously referenced *Gulag: A History,* by Anne Applebaum, which provides additional Pulitzer Prize winning scholarship to our understanding of what transpired in these dreadful places. While Solzhenitsyn is valuable for his first-hand account of what went on the such camps, Applebaum provides an intricate, well documented historical narrative. Both works will be relied upon to recapitulate the life in a Soviet Gulag.

First, a relevant caveat from Ms. Applebaum in *Gulag*, where she begins Chapter 10 with a summary of the number of camps estimated to have existed, and in so doing, provides the important qualification that there was significant variation in the living conditions from camp to camp, and within camps at different times.[131] Furthermore, not all camps were equally horrific, with some

---

[130] Ibid.

[131] Applebaum, *Gulag*, 183-184.

being run by "relatively" humane boss versus the many sadists in the system.[132] With that caveat acknowledged, she does state that, especially in 1937-38 Stalin and his lieutenants had allowed some of the Gulags to function as death camps, with all the dreadfulness that implies.[133] For the remainder of this chapter, it is the death camp aspect of the gulag that we will focus on, particularly as recalled by Mr. Solzhenitsyn in his capacity as one of history's eye-witnesses to the horror of it all.

I see this as a highly relevant exercise due to the fact that many millions of American young people in the early decades of the 21st Century are being seduced by the Marxist utopian ideal which formed the political impetus for the gulag in the first place (i.e., had there been no Marxist driven forced collectivization where private property was seized by the state, there would not have been anywhere near the resistance to Bolshevism). As the reader will see, these young and often uniformed Americans have absolutely no idea of the madness and destitution they are flirting with. Here is where Mr. Solzhenitsyn can help.

In Chapter 7 of The *Archipelago (abridged version)*, Solzhenitsyn describes the harshness of daily living in these repulsive places. Essentially the daily life of a "native" as he called them (we would consider them 'inmates'), is one of work, work, more work, and then of more work after that.[134] As for the conditions of such work, he was straightforward – starvation, frigid cold and cunning; subtle atrocities were common, as prisoners were made to do manual labor such as unloading bricks without gloves where the skin wears off the fingers and hands rather quickly. To haul the heavy bricks with a shoulder barrow, to dig peat in a bog, waist deep in mud, mine coal by manually digging, ditto with copper and lead where the toxic soot lines the mouth and nose. He writes of logging where men labor through snow that comes up to the chest, feeling out the branches through the snow which must be cut off before the tree can be cut up.[135] All of what is described is backbreaking work under the most inhospitable circumstances. Prisoners were worked up to 10-14 hours in the bitter cold, extremely malnourished or starving outright. It was not uncommon for the prisoners to be made to work in weather as cold as 60 degrees below 0; those who froze to death on such days were ascribed another cause of death by the camp authorities. Those literally crawling back to the camp, no longer able to walk were simply shot by the guards.[136] The prisoners were dressed in rags, if they had shoes at all, they were often makeshift items such as taking a used automobile tire and tying it onto bottom of the bare foot with a wire or electric chord.[137] No insulation from the frigid cold, or from the wet snow or mud.

Solzhenitsyn describes the physical appearance of his fellow Archipelago inhabitants as "…bronze-gray camp faces …. Eyes oozing with tears, red eyelids. White cracked lips, covered with sores. Skewbald, unshaven bristles on the faces. In winter … a summer cap with earflaps sewn on.[138] He also admonishes his reader that what is described is in reference to an established camp already in operation. As for building an entirely new camp, the prisoners ("zekes" as he

---

[132] Ibid., 184.

[133] Ibid.

[134] Solzhenitsyn, 220.

[135] Ibid., 220 – 223.

[136] Ibid.

[137] Ibid., 224.

[138] Ibid.

often refers to them) would arrive at a desired location in the cold snowy forest, start stretching wire from tree to tree and start the process of constructing the barracks.[139] He then chillingly states that whoever managed to survive this construction process until the first barracks knew that the structure would be for the guard and not the prisoners, who were often left to sleep in a dugout in the ground or a tent – no matter the temperature conditions.[140] He ascribes the entire experience as "the special process of narrowing the intellectual and spiritual horizons of a human being, the reduction of the human being to an animal and the process of dying alive."[141]

Gulag Archipelago, enumerates the ghastly detail of the effects of starvation on the inmates. Solzhenitsyn painstakingly describes the fighting between inmates to get sloppy food waste, sometimes getting killed in the process; he talks of emaciated humanity or "bags of bones which are still joined together," dying on hospital beds.[142] Inmates did not dare even to pretend to be sick. If one was ill, he or she worked anyway, under any conditions. Solzhenitsyn describes the gruesome physical conditions prisoners often worked through, such as scurvy, where the mouth bleeds when taking even a bite of bread, teeth fall out, gums rot, and ulcers appear on ones legs; or pellagra, where the face turns dark, diarrhea sets in, the skin begins to peel and fall off in whole chunks, and one begins to smell like a corpse.[143] According to Solzhenitsyn, they worked through it all nevertheless. To illustrate the dreadful last stages of those who were ill, yet still carried by fellow inmates out of the camp to work, I will quote the following passage:

> "The man grows weaker, weaker, and the bigger he is, the faster it goes. He has already become so weak that he cannot climb to the top bunks, he cannot step across the log in his path; he has to lift his leg with his two hands or else crawl on all fours. The diarrhea takes out of man both strength and all interest – in other people, in life, in himself. He grows deaf and stupid, and he loses all capacity to weep, even when he is being dragged along the ground behind a sledge. He is no longer afraid of death; he is wrapped in a submissive, rosy glow. He has crossed all boundaries and has forgotten the name of his wife, of his children, and finally his own name too. **Sometimes the entire body of a man dying of starvation is covered with blue-black pimples like peas, with puss-filled heads smaller than a pinhead – his face, arms, legs and trunk, even his scrotum. It is so painful it cannot be touched. The tiny boils come to a head and burst and a thick wormlike string of pus is forced out of them. _The man is rotting alive_.**[144] (Emphasis added).

The next time you engage with someone pre-disposed with Marxist tendencies, feel free to recall this passage. The next time you hear an imbecile like Michael Moore or some other Hollywood drip case espouse the virtues of socialism, feel free to refer him to Solzhenitsyn and the above passage. We owe it to those who suffered this horrid mistreatment at the hands of Marxists to never forget their plight, and to be willing to die preventing it from ever occurring

---

[139] Ibid., 225.

[140] Ibid.

[141] Ibid.

[142] Ibid., 226-227.

[143] Ibid., 227.

[144] Ibid., 227-228.

again. Millions of innocent peasants and their better off Kulak brethren suffered unimaginable physical hardship because of the threat they were perceived to have posed. If you want an idea of the agony of these camps, imagine you are in a large Midwestern city like Chicago or Minneapolis, or in a Northeastern one like Boston, and you happen to be there in the middle of winter. Imagine putting on a *light j*acket to go out in 0 degree weather for fifteen minutes and do a chore with no gloves on. Then think of the starving, scantily clad Kulak doing the same work in such weather – or even much colder, all while under the threat of instant execution or a brutal beating if they did not comply. And then think of what it would be like to be violently coerced to do your chore under those conditions for up to 14 hours each day. No relief, no warm clothes, no warm barracks to go back to in order to escape the pain. You have only the knowledge that this is your fate until your body gives in. If the Soviet gulag was not hell on earth, then what would be?

Not to belabor the point, or to dwell on the macabre details, there is one additional chapter from Solzhenitsyn's *Gulag Archipelago* that I will cover, even though it pertains to a period in the history of the gulag camps that would transpire well after the liquidation of most of the Kulaks (by about five years). The reason for discussing these events is that his description of events so meticulously embodies the *intentional* evil of the Stalinist era and appalling brutality of these camps. What happened in them during this period was no accident, as will be explained momentarily. This is the phase where the gulag began to take on a more formal and explicit role as murder camps. The "katorga" phase of these camps, which begins in the middle of the Second World War would, as Solzhenitsyn himself would say, came to combine all the worst of the gulags with the worst of the Soviet prisons.[145]

We start with Part V of the *Gulag Archipelago*, which is entitled, as you might expect – *Katorga*. Chapter one of this part is entitled quite simply "The Doomed." What I am about to synopsize for you is every bit as sickening as any other excerpt from *Gulag Archipelago* that I have already covered. Here Solzhenitsyn defines the word katorga, which means "hard labor" or "penal servitude".[146] Stalin had formally reintroduced this concept for the gulag in 1943.[147] Whatever the gulag was in terms of its severity before 1943, its purpose would become literally to work inmates to their death; and Solzhenitsyn describes the katorga camps as unconcealed murder camps, where death was to be prolonged as long possible with maximum suffering.[148] Two-hundred prisoners were crammed in physical structures or "huts" built for 80, they were worked for 12 hours per day, in two shifts, with no days off.[149] While working the prisoners were quarantined by guards with dogs; suffered routine beatings, often without cause; and when returning from work, guards would periodically fire on the prisoners with their automatic battlefield weapons, again usually without cause, and not be held responsible or accountable for any casualties.[150] The prisoners were most expendable.

---

[145] Ibid., 332

[146] Solzhenitsyn, 331.

[147] Ibid.

[148] Ibid.

[149] Ibid.

[150] Ibid.

The following except is taken from this Chapter and depicts prison transfers from one camp to another. He writes:

> "…Part of these twelve [rest] hours went to moving [the prisoners] form one camp area to another, parading them, searching them. Once in the living area, they were immediately taken into a "tent" which was never ventilated – a windowless hut – and locked in. In the winter a foul sour stench hung so heavy in the camp air that no one unused to it could endure it for two minutes. The living area was even less accessible to the *katorzhane* than the camp work area. They were never allowed to go to the latrine, nor to the mess hut, nor to the medical section. All their needs were served by the latrine bucket and feeding hatch. Such was Stalin's katorga as it took shape in 1943-44: a combination of all that was worst in the camps with all that was worst in the Prisons. … According to the camp records, which were not meant to preserve for history **the fact that political prisoners were also starved to death,** they were entitled to supplementary "miner's rations" and "bonus dishes," which were miserable enough even before three lots of thieves got at them." … So that out of twelve leisure hours in the cell, barely four remained for undisturbed sleep. Then again, *katorzhane* were of course paid no money, nor had they any right to receive parcels or letters. **The *katorzhane* responded nicely to this treatment and quickly died.** (Emphasis added).[151]

This orchestrated massacre, described so vividly by a survivor, is an eye-witness testimony of what had become formal Soviet policy. Solzhenitsyn goes on page after page with the atrocious details of the murder of millions of peasants, political dissidents, prisoners of war, or other "enemies of the state", and to read it all requires a "cast-iron stomach", as my grandfather might have said. But as tough a read as it may be, it is essential that the civilized world be constantly reminded of how uncivilized even a developed country can be.

In fact, an argument can be made that once a well-developed industrialized country is lost to a mad man, the sophisticated infrastructure available to him amplifies the tragedy by orders of magnitude. Solzhenitsyn, reminds his readers that nothing whatsoever in relation to the gulag system was happenstance or random. It was official state business planned out in painstaking officious detail. He notes the formal position of the Soviet government, by way of a March 26, 1928 Council of People's Commissars (the "Council') recommendation that the gulag and prison systems, originally amped up under Lenin, had become inadequate and needed to be more severe.[152] Specifically, the Council decreed that harsh methods of subjugation should be administered on enemies of the Soviet state (i.e., class enemies), basically anyone deemed a threat to the order, and expressly that forced labor would be a key component of this control, and therefore, admonished that the forced labor camp capacity should be expanded.[153]

As the camps themselves were intentionally treacherous for the prisoners, Applebaum in *Gulag* provides some additional grimm color on the atrocity of the Gulag system by just describing the

---

[151] Ibid., 332 - 33

[152] Ibid., 193.

[153] Ibid.

conditions in which prisoners were *transported* to the camps and between them. It wasn't enough just to be inhumane in the camps themselves, getting to them and between them had to be merciless as well. She writes:

> "…but the prisoners who came after [Princess Volkonskaya] could not even hear the word *e'tap* – prison jargon for "transport" – without feeling a jolt of mouth-drying fear, even terror. Every journey was a wrenching leap into the unknown, a move away from familiar cell mates and familiar arrangements, however poor those might be. Worse, the process of moving prisoners from prison to prison, from transit prison to camp, and between camps within the system, was physically grueling and openly cruel. In some senses, it was the most inexplicable aspect of life in the Gulag."[154]

Applebaum describes the unspeakable stomach-churning details in page after page.[155] She recalls stories of ordeals that tear at the readers heartstrings and others that put butterflies in the gut. It was not uncommon for prisoners to be placed in absurdly overcrowded holding cells, crammed in with other inmates and not given any opportunity to use a latrine. When a prisoner's organs could no longer hold back, they would soil themselves to the point of soiling those immediately next to them. She documents the melancholy fact of gang rape on these journeys and voyages, sometimes to the point of death. Political prisoners were often put at the bottom of cargo holds on transport ships, and when prisoners directly above them vomited due to sea-sickness, the putrid fluids would reign down through the grated floors onto these political prisoners. There were common instances of starvation, of being crammed into overcrowded rail cars in sweltering heat or bitter cold; of the sick being denied medical treatment and needed medications. No accommodations were made for small children, adolescents or the frail elderly, all of whom often died due to the conditions. And on and on go the sordid sorrowful details and the utter inhumanity of it all.

The gulag then, was official state policy. Those who died in them were either intended casualties of the Soviet regime or they were prisoners who died due to their reckless neglect while in government custody. Therefore, there can be nothing about this atrocity that was given to chance. Things didn't just "get out of control". There were not just "a few bad apples" in the Soviet government. This was Marxist Tyranny, from top to bottom, at least where Lenin and Stalin were concerned. Those who resisted the Soviet coercion were "disposed of", brutally, systematically, and ruthlessly. Period. Applebaum notes that at the earliest points of the Bolshevik Revolution itself, these labor camps were contrived by Vladimir Lenin, even suggesting that he had been "sketching out" a plan to organize "obligatory work duty" for wealthy capitalists.[156] When resistance to Bolshevism intensified, he became even more fervent regarding the need to develop a forced labor form of punishment.[157] For Lenin, old fashioned crimes such as larceny and murder were a function of class exploitation and would presumably disappear once capitalism was overthrown; moreover, he believed there would be new form of crime, that of a "class enemy", one who resisted the Revolution and the Soviet grand plan.[158] The class enemy was a greater

---

[154] Applebaum., 168.

[155] Ibid., *see generally*, Chapter 9.

[156] Applebaum, *Gulag.,* 5.

[157] Ibid.

[158] Ibid.

danger to the Soviet grand dream because he was often difficult to identify and even more difficult to reform; therefore, warranting harsher punishment than a more conventional criminal.[159]

This last point is incredibly salient towards the purpose of writing *American Kulak*. It is because people do not naturally collectivize, and it is not a normative instinct for a person to give up life time accumulated wealth for some abstract notion of the "greater good," hence they are not at all likely to acquiesce to a collectivist ideal or to abide the nationalization of private industries. As people are very likely to be inclined to have antipathy towards forced collectivization, they will in many cases naturally resist. And when they do, the fervent Marxist views them as an impediment to the socialist utopian dream, an obstacle that must be removed at all costs. Viewing them as some kind of "enemy" of the state is most often the primary intellectual vehicle to justify the harshest possible treatment against them. No one knew this better than the Kulaks, and the Soviets had an answer for them. It was a combination of violence, contrived starvation in the form of famine, and the hell on earth known as the Gulag Archipelago. By 1938, there were basically no more Kulaks, or the ones that were still alive had been deported to desolate relocation villages in the Siberian "no man's land".

SUMMARY OVERVIEW: PUTTING EVENTS AND PERSPECTIVE TOGETHER

By 1974 Solzhenitsyn had been exiled from Russia and was living in the United States. In the summer of 1975 he gave three speeches which are summarized in a book entitled *Warning to the West*.[160] The same book also contained two speeches to the British the following summer. In a speech on June 30, 1975, delivered in Washington DC at a dinner given in his honor by the AFL-CIO, he concisely synopsizes the entire history of the Soviet persecution of the peasantry in a few short paragraphs. Let's enumerate each step summarized by Mr. Solzhenitsyn: (1) The Bolshevik system was installed by an armed uprising; (2) it disbursed Constituent Assembly; (3) it surrendered to the common enemy Germany; (3) it commenced Cheka, which is punishment and even execution without due process (trial); it violently disbursed worker strikes; (4) it looted the peasant countryside to a degree that incited a peasant uprising; (5) when the peasants rebelled, the Bolsheviks slaughtered the peasantry using the harshest most violent methods possible; (6) it routed the Church; (7) it intentionally inflicted total and complete famine throughout the Ukraine in 1921, and 1932-33; (8) the Bolsheviks initiated the first concentration camps in world history; (9) they used family members as "hostages" to get to dissidents; (10) they required "enemies" of the state to "register" and murdered those who complied; (11) they killed these innocent registrants by putting them on a barge, 100 – 1000 at a time and then sinking it; (12) they massacred all non-communist party members; and (13) this was the system that ultimately killed at least 15 million peasants.[161] As we know, the Kulaks were among the first of the peasantry to face formal extirpation, but in the end, they were accompanied by millions more.

The height of the Stalinist purges against the peasantry and other enemies of the state, Solzhenitsyn estimates that the communist terror tactics killed more than 40,000 human beings

---

[159] Ibid., 5-6.

[160] Aleksandr Solzhenitsyn, *Warning to the West* (Farrar, Straus and Giroux, NY 1976).

[161] Ibid., 14-17.

each month.[162] The relevance of the Kulak is not necessarily the magnitude of their genocide, indeed, it numbered in the millions, but it was part of a much larger holocaust; rather, the salience of the Kulak experience for the American affluent class in terms of the similarities between the two, which I will detail in the next chapter. The Kulaks had largely vanished from this earth by the early 1940s, the question before us now, is whether there will be some version of an American Kulak 80 years later. In the event the American government finds itself a Marxist regime, we can expect that what happened to the Kulak will be a blue-print for any affluent professional or small business owner who refuses to formally and affirmatively give up a life's work and drink the communist cool aid. Dekulakization will be given a new context and a new lease on life. Chapter five will explore the current dekulakization trends already under way for America's affluent, and then explore what may follow. Admittedly, while these trends are not yet of a violent nature, once America starts down the road to official collectivism under the mind-altering allure of utopian Marxism, there is no telling where it will end. History has shown that it can end in a very bad place.

---

[162] Ibid., 19-20, 30-31.

CHAPTER IV

AMERICAN KULAK

—————————

The Middle Class is the best social class in the world because nobody messes with the middle class. Politicians endlessly pander to the middle class in order to gain votes to stay in power. When you are in the upper class, you become a target for hate groups who can't stand success in the great USA. If you are poor, well that just stinks. But what about the mass affluent?[163]

So what is mass affluence anyway? And who are the mass affluent? That is the explicit goal of this chapter – to leave the reader with a crystal-clear view on what attributes and traits would make someone part of this group. Once we understand who is "affluent" in America, we can begin to compare them to the better-off Soviet peasants who came to be known as the Kulaks. We will begin the conversation with the supposition that the affluent American is by definition not middle class, nor is he outright wealthy. We will explore government data and other authoritative sources that help us define the mass affluent and then we will examine the occupations that fall within the defined mass affluent category, and compare their attributes to the legal definition the Soviet government prescribed in identifying a Kulak peasant. Trigger warning: you will find this comparison disturbing, especially if you are one of the millions of Americans who fall in this category. If you are reading this and are affluent as defined in this chapter, you will hopefully be left with a clear understanding the similarities between how a Kulak was defined by law and how your own personal situation stacks up against that definition, chilling as that might be. It is a grotesque understatement to recall that things did not work out well for the Kulak, and it is altogether in the realm of possibility that an American Kulak may face a bleak future. If you are not frightened by this chapter and the next, you are not paying very close attention.

As I have asserted elsewhere, there is a shifting political sentiment in American politics over the past 40 years that is pulling the country in a radically different direction, one that has no precedent in American history. If the nation crawls ever so continuously towards a form of collectivist Marxism, life as we have come to know it will be very different unless we quickly alter

---

[163] Internet Blog Posting by *Financial Samurai*, as of 2/6/2019. See, www.financialsamurai.com/what-is-considered-mass-affluent-definition-based-off-income-net-worth-investable-assets/.

course. If we do not, and wind up in a Marxist based economic system, who will be the initial target? The super and mega rich will be able to fight off (or perhaps "buy off") any Marxist threat, at least initially, and be in a position to flee the country if things get really bad. Those Americans with little or no net worth will be left alone as they may be middle class in terms of income but they essentially live paycheck to paycheck. It is the affluent that will be a prime target. The super-rich, who are rich enough not to have to care about taxes, will grudgingly pay higher – perhaps much higher taxes than they would like, and when it gets too uncomfortable, they will flee to safe havens and be fine. The merely "affluent" will have no such opportunity.

Attributes of the American Kulak: Comparing the Affluent American to the Decree of the Sovnarkom Resolution of May 21, 1929

The best and most concise definition of mass affluence in America that I could find came from a blogger who posts under the name *Financial Samurai*. According to this blogger, it is first important to understand that the member of the mass affluent class did not inherit his or her money, they are active in the workforce, not idle trust fund babies.[164] There are three thresholds that can be used to identify the mass affluent, income, investible assets and net worth.[165] According to this blogger, to be considered part of the mass affluent, one must earn an income that is 150% of the median per capita income of their surrounding geographical area (best represented by the HUD median income for the area).[166] So if you live in a Connecticut suburb of the New York Metropolitan area, and the area's median household income is say - $100,000 per year; to be considered "mass affluent", your income would need to be at least $150,000 annually. *Financial Samurai* asserts that an individual or household must have investible liquid assets of between $100K and $1MM to fall within the "mass affluent category.[167] Finally, if your net worth is between $500,000 and $5MM, you fall in the mass affluent class.[168] Hit any one of these three targets, and he views you as mass affluent. A moderate-income household that is not affluent often land in the mass affluent class by virtue of astute investing acumen and prodigious saving and investing habits. In contrast, a high-income earning executive who spends like the dickens and has comparatively little in net worth or investible assets is still considered among the mass affluent by virtue of his income. The *Financial Samurai* blog goes into greater detail and covers some of the nuance of it all, but these are the broad contours.[169]

The afore-referenced blog cites data from 2017, so it is relatively recent. Its results are very much in line with results from a *Nielsen* study published in 2012. For those who are not familiar

---

[164] Ibid.

[165] Ibid.

[166] Ibid.

[167] Ibid.

[168] Ibid.

[169] In addition to *Financial Samurai*, a 2014 newsletter from marketingcharts.com entitled *Who Are America's Affluents, and What Are Their Top Spending Categories?*, dated September 22, 2014 was a bit more inclusive regarding what is mass affluence. The newsletter describes some 67.5 million adults living in households with incomes of at least $100,000 – the newsletter's threshold for affluent, translating to 28% of adults and 23% of households in this category. Importantly, this newsletter points out that America's affluent and wealthy are far more likely to have achieved an advanced degree ***and are concentrated disproportionately in managerial and professional positions.*** According to the newsletter, 63% of affluent adults and 66% of wealthy adults fit into these job categories. For the full newsletter, see, https://www.marketingcharts.com/industries/non-profit-46221.

with *Nielson*, they are a world renown data analytics company whose databases are widely used in a variety of industries. I have personal experience with using data from *Nielson* in the consumer products industry and the financial services industry. *Nielson* ratings are also used widely in the broadcast television industry. When you hear someone boast that the "ratings" were excellent for this show or that, the ratings are often tabulated and provided by Nielson. The *Nielson Report* I refer to is entitled *Affluence in America: A Financial View of the Mass Affluent in America.*

The *Nielson Report* has similar thresholds in defining mass affluence as does *Financial Samurai*. The *Neilson Report* depicts the average income for those deemed to be part of the mass affluent at $105,500, more than double the average income for those considered part of the "Mass Market" class.[170] *Nielson* also notes that those who have income producing assets between $250,000 and $1MM. fall within the mass affluent range[171] This is a tighter range than *Financial Samurai*, whose bottom range went down to $100K. It is interesting to note that the *Nielson Report* shows that 58% of the mass affluent make $100K or less annually.[172] This reinforces the notion that those who have invested well on a non-six figure income very often fall in the category of mass affluence. Nielson notes that only 6% of US households have income producing assets in an amount greater than $1MM.[173]

Taken together, *Financial Samurai* and *Nielson* set reasonable parameters around the attributes commonly associated with being among the "mass affluent". Next question, how many Americans actually fall within this category. *Financial Samurai* puts the number at 33 million Americans (11% of the population).[174] Nielson puts the number at 13 million households (instead of individuals), and arrives at the same 11% figure (84.55% Mass Market v. 11.1% Mass Affluent v. 4.4% Affluent.)[175] Finally, as noted previously, there is evidence that the affluent are disproportionately concentrated in managerial and professional occupations and have advanced degrees which enabled them to occupy such jobs. If we compare these two sources to IRS data, we see the total number of individual income tax filings for 2017 (the latest data available), there were over 150 million total filers, of which there were 14,329,516 (10th percentile), that had at least $145,135 in adjusted gross income.[176] As income of $145K in places like the Bay area or New York City would not constitute "affluent", the definitions provided by *Financial Samurai and Nielson* are probably more reliable to pinpoint who exactly would constitute "affluent" anywhere in America. With that acknowledged, the definitions provided by these two sources are relatively "in line" with IRS tax filings because the difference between the 11% total number they derived are corroborated by the 10% total number of IRS filings with at least $145K – with the difference being *Nielson* and *Financial Samurai* methods account for high cost metro areas. The position we take for this book is that the three sources sufficiently validate each other enough to accept their definition of what is "mass affluent" in America today. The discussion below will

---

[170] The Nielson Co.: Report, *Affluence in America: A financial View of the Mass Affluent in America.* 2012. P. 2

[171] Ibid.

[172] Ibid.

[173] Ibid.

[174] *Financial Samurai*, as of 2/6/2019. See, www.financialsamurai.com/what-is-considered-mass-affluent-definition-based-off-income-net-worth-investable-assets/

[175] Nielson, 3.

[176] Alexander Tanzi and Ben Steverman, *Americans Now Need at Least $500,000 a year to Enter Top 1%,* (Bloomberg.com, October 16, 2019) citing 2017 IRS data.

drive home the point that annual incomes between \$100 – \$200K are smack dab in the middle of the American professional class. You routinely deal with mass affluent every time you visit a doctor, go to the hospital or the dentist and many of the products you consume were created by managers in this class.

Now that we have some common understanding regarding what is referred to by the term "mass affluence" in the United States, we proceed with recalling the formal definition of Kulak that the Soviet government derived in the late 1920s, discussed in Chapter 2. Recall that definition was as follows: Under the decree of the Sovnarkom Resolution of May 21, 1929, any of the following would be considered attributes of a Kulak: (1) use of hired labor; (2) ownership of a mill, a creamery, *other processing equipment*, or *a complex machine* with *a mechanical motor*; (3) systematic renting out of agricultural equipment or facilities; and, (4) involvement in trade, money lending, commercial brokerage, or other sources of non-labor income. These attributes are very easily ascribed to a 21st Century American affluent professional, even though they were targeted in 1929 towards peasants, and in particular Kulak peasants. How many small manufacturers, warehouse owners, doctors, dentists and lawyers would fall with in element number 1 and 2 above (employing the labor of others and owing advanced mechanized equipment)? Do they hire labor and have a payroll? Check. Do they all not own or direct the use of complex machines with a mechanical motor? Check. For example, my Doctor has ordered 10 CT and MRI scans on me in the last five years. Those are extremely complex machines costing millions of dollars. My dentist has complex x-ray machines in his office. Small manufactures use complex machines to make other machines. Warehouse owners store all the parts and finished products during the manufacturing process. Get the point? Even though today's small businessman or professional is not a farmer, the Soviet Labor Code terminology would at most need only minor modifications to be applied to the 21st Century affluent professional – the American Kulak.

Examples of Occupations and Income Levels that would Fall Within the "Kulak" Definition

I can easily go through the US Department of Labor statistics occupational categories, select those with six figure average incomes and start applying these Soviet era definitional attributes for what was considered a Kulak in 1929 and get a credible resemblance without even having to tweak the language of the old Soviet labor code. By now if you are an affluent professional, and this isn't already making you nervous, then you may have to learn the hard way that Marxism will not likely be your friend. I order to help you crystalize the comparison, I will analyze 15 occupations, which in 2018 commanded the highest salaries in the United States, describe them in some detail, then compare the nature of the occupation to the former Soviet labor code identifying Kulaks, and you will see all of them fit nicely into one of the elements of this definition. The list is taken from the 2019 list of best paying jobs published by US News & World Report, which derives the "median salary" figure from the Bureau of Labor Statistics tallies.[177]

---

[177] See, https://money.usnews.com/careers/best-jobs/rankings/best-paying-jobs. Rankings are based on analysis of BLS data by USNews.

1) <u>Anesthesiologist</u>:

An anesthesiologist is a medical doctor who administers general anesthesia during surgeries allowing for medical procedures, which would otherwise be excruciating to the patient, to be administered pain free. The 2017 median Salary was $208,000.[178] An anesthesiologist can be employed by a hospital or medical group as a salaried employee with income reportable as W-2 income for federal tax purposes. With more experience, this type of doctor often joins forces with other anesthesiologists and create a partnership or limited liability company and contract with hospitals and other medical groups for their services.

<u>Would an Anesthesiologist be Considered A Kulak?</u>

Set aside the fact that the Kulak was a farmer, and an anesthesiologist is a medical professional with an advanced degree, the job is none-the-less analogous to how "Kulak" was defined by the soviet labor code, which would render it a 21st Century "American Kulak". Certainly, if the anesthesiologist is a partner in a medical group he or she would fall squarely within the first category – one who employs others (use of hired labor). Even if the anesthesiologist does not employ others, and is employed by others, a militant Marxist could easily ascribe them Kulak status on the basis of their involvement in the medical trade (a component of the fourth element). If the anesthesiologist is employed by a medical practice group but is given any kind of equity stake in the firm, and the firm owns any kind of advanced equipment, then that anesthesiologist would trigger the second element of the Soviet labor code due to the ownership of complex machinery.

In the event America opts for a formal form of socialism, and that triggers a series of events similar to that of Hugo Chavez in Venezuela from 1998 to the present day, and the benign level of socialism metastasizes into a formal state ownership of the means of production (nationalization) over time, then I would submit to you the anesthesiologist would be a prime target for Kulak treatment given the very high, and therefore, plunderable income. As noted previously, the median income for an anesthesiologist is $208,000 in 2017. Contrast that with the recently reported Census Bureau median family income figure, which was $61,372 for 2017.[179] As one can see, the anesthesiologist's median salary is roughly three-and-a-half times the median *household* income. That means that the anesthesiologist is typically earning about 3.5 times what households earn – many of whom have two incomes! Given the foregoing, with this level of income, it is without question that the anesthesiologist would most certainly fall within the definition of "mass affluent" we discussed earlier in the chapter.

The conclusion would have to be that the anesthesiologist would almost certainly be considered an American Kulak should America fall to the hard-core Marxists. Interestingly, one of my best friends is an anesthesiologist. He once told me that he had a family member over for dinner who brought a friend with them who had very "Marx-friendly" viewpoints. This "friend" wound up commenting to her anesthesiologist host that "no one should be allowed to own or live in a house

---

[178] Ibid.

[179] Jonathan Rothbaum, *Income and Poverty: Highest Median Household Income on Record?* (U.S. Census Bureau, September 12, 2018). Mr. Rothbaum is Chief of the Income Statistics Branch in the Social, Economic, and Housing Statistics Division of the Census Bureau.

this big." Never mind the chutzpah of being a guest in someone else's house and popping off with an obnoxious comment like that (lefties are not exactly known for their diplomatic elegance); such a comment is more than sufficient to give you an idea of the perspective a hard-left socialist American government will bring. At their core they do not respect the notion that one should be the ultimate beneficiary of the fruits of their labor. One recalls the 2012 Presidential campaign where former President Obama exhorted "you didn't build that" in reference to successful businesses started by entrepreneurs; "somebody else built that" the President insisted. Suffice it to say that when this mind-set is firmly in control of all institutional levers of American governance, the affluent will be pushed back on their heels politically and will be fighting to retain whatever scraps of wealth and savings they were able to accumulate. Perhaps a condominium and a bank account in Australia or New Zealand might not be a bad idea for someone in this line of work.

2) Surgeon:

A surgeon in the U.S. has a very similar economic profile to the anesthesiologist standing next to her in the operating room. They both have the same median income of $208,000,[180] and are both medical professionals, albeit with a markedly different task orientation. The surgeon does the slicing and cutting and cauterizing, the anesthesiologist ensures the patient isn't screaming in agony the whole time. A surgeon can be employed the same way an anesthesiologist can, either by being an employee earning a very high W-2 reportable income, or they can form practice groups as partnerships or LLCs like other doctors. The analysis of the surgeon would be identical to the anesthesiologist in terms of whether they would fall with in the Soviet definition of a Kulak – as they are part of a trade, and if they form an entity where they have an equity stake, and that entity employs the labor of others, and owns complex machinery, well – the result would be the same for the surgeon as it is for the anesthesiologist. The surgeon fits the definition of a Kulak. Moreover, just as with the anesthesiologist, the surgeon's income would place her well within the "mass affluent" category. If America ever becomes "Amerika" and the hammer and cycle replaces the stars and stripes, the surgeon should look out, as they will be deemed American Kulaks and have a target on their backs.

As a matter of fact, the next four occupational categories listed on the US News Best Paying jobs list are all medical professionals along with the anesthesiologist and surgeon; and interestingly, all have the same $208,000 median salary.[181] These occupations are as follows:

3) Oral and maxillofacial Surgeons
4) Obstetricians and Gynecologists
5) Orthodontists
6) Psychiatrists

---

[180] https://money.usnews.com/careers/best-jobs/rankings/best-paying-jobs
[181] Ibid.

In my view all would follow the analytic framework of the anesthesiologists and surgeons. All would likely fall within the soviet labor code definition of a Kulak (either by being engaged in a medical trade, or owing an equity interest in a medical practice group in their field). All would certainly be members of the mass affluent class in America by virtue of their large salaries alone. When the ultra-left assumes control of American governance, and the American Bolsheviks are done plundering the mega rich and outright wealthy, they will get to the American Kulaks – and each of these occupational categories will be prime fodder. There is only so much wealth that can be confiscated from billionaires, of whom there are less than 1,000 in the US. As we have seen in the Preface to this book, there are only 0.055% of the 150,000,000 individual income tax filers in the US have a net worth of over $50 million. There is simply not enough of them to pay for a $33 Trillion Medicare for all socialist utopian dream, on top of a multi-trillion "Green New Deal" on top of "Mandatory Employment for all", and all the other promises being made by the Bernie Sanders and Elizabeth Warren wing of the Democratic Party.

7) Physician:

You may be wondering why I didn't include physician with the other occupational categories that require a doctorate in the medical health sciences. The reason is that the garden variety physician is the first occupational category on the US News Best Paying Jobs list with a median income of less than $208,000 – for physicians, that number is $192,930 for 2017.[182] While this is the median salary for the average medical doctor, there is a bigger range of income in this category, with the bottom 25% earning a salary of $109,000; to the 75% percentile and higher earning $208,000.[183]

Nevertheless, the analysis would be the same for the physicians as it is for the other medical profession occupations. They are likely to fall within the Soviet labor code definition of a Kulak because they are involved in a trade – the medical services trade; and they often practice in a partnership group or LLC arrangement. They often have expensive equipment or complex machines used in their offices, which their practice entity either owns or leases. I personally have had an EKG administered to me in the Dr. Office (a procedure once upon a time reserved exclusively for the emergency room and hospitals), as well as advanced breathing tests with sophisticated equipment. The list could go on. The median income of $192,000 would most certainly place them in the mass affluent definition we covered early in this chapter. Sorry to say, but your family doctor, allergist, ear nose and throat specialist and so on are all likely to be considered American Kulaks by American Marxists.

8) Prosthodontist:

The prosthodontist is a dental professional with a doctorate in the dental sciences whose main mission is repairing a person's smile. Think of it as a specialized area of dentistry where your teeth are restored or replaced as necessary. The median income for this occupational category was

---

[182] Ibid.

[183] Ibid.

$185,150.[184] Like most dentists and dental specialists, they have their own practice, rent their own space, and use highly complicated and advanced equipment from the x-ray machines that can see cavities between your teeth to equipment used in dental surgeries. Their income will certainly put them in the mass affluent category as we have defined earlier in this chapter.

The fact that the prosthodontist is very likely to employ support staff in her office, use complex equipment and machinery and is involved in a trade/profession means the 21st Century American communists will likely be treating them as Kulaks, ready for plundering.

   9) Pediatrician:

The pediatrician is the Dr. specializing in care for children. The median income for this occupational category was $172,650 for 2017.[185] The analysis would be identical for the other occupational categories with medical doctorates in the health sciences. It is very difficult to see how a pediatrician would not receive the same Kulak treatment other doctors would under an American communist dictatorship. The median salary for a pediatrician is most certainly going to be mass affluent.

   10) Dentist:

The dentist is the one who lets us keep chewing solid food for the entirety of our lives. Listen to the dentist, do what he says, and you will keep your teeth. And they can even whiten them up for you, give you an extra deep clean or the standard cleaning you've had since you were old enough to remember. Most American's do not even remember what a toothache feels like. I dare say the vast majority of the 328 Million of us have never even had a toothache. Whereas our forefathers lost most of their teeth before their 40th birthday (if they lived that long), most Americans die with their original adult teach they've had since they were 13 or 14. There is a reason for that. Sure fluoridated water in most urban areas played a key role, but so too did the advances in the dental sciences over the course of the 20th century. The preventative care the standard dental practice engages in is the ounce of prevention that is worth literally tons of cure. Indeed, Dentists do their job very well and millions upon millions upon millions of beautiful smiles are the proof.

And for their good work, the median income for the dentist is $174,110 according to the US News analysis of Bureau of Labor Statistics data.[186] In that sense, the analysis for the dentist is the same as for the prosthodontist, just with a little less annual income. So, would a dentist dare ever get treated as an American Kulak? Well, they fit the definition. They hire people such as dental hygienists and office staff. They own or lease very complex equipment. They are engaged in an advanced medical trade just as any of the doctors do. I'd say they fit right in. And with a median income of $151,000+, they fall quite comfortably in the mass affluent category in all but a tiny handful of very expensive zip codes. I think if America falls to hard left Marxists, as unlikely as that may be (but certainly not impossible), your family dentist would have the "Kulak" target

---

[184] Ibid.

[185] Ibid.

[186] Ibid.

on their back. Too much income for a cash hungry communist to ignore, but not rich enough to influence politicians, command a private army to defend themselves, or flee the country in style. The purest form of Kulak.

11) <u>Nurse Anesthetist</u>:

As we leave the top 10 best paying jobs, coming in at number 11 is the Nurse Anesthetist, the first position on the list that does not require a medical or dental doctoral degree to hold the job. This specialized nurse; however, does require specialized training and a degree in this field before they can assist an anesthesiologist, surgeon, dentist or other professionals with their work. And for good reason, botch the anesthesia, and you can put a patient in a permanent coma or cause severe and permanent injuries to their central nervous system.

According to the US News study, the Nurse Anesthetist median income is a tad over $160,000. This is squarely within the mass affluent range as defined earlier in the chapter. But for a nurse anesthetist to qualify as a Kulak under the old Soviet Labor Code, it would be on the basis of being in a trade, as this role is very likely to be an employee rather than an owner of a business entity. No matter, with income that high, when the new American Bolsheviks arrive with their Marxist agenda, which will require trillions stacked on top of trillions, stacked on top of yet more and more trillions, the Bolsheviks will search for revenue wherever they can find it. And the Nurse Anesthetist would serve just fine.

12) <u>Petroleum Engineer</u>:

As we arrive at the number 12 slot, we have our first job outside the medical profession entirely. While all engineering professionals are usually paid handsomely for their highly technical skills, the petroleum engineer is especially well paid given the demand for their skill set. The entire global economy is still largely driven by fossil fuels and will be for much of the remainder of the current century, the petroleum engineer is well situated for affluence for the foreseeable future.

As for their income, they can easily earn six figures literally right out of college. There are only a handful of mining technical schools that offer the degree (you read that correctly, drilling for oil is technically considered a mining activity). The median salary for all petroleum engineers is $128,230.[187] In all but the most expensive Metropolitan Statistical Areas like New York and San Francisco, this level of income will be considered mass affluent. And if we adhere to the definition provided in the Nielson report cited earlier in this chapter, they would be comfortably in this category. As they are most certainly operating in an engineering trade and industry, the cash hungry Marxist will absolutely view this professional category as a target. Should the petroleum engineer resist any mandatory collectivization effort, they should expect to be treated just as a Kulak peasant would be – taxed to financial and economic oblivion, then who knows what else.

---

[187] Ibid.

12) <u>IT Manager</u>:

The Information Technology manager is usually pretty well educated. Typically, they are proficient in many of the newest programming languages of the internet age, they often have BS degrees, or even MS degrees in Computer Science, or Software Engineering. Both are fields which require extensive skills in very advanced mathematics. The "coding expert" is most familiar with advanced algorithms that have to be deployed to enable the software language to perform the literal miracles that modern American designed software does on a routine basis. Often the IT manager manages the entire network of a business or other entity such as a hospital, museum, university or library; or, they can manage departments that have a portion of the overall IT function in an organization.

According to the US News Study, the IT manager's median salary is $135,800 which will comfortably place them in the mass affluent category noted by the Nielson Report. They practice the trade of software engineering or other information technology management skills such as keeping a network functioning or repairing a server that has gone down. As with the previous 12 occupational categories, in a Marxist society, these affluent professionals would most certainly be squarely within the category of "Kulak" due to their participation in a trade. If they were not 100% on board with the collectivization efforts, they would have a bullseye on their back. They may not even need to resist. As we saw with the previous two chapters that all the Marxist regime needs to persecute is to feel threatened. The threat will then be pillaged, usually through taxation to start, then whatever else it takes. The IT manager would not be exempt from this unless they find themselves literal party members. Even being a party member doesn't guarantee safety (remember Leon Trotsky?).

13) <u>Marketing Manager</u>:

In just about every type of business, whether selling a tangible product, or a service, there is a need for a marketing. Having been in the financial services industry for a quarter century, I can personally attest to the relevance this skill set provides any business. If the marketing effort is unsuccessful, then customers don't even know the company, service or product exists. If the marketing professional does his or her job well, then the marketing effort literally drives customers to the business. I have seen this first-hand. There is the basic-level marketing such as the salesman touching buyers and consumers directly. Then there are sophisticated direct mail campaigns that started to gather steam in the 1970s, and got perfected in the ensuing decades. By the first part of the 21 Century, direct mail campaigns done correctly with good statistics behind them, could drive rather large volumes of business to the desired business channel. The advent of social media and search engine technology has opened up an entire new frontier of marketing managing driven by complicated mathematical algorithms that predict consumer tastes and preferences. Marketing managers with their technologist partners turn this into a space aged advertising endeavor.

The well-established marketing professional is worth every penny of their service, and a good marketing manager will earn a median salary of $131,180.[188] This is definitely Kulak territory. There is mass affluent level income, and there is the engagement in a trade or business. There is

---

[188] Ibid.

no reason this occupational category would escape the inglorious Kulak treatment the other occupations are sure to reap in the event America ever falls to the Marxist collectivist purists.

14) <u>Podiatrist</u>:

As we arrive at number 15, we are back to the medical profession, which has 12 of the 15 top paying jobs in the US according to the US News *Best Paying Jobs* list. The podiatrist is another specialization in the medical profession focusing on foot related disorders. They are doctors with medical doctorates and the additional training required to practice a specialty.

According to US News, their median income is $124,830.[189] This level of income still qualifies as mass affluent according to the Neilson Report, and for the same reasons as apply to the other similar medical professional occupational categories, this one would likely be considered a modern Kulak as they are engaged in a medical practice trade, and if they have an equity ownership in a limited liability entity for their practice, then they would almost certainly be afforded the Kulak treatment based on the how the former Soviet Union went after the affluent peasants. Tax them to oblivion, then focus on oblivion. If there are podiatrists voting for hard left candidates in American elections from 2018 to the present day, all I can say is be careful what you wish for, as you might just get it and a whole lot more than you ever thought you bargained for!

Examples Across Industries:

Thus far we have looked at specific high paying occupations as surveyed by US News & World Report to analyze how an American Kulak may be determined, perhaps another angle for review that warrants discussion would be to look at data specific to entire industries. We could do this analysis in many industries; the energy industry, the tech industry, consumer products, aerospace and defense, and on and on. The analysis would reveal the same result no matter the industry. The managerial and professional job categories in nearly all industries would likely satisfy the definition of American Kulak that is reasonably defined as affluence coupled with one of the four attributes from the old Soviet Labor Code.

Four our illustrative purposes, we will look at three industries, all with large numbers of well-paid employees and see how the analysis lines up with the job-specific view. The three industries will be Financial Services, Energy, and Entertainment.

1) <u>Financial Services</u>:

A hard-core Marxist applying the Soviet code listed at the outset of this chapter would have field day with most of the occupations within this industry. Almost all the management jobs in the financial services industry would fall within the first and fourth element of the former Soviet labor code in that they employ other people and have involvement in a trade and the nature of the business is money lending. Of the 8.6 million jobs in the industry classified as Financial Activities by the Bureau of Labor Statistics (hereafter "BLS") as of January 2019; approximately 1.9 million of those jobs would be classified as supervisory employees, leaving roughly 6.6 million as

---

[189] Ibid.

production and non-supervisory employees. Details are noted in Figure 1 below.[190] So there are almost two million supervisory or higher positions in the financial services industry, which means these employees automatically satisfy the first element of the Soviet Labor code of 1929 – they employ the labor of others. I will argue that even if an institution is the ultimate "employer", the supervisor or manager is part of the "employer" class as they make the routine day-to-day decisions regarding hiring and firing (typically with input from a Human Resources Department). A Marxist regime would probably treat them as American Kulaks on that basis alone.

If we drill down a little deeper and isolate the financial managerial job class, we get the added color of income, which brings in the mass affluent component of this analysis. Here the BLS has an entire job category entitled "11-3031 Financial Managers" under the "Occupational Employment and Wages, as of May 2017" subheading under their "Subjects" tab on the BLS main page.[191] The BLS has published some useful information regarding these Financial Manager positions. To illustrate, please see Figure 2, which contains the BLS estimate of the total number of employees with this job category at 569,000+, and the table also notes the BLS estimate of their mean or *average* annual income – at $143, 530 as of 2017.[192] This would be mass affluent pretty much any way you look at it given the discussion we had at the beginning of this chapter. It is hard to see how the Financial Manager occupation would not be squarely within the sights of the Marxist purist as either an American Kulak or outright bourgeoisie.

FIGURE 1: Total Employment in the Financial Activities Industry

Employment, Unemployment, and Openings, Hires, and Separations

Data series	Back data	Oct. 2018	Nov. 2018	Dec. 2018	Jan. 2019
Employment (in thousands)					
Employment, all employees (seasonally adjusted)		8,611	8,614	(p)8,618	(p)8,631
Employment, production and nonsupervisory employees (seasonally adjusted)		6,669	6,668	(p)6,676	(p)6,686

---

[190] U.S. Department of Labor, Bureau of Labor Statistics, *Industries at a Glance,* Financial Activities. See, https://www.bls.gov/iag/tgs/iag50.htm. Figure 1 was taken from this site and modified to depict only the total number of industry jobs and the production and non-supervisory jobs. No other change was made to this table.

[191] *See.,* https://www.bls.gov/oes/2017/may/oes113031.htm.

[192] Ibid.

FIGURE 2: Financial Managers

Employment estimate and mean wage estimates for this occupation:

Employment (1)	Employment RSE (3)	Mean hourly wage	Mean annual wage (2)	Wage RSE (3)
569,380	0.6 %	$69.01	$143,530	0.3 %

2) The Energy Industry:

Another industry in America employing literally millions of people, many of whom with compensation far above median family income, would be the Energy Industry. From oil and gas extraction to managing utilities and the electric grid, this now centuries-old industry is one of the most established in the country. The Bureau of Labor Statistics tables for the Oil and Gas Extraction Industry alone had 276 Occupation Code Entries from the Chief Executive Officer (250 employees in this category) to Wellhead Pumpers (8,130 positions as of May 2017).[193] Figure 3 below is taken directly from the BLS Occupational Employment Statistics for the Oil and Gas Extraction Industry (May 2017 data), and it is taken from the table containing all 276 occupational entries, but I have sorted the top 10 paying occupations in the industry from the highest paying to the lowest.

---

[193] U.S. Department of Labor, Bureau of Labor Statistics, *Occupational Employment* Statistics, Oil and Gas Extraction. *See.* https://www.bls.gov/oes/2017/may/naics4_211100.htm#23-0000.

BLS NAICS 211100 - Oil and Gas Extraction

Occupation code	Occupation title (click on the occupation title to view an occupational profile)	Group	Employment	Employment RSE	Percent of total employment	Median hourly wage	Mean hourly wage	Annual mean wage	Mean wage RSE
11-1011	Chief Executives	detail	250	12.6%	0.18%	(5)	$105.51	$219,460	6.5%
11-9041	Architectural and Engineering Managers	detail	1,200	7.9%	0.89%	$86.22	$94.92	$197,440	3.9%
11-2021	Marketing Managers	detail	190	7.0%	0.14%	$86.88	$94.71	$197,000	5.3%
11-2020	Marketing and Sales Managers	broad	390	12.8%	0.29%	$87.59	$93.87	$195,250	5.5%
11-2022	Sales Managers	detail	190	24.1%	0.14%	$88.12	$93.03	$193,500	9.3%
11-9121	Natural Sciences Managers	detail	120	14.5%	0.09%	$74.65	$90.03	$187,260	11.3%
11-2000	Advertising, Marketing, Promotions, Public Relations, and Sales Managers	minor	480	11.8%	0.35%	$82.19	$89.08	$185,280	5.0%
23-1000	Lawyers, Judges, and Related Workers	minor	1,320	15.9%	0.97%	$78.51	$88.98	$185,090	5.8%
23-1010	Lawyers and Judicial Law Clerks	broad	1,320	15.9%	0.97%	$78.51	$88.98	$185,090	5.8%
23-1011	Lawyers	detail	1,320	15.9%	0.97%	$78.51	$88.98	$185,090	5.8%

It is worthy to note that all 10 occupations have an annual mean/average compensation of over $185,000. This makes all 10 comfortably within the definition of Mass Affluence noted at the outset of the chapter. In fact, the first 50 occupations on the full table have an average annual income of in excess of $115,000.[194]

Furthermore, if we were to apply the decree of the Sovnarkom Resolution of May 21, 1929 to any of these occupations we would have no trouble encompassing them under that the law. Many of them are management positions by definition, meaning they engage in hiring and firing. They are all performing duties that are trade specific; specific to the oil and gas industry and specific to other related trades and professions like marketing, engineering and law. As we saw from Robert Conquest previously in Chapter 3, this code was liberally applied, so, from my point of view, all the positions in the top 50, and certainly the top 10 could logically be deemed a Kulak under this law. To put it differently, these are not "worker bees" so to speak, they are the management and professional class, or the highly technical class, and in all cases they are much more affluent than the average American. While the top ten list in Figure 3 covers approximately 6,800 employees, the top 50 covers tens of thousands.[195] For example, in the top 50 compensated occupations, there are 13,000 engineers, and there are 8,150 Life, Physical and Social Science Occupations (with an average income of 118,560).[196] Suffice it to say, it is not irrational to argue or assert that if American Civilization goes the way of Venezuela, there will be scores of thousands of highly paid

---

[194] Ibid.

[195] Ibid.

[196] Ibid.

oil and gas managers and professionals who may find out what it means to be treated as a 21st Century American Kulak. And it is worth bearing in mind that the Oil and Gas Extraction industry is only one subset of the entire energy industry!

3) The Entertainment Industry:

The story with Arts, Entertainment and Recreation is much the same as Financial Services and Energy. There are tens of thousands of highly paid managers and professionals who would have no difficulty passing as modern-day Kulaks. Here are the specifics. This BLS category includes three main sections; (1) performing arts, spectator sports and related industries; (2) museums, historical sites and similar institutions; and, (3) amusement, gambling and recreation industries.[197] This category has a total of 2,370,160 as of May 2017.[198] Figure 4 depicts the top 10 occupations in terms of annual compensation, sorted from highest to lowest.

Before digesting the results of Figure 4, it is worth a moment to digress for a moment and consider the irony associated with this particular industry. There is no industry in American more dedicated and committed to the progressive left agenda in all respects, save perhaps for unionized government employees. Affluent professionals in this industry reside in large numbers in well know uber-liberal cities like greater Los Angeles, metropolitan New York and the San Francisco Bay Area. These professionals were among the most ardent supporters of Barak Obama, Hillary Clinton and Bernie Sanders. They routinely vote for candidates up and down the ballot who advocate for radical progressive policies that include huge tax increases on the "wealthy", and for massive increases in government spending (free college tuition, Medicare for all, a Green New Deal, and on and on). Perhaps these voters believe the stifling increases in taxation will only be wielded upon those unfortunate enough to have earned economic success measured in the millions, but if history is any guide, anyone who is merely affluent, where there income is above the average or median nationwide will be fodder for tax increases, which of course will include these very same voters.

Once a radical progressive agenda is in place, funding for it with the existing tax structure will quickly prove to be inadequate, even with large tax increases on the "rich." It will take very little time for the tax increase proposals in a hard-core Marxist government to work their way down to bite these very professionals in the Entertainment Industry. Lord only knows how their attitudes will adjust. Nevertheless, the irony will be palpable. You wouldn't expect the affluent to walk down a path that will clearly lead to their own economic annihilation, but cognitive dissonance, the ability to entertain two mutually conflicting ideas as part of one's believe system, is a powerful emotional condition. But enough with the Digression, and back to evaluating Figure 4.

---

[197] U.S. Department of Labor, Bureau of Labor Statistics, *Occupational Employment* Statistics, Sector 71 – Arts, Entertainment and Recreation. *See.*, https://www.bls.gov/oes/2017/may/naics2_71.htm.
[198] Ibid.

Sector 71 - Arts, Entertainment, and Recreation

Occupation code	Occupation title (click on the occupation title to view its profile)	Level	Employment	Employment RSE	Percent of total employment	Median hourly wage	Mean hourly wage	Annual mean wage	Mean wage RSE
29-1060	Physicians and Surgeons	Broad	40	22.7%	(7)	$96.24	$100.61	$209,280	7.8%
11-1011	Chief Executives	Detail	3,570	6.6%	0.15%	$88.05	$94.32	$196,180	2.4%
41-9022	Real Estate Sales Agents	Detail	90	15.3%	(7)	$56.18	$79.33	$165,000	23.9%
23-1000	Lawyers, Judges, and Related Workers	Minor	490	9.3%	0.02%	$68.76	$78.20	$162,650	3.3%
23-1010	Lawyers and Judicial Law Clerks	Broad	490	9.3%	0.02%	$68.76	$78.20	$162,650	3.3%
23-1011	Lawyers	Detail	490	9.3%	0.02%	$68.76	$78.20	$162,650	3.3%
41-9020	Real Estate Brokers and Sales Agents	Broad	100	15.0%	(7)	$53.02	$78.00	$162,250	24.3%
11-9041	Architectural and Engineering Managers	Detail	180	13.8%	0.01%	$70.12	$73.90	$153,720	3.9%
23-0000	Legal Occupations	Major	620	8.5%	0.03%	$56.57	$68.26	$141,970	3.6%
29-1128	Exercise Physiologists	Detail	(8)	(8)	(8)	$83.03	$64.05	$133,220	22.1%

Of these ten occupational categories, all are above $133,000 in average annual compensation. All would easily fall within the definition of Mass Affluent based on how it has been defined by Nielson and Co., and all would satisfy the Sovnarkom Resolution of May 21, 1929. It is important to note that there were 575 occupational entries in this BLS occupational table, with the top 25 entries all having over $103,560 in average annual income.[199] There were tens of thousands of occupants in these jobs. As noted in the digression above, managers and professionals in these particular industries have wished for and voted for the militant progressive agenda for most of my adult life and they appear on the cusp of achieving their stated goal. The betting is that they won't like the outcome all that much once they've had a taste of true-blue Marxism. They will all be treated as Kulaks.

What to Conclude: We Have a Pretty Good Idea of What Would Constitute an "*American* Kulak" in the 21st Century

The point to be made from this exercise, is that one can easily take high paying occupations from a variety of industries, trades and professions, and apply the characteristics of the job and income to the old Soviet Labor Code that was used to identify and persecute Kulak peasants, and find many American job categories would have fallen within the literal terms of the definition. Furthermore, if we expand beyond the occupational categories covered in the US News list we cataloged above, we find the same is true in a myriad of other industries. There is surely a very

---

[199] Ibid.

large population of well-paid managers and professionals across the American workforce would be susceptible to falling within the 21st Century American Kulak characterization.

If the day ever comes where America finds itself in the grip of Marxist totalitarianism, then this old code could be dusted off and revised as necessary for the modern day affluent, and away we would go to full-on American tragedy. We assert that if developments like those of the early 20th Century Soviet Union ever came to be, no-one in the mass affluent category would be immune from a Kulak style eradication. We have seen that the total number in the mass affluent category is easily estimated to be approximately 10+% of the U.S. population, or 33+ million people. And, as I have shown, even a cursory review of job categories and multiple industries supports the notion that there multitudes of affluent professionals working in them that would fit nicely into the notion of an American Kulak, which we shall conclude, is one that encompasses affluence along with traits that align with the old Soviet labor code – employing others, involvement in a trade, engaged in money lending or commercial leasing, and so on. Tens of millions of our fellow citizens will fall into this category.

If America can avoid hard left progressivism, perhaps we can avoid the potential calamity that will await if we rush into the arms of tired, long discredited Marxist rubbish. I have my doubts. As I will explain later in the book, I have witnessed over a 25-year career a steady, seemingly unstoppable leftward drift in American politics. When I first entered the workforce a quarter century ago, America was a center right country politically. I do not think that can be said of America today. Since 1992, Republicans, our center right party, has won the popular vote for the Presidency only once, in 2004, and that didn't even hit a full 51% (it was closer to 50.8%)! The left has taken firm control of our cultural institutions, our colleges and universities, our major cultural endowments, the entertainment industry and the mainstream media. America's center of gravity is moving to the left. We saw in the Preface and first chapter that young people under age 40 are increasingly telling pollsters they prefer socialism over capitalism. And why would we expect any different, with a steady stream of left leaning propaganda coming from all sources but for a few right leaning outlets, why wouldn't the Marxist world view gain steam?

To further this point, there is an excellent article written by Jay Cost, for the *National Review*, where he notes that it is altogether possible that Trump will not win re-election in 2020 due to his relative unpopularity, and that may well bring a true-blue (or should we say – redder than red) socialist to the Presidency.[200] Mr. Cost posits that the American People may for the first time in our history, elect an outright Marxist in preference over voting for Trump.[201] Mr. Cost persuasively writes:

> "I am worried that voters are willing to elect a would-be socialist over a President they never actually liked. More important: I am worried that they won't even recognize this is what they are doing. This is how little confidence I have in the discernment of American voters – they won't connect the dots and realize that the Democrats are calling for a government takeover of pretty much everything. I am worried that the people have ceded

---

[200] Jay Cost, *Are We Really on the Brink of Electing a Socialist President,* (National Review, February 11, 2019).
[201] Ibid.

the ideological fringes of both parties the power to select the two-party nominees, and then choose between them based on their view of the incumbent administration – whether that means electing a celebrity television star like Trump, or a socialist like Bernie [Sanders]."[202]

Josh Kraushaar, writing for the National Journal, is even more emphatic when he writes that Bernie Sander's chances of victory are improving for the same reasons Donald Trump's improbably candidacy won in 2016, a dedicated base of support amidst splintered and fractured opposition.[203] Kraushaar concludes the article by noting that:

> "We live in an age of grandiose promises and ideological extremes. The rise of social media has widened the range of public discourse, allowing for political conversations that were once well outside the political mainstream. These dynamics paved the way for Trump's unlikely election, and are now making it the prospect of a Bernie Sanders presidency more plausible than ever before."[204]

We could just as easily ascribe these concerns to the election of Elizabeth Warren should she be successful in her 2020 campaign. She is essentially "Bernie Light", and overtook him in polling beginning in the summer of 2019. An Elizabeth Warren Presidency is very much a possibility. An even more ominous warning comes from Thomas Sowell in a 2019 interview with David Asman on Fox Business Network.   Mr. Sowell, a prize-winning economist, was uncharacteristically blunt in his assessment of the trend towards outright socialism in the United States. He pessimistically outlined his fears that America may go down the path of financial ruin due to "wonderful sounding" [socialist] rhetoric. Specifically, Sowell said in the interview:

> "So many people today, including in the leading universities, don't pay much attention to evidence. When you see people starving in Venezuela and fleeing into neighboring countries and realize that this is a country that once had the world's largest oil reserves, you realize that they've ruined a very good prospect with ideas that sounded good but didn't turn out well."

> …

> I do have a great fear that, in the long run, we may not make it, I hate to say that. The one thing that keeps me from being despairing is that we don't know. There are so many things that we can't possibly know. And so, we may make it, but I wouldn't bet on it."[205]

---

[202] Ibid.

[203] Josh Kraushaar, *The Case for Bernie Sanders*, (National Journal February 26, 2019).

[204] Ibid.

[205] Douglass Ernst, *Thomas Sowell Warns U.S. May Not Resist Siren Song of Socialism: "I wouldn't Bet On it."* (Washington Times, Tuesday March 5, 2019). *See,* https://www.washingtontimes.com/news/2019/mar/5/thomas-sowell-warns-us-may-not-resist-siren-song-o/.

Perhaps the most menacing assessment of all comes from Victor Davis Hanson, a Senior Fellow at Stanford University's Hoover Institution and a professor of Classics (Emeritus) at California State University. In a 2019 interview with Rebecca Mansour and Joel Pollack on SiriusXM's *Brietbart News Tonight,* Professor Hanson articulated the Democrats escalating antipathy towards American History in their efforts to excavate traditional American values and institutions as a first step in constructing a socialist/Marxist economic and political system. Brietbart's transcript of Professor Hanson's comments is as follows:

> "There's always a choice — the conservative intellectuals say no — but it always is a Manichean choice in our system, and in 2020, ***it's going to be not just socialism of redistribution and high tax rates, a wealth tax, abolition of student debt, it's going to be more of a Maoist all-inclusive let's tear down statues, let's rename streets, let's tear down Christopher Columbus's images, let's tear down the wall on the southern border, let's abolish ICE and ban the internal combustion engine, let's let 16-year-olds vote. It's kind of Maoist that we're trying to destroy the middle class and the traditions of America as we've understood them.***
>
> …
>
> When Ocasio-Cortez says that all she can say about Roosevelt and Reagan is that they were racists, **and she has such *animus*,** you can see where this thing is going. She has no appreciation — she has no knowledge — of people dying at Guadalcanal or being blown up in B-17s over Germany so her parents could immigrate here, or what people died in Korea doing fighting global communism. ***It's a pretty scary effort to really destroy the United States as we've known it and remake it in some kind of strange identity politics socialist image.***"[206] (Emphasis added)

With this passage we can see Professor Hanson make an absolutely crucial point that has not been made in the other previously referred literature. He expressly calls out the fact that Alexandria Ocasio Cortez and her ideological ilk in congress and elsewhere are not simply seeking to merely transform the US into a Marxist political and economic regime, they are simultaneously attempting to mutilate and then disintegrate American heritage in all respects so that it can be replaced with something utterly different than anything that has ever existed on the North American continent. There is absolutely no better articulation of what I have been alluding to throughout this book. I have said many times the risk is not that America is led down the path of a bloated European welfare state, although that will be problematic enough. The real risk is that the ostensible agenda of AOC and like-minded Democrats is not the actual agenda. The risk is that the true agenda is something much MUCH more sinister and potentially catastrophic – a Soviet or Maoist style communist state. Professor Hanson perfectly expressed the apprehension that I have long felt inasmuch as this leftward lurch by the Democratic Party may indeed not be benign or well

---

[206] Robert Kraychik, *Victor Davis Hanson: AOC Democrats Want 'Maoist' Cultural Destruction Not Just Socialist 'Redistribution',* (Breitbart.com, March 13, 2019). To listen to the interview in its entirety, *see,* https://www.breitbart.com/radio/2019/03/13/victor-davis-hanson-aoc-democrats-want-maoist-cultural-destruction-not-just-socialist-redistribution/.

intentioned. There is every possibility that this movement is menacing and baleful, with the purpose of destroying the United States in its current political and economic configuration.

Indeed, shortly after Vermont Senator Bernie Sanders declared his 2020 Presidential Bid, the media began doing something it did not do in 2016, it started uncovering the truth of what Senator Sanders has stood for from the beginning of his career in U.S. national politics, and it is anything but the benign soft European Welfare state. For example, in March of 2019, CNN posted an article detailing the fact that Mr. Sanders explicitly urged nationalization of most major industries in the U.S. during the 1970s.[207] On the list were the energy industry, banking, telephone electric, pharmaceutical and manufacturing industries.[208] Sanders took these positions when he was a "leading member" of the *Liberty Union Party,* which was by his own admission a radical political party.[209] Sanders continued with his radical leftist activism through the 1980's, as the *New York Times* has reported. In 1985, then Mayor of Burlington Vermont, Sanders made a 14-hour journey to Nicaragua, to listen to a speech by, and then meet with, President Daniel Ortega, the leader of the Sandinista Revolution that took power six years prior.[210] For anyone old enough to remember, the Sandinista's were a brutal communist backed regime and Ortega was one of the staunchest communists in all of Latin America. The *Times* article goes on to conclude as follows:

> "A New York Times review of Mr. Sanders's mayoral papers – including hundreds of speeches, handwritten notes, letters, political pamphlets and domestic and foreign newspaper clippings from a period spanning nearly a decade – revealed that from his earliest days in office Mr. Sanders aimed to execute his own foreign policy, repudiating Mr. Reagan's approach of aggressively backing anti-communist government and resistance forces, while going further than many Democrats supporting socialist leaders."[211]

So we know with increasing certainty that Sanders has been a committed Marxist from his earliest days in politics. The NY Times article also notes that Sander's activities as Mayor of Burlington routinely displayed a worldview that was highly sympathetic to towards Marxist-inspired movements in the developing world.[212] Clearly, throughout the 1970's and 80's, Sanders was in no way any kind of "New Deal Liberal" or "Liberal Democrat." He was a Marxist. Period.

Over the decades since then Sanders has moderated his positions, but ask yourself; was that due to a true epiphany in realizing the dangers of formal collectivization, or was that political expediency? Perhaps the real Bernie Sanders has just been hiding behind a more moderate soft socialism façade, waiting for the right opportunity for the real Bernie Sanders to reveal himself to

---

[207] Andrew Kaczynski and Nathan McDermott, *Bernie Sanders in the 1970s Urged Nationalization of Most Major Industries,* (CNNpolitics, Thursday, March 14, 2019).

[208] Ibid.

[209] Ibid. The authors, Kaczynski and McDermott note that many of Sander's positions while at the Liberty Union had already been reported on and known, but that a comprehensive review, in addition to hundreds of newly digitized newspapers and files from the Liberty Union Party archived at the University of Vermont paint a more complete depiction of Sander's views regarding nationalization of industry at that time.

[210] Alexander Burns and Sydney Ember, *Mayor and 'Foreign Minister': How Bernie Sanders Brought the Cold War to Burlington,* (New York Times, May 17, 2019).

[211] Ibid.

[212] Ibid.

the nation. Assuming a benevolent intention behind the policy proposals advocated by Mr. Sanders, given what we know today, is one of the most dangerous suppositions one could make in the voting booth in the year 2020.

We can conclude from this analysis, that an increasing number of mainstream commentators are independently concluding there is an evolving consensus that the American political discussion, particularly on the left, is presently normalizing ideological positions that would have been categorically rejected by the American Electorate as recently as a decade ago. The goal posts are indeed moving, and within the Democratic Party, they are moving sharply to the left. But one of the primary forces moving the goal posts is Senator Bernie Sanders himself, who is now factually demonstrated to have at the start of his political career, publicly espoused nationalization of private industry, one of the purest principles of Marxism there is. This is a man who wishes to occupy the Oval Office, running a country that, until now, has rejected Marxism for the better part of a century.

The tragedy of it all is that, while an apathetic public drifts dangerously towards a purist form of socialism, there is so much information available from a myriad of sources that sheds light on the true nature of Marxism, which is an unalloyed totalitarian ideology. As has been reasserted multiple times in this book, people do not naturally collectivize on a mass scale. It is not a natural instinct. People desire to accumulate the fruits of their efforts – not be the one diligent and industrious "sucker" working in a regiment of unmotivated sloths getting the benefit of someone else's sweat and toil. People naturally ascertain when they are the only ones exerting effort for no apparent gain relative to the citizen standing right next to him. They will adjust their expectations and their desires accordingly. If they are in a system that does not reward individual achievement in any meaningful economic way, these naturally hard-working souls will not naturally step forward to be the martyr, the one that works like a horse only to be in exactly the same position as those doing nothing.

History has so many examples of this axiom, an enumeration is very easy. If Marxism is so effective, why did the Chinese abandon its' economic aspects in the late 1970s? If communism works so well, why did the USSR collapse? Why did Cuban and Cambodian communism fail? If democratic socialism and communism worked so well, why did Venezuela collapse leaving citizens who could not flee the country's disintegration to literally have to drink sewer water amid electrical black-outs?[213] If Marxist based economics is so worthy, why is North Korea a literal hell on earth, complete with its own atrocious gulags of the modern era? Suffice it to say I am not embellishing with my assertions that America is flirting with catastrophe. There is a more than reasonable basis to believe that America is seriously dallying with a hard-leftward lurch towards

---

[213] Natalie Musumeci, *Venezuelans Turn to Drinking Sewer Water Amid Blackouts,* (New York Post, March 12, 2019). Ms. Musumeci writes: "Desperate Venezuelans were forced to turn to filthy sewage drains and polluted rivers as the country's nearly weeklong power outage left many without water. I've never even seen this before. It's horrible, horrible," said Lilibeth Tejedor, 28, one of dozens who flocked to a drain pipe that runs into a river carrying sewage through the Venezuelan capital, Caracas, Reuters reported." Ibid. The fresh water situation has become so bad in many Venezuelan cities where basic infrastructure is so degraded that drinking the fresh water when it actually does come from the faucet (when the electricity is running) exposes the citizen to water contaminated with dangerous levels of bacteria. See Anatoly Krumanaev and Isayen Herra, *Venezuela's Water System is Collapsing,* (New York Times October 19, 2019).

a toxic Marxist ideology that could literally blow this country apart, resulting in a genuine loss of freedoms we have enjoyed for generations.

The risk the American People will scratch the totalitarian Marxist itch is so acute at this point, that even the Wall Street Titans are weighing in on the possibility we could be heading for some good old-fashioned class warfare. In a *60 Minutes* interview in April of 2019, hedge fund guru and multi-billionaire Ray Dalio went on record publicly estimating there is a 60-65% probability the US will experience "conflict" between the rich and the poor versus successfully reforming the system.[214] He does not define what he means by "conflict", but we can reasonably presume that it will not be an especially pleasant experience. Mr. Dalio has been giving an increasing number of interviews bemoaning the wealth gap and income inequality. He is correct of course, and he is even more on the point when he asserts, as he often does, that the answer is most certainly NOT socialism/Marxism. While it is encouraging that the moneyed elite in this country now seem to have a sense that they overplayed their hand over the past four decades, the horse may be out of the barn so to speak. The American people, especially young people are so fed up with what they perceive as a rigged and corrupt system that any "reform" will come in the form of political carpet bombing. I dare say the likes of Mr. Dalio will ultimately weather the storm unless it spirals out of control and something horrendous like the Bolsheviks actually does materialize; aside from that, it will be the affluent professional class that gets ultimately crushed.

And if the foregoing isn't proof enough, even the Federal Reserve is jumping in the discussion with recent comments warning of potentially destructive consequences of wealth inequality.[215] Specifically, Fed Governor Lael Brainard had publicly stated that "the long term vigor of the U.S. economy may be at risk as middle class households are squeezed by slow growth in income and wealth and rising costs for housing, health care and education."[216] She goes on to warn that the increasing share of income going to high-wealth households could result in muted consumer demand.[217] The article also recapitulates the point that Brainard made with respect to the sobering fact that middle class families still have not fully recovered the wealth they lost in the Great Recession, which ended over 10 years ago.[218] So a decade after the end of the last economic downturn, middle income America has yet to recoup their losses in the aggregate, and their incomes, even with modest gains since 2014, are still not keeping up with the rising costs associated with critical necessaries like education, health care and housing.

Corroborating Ms. Brainard's comments is a recent survey conducted by Charles Schwab showing that 62% of Millennials say they are living paycheck to paycheck.[219] A recent study by Deloitte, the well regarded accounting firm, shows the average Millennial has a net worth of a

---

[214] Ian Schwartz, *The American Dream is Lost; Capitalism Must Be Reformed, Not Abandoned,* (RealClearPolitics.com, April 8, 2019)

[215] Rich Miller and Matthew Boesler, *Fed Officials Warn Rising Inequality Threatens U.S.'s Long-Term Economic Strength,* (Bloomberg, May 10, 2019).

[216] Ibid.

[217] Ibid.

[218] Ibid.

[219] Megan Leonhardt, *62% of Millennials Say They're Living Paycheck to Paycheck,* (CNBC, May 13, 2019).

paltry $8,000.[220] An independent research institution at the University of Chicago adds still further support to the notion that the average American is in an unstable financial situation. The study shows that millions of Americans would face 'financial disaster' if they miss even a single paycheck.[221] The study shows that 40% of US households "lack a basic level of savings," and that these 'liquid asset poor' households do not have sufficient savings to live even three months at the poverty level should their income be disrupted.[222] In short, an astonishingly large number of US households will turn to financially dangerous fallback measures to cover basic living expenses in the event even one paycheck is missed; with resorting to credit card debt being one of the most often cited options.[223]

Given this unfortunate backdrop, I will siren a more urgent call than what Fed Governor Brainard is apparently prepared to do. This economic environment is a prescription for economic and political disaster. If the current economic system in the United States cannot be made to once again foster a vibrant and growing middle class, then the allure of Marxism will only intensify and accelerate. According to well-known pollster Frank Luntz, facts like those summarized above have made the term "capitalism" effectively "a dirty word" for substantial majorities of Democrats who will choose their next Presidential nominee.[224] Luntz is adamant that Bernie Sanders will ultimately win the Democratic nomination but believes that socialism is still a tough sell for a majority of Americans, and that the voters still respond well to the notion of "economic freedom" as capitalism has come to be associated with the excesses of big business, big tech and Wall Street.[225] It turns out American's really don't like living a paycheck away from financial oblivion while a relatively small number of business tycoons and celebrities drench themselves with wealth.

And now even former bank regulators are starting to weigh in on the potential for social and political conflagration in the offing due in large part to the financial precarious position the bottom half of American income earners find themselves. Eugene Ludwig, a high ranking Treasury Department official serving under former President Clinton recently penned a piece in *The Hill* acknowledging that looking at the dark underside of the seemingly robust Trump economy are millions of lower middle income American's living "on a knife's edge" one paycheck away from financial disaster.[226] Ludwig points out that the lower end of the economic spectrum is basically a "hand to mouth" living situation in America, with no savings, and an over reliance on debt to secure basics.[227] More importantly, he reminds the reader that in the event of the inevitable economic downturn yet to come, these over-leveraged consumers will lack the resources to repay this debt, potentially triggering another credit crisis, ensnaring banks in the near certain

---

[220] Abha Bhattarai, *The Average Millennial Has A Net Worth of $8,000. That's Far Less Than Previous Generations,* (Washington Post, May 31, 2019)

[221] Jacob Passy, *Millions of Americans are Just One Paycheck Away From 'Financial Disaster',* (Marketwatch, May 17, 2019), citing the study of NORC at the University of Chicago.

[222] Ibid.

[223] Ibid.

[224] Tim Hains, *Frank Luntz: Sanders Most Likely to Win Democratic Nomination, Capitalism Has Become a Dirty Word for the Left,* (RealClearPolitics, May 12, 2019).

[225] Ibid.

[226] Eugene Ludwig, *Rosy Economic Data Belies a Harsh Reality for Many Americans,* (The Hill, May 15, 2019). Mr. Ludwig was Comptroller of the Currency under President Clinton. The Comptroller is the primary regulator of all National Banks.

[227] Ibid.

backlash.[228] He describes the "future abyss" in terms that depict a popular clamoring for harsh retribution for business leaders, wealth redistribution and "particular venom for lenders."[229] And why wouldn't they? After all, the basic economic situation in America today is that half the 159 million-member workforce has effectively been told that there is no place for them at the table of prosperity.

As it stands today, with these political and economic realities, the American People are giving a good hard look and many campaign dollars to Bernie Sanders, the self-avowed democratic socialist whose views, as we have shown, are now empirically known to be purest Marxism. This is the same Senator who took his honeymoon in the USSR during 1988 (as an ideological foreshadow or intimation perhaps?).[230] And we now know increasingly more about what transpired on that "honeymoon" to the former Soviet Union. The Washington Post recently ran a full-length article covering what is now known to have occurred during that visit, based interviews with five attendees on top of audio and video recordation of that trip. It is not an exaggeration that Mr. Sanders stood on foreign soil of his country's arch-enemy, and bashed the United States while extolling the virtues of Soviet communism.[231] The lone Republican in Sander's "delegation" was so offended by Sander's conduct at a banquet attended by 100 or so people, that he walked out of the event.[232] When confronted by an audience member in an April 2019 CNN Town Hall event on his seeming affection for the former USSR, Mr. Sanders was indignant. He challenged her to identify when he'd ever condoned authoritarian communism under the USSR.[233]

His indignance evidences that (to paraphrase George Will and William F. Buckley) he is a pyromaniac in a barn full of straw men. No one is challenging the fact that Sanders has for 20 years espoused socialism in the context of democracy. What his critics (including me) are saying is that: (1) socialism in the context of "democracy" has failed as much as it has under authoritarian rule (see modern day Venezuela); and, (2) the fact that he has formally endorsed the nationalization of many private industries earlier in his career calls into question his sincerity when he toots the horn of democracy in his socialist pursuits. Does he really think nationalizing industries could be done peacefully? It seems to me that the only time nationalization occurs is when authoritarians shove it down the throats of unwilling participants, and if it is done using democratic means at the outset, it almost always results in authoritarianism at the end (again, see modern day Venezuela for Exhibit "A"). One of the most succinctly stated assertions for the improbability of socialism in the context of democracy comes from the left leaning *New Republic*, a stalwart intellectual

---

[228] Ibid.

[229] Ibid.

[230] Will Cabanis, *George Will Describes Bernie Sanders' Soviet Union Honeymoon,* (Punditfact, August 12th 2015). Sanders himself referred to his trip with his new wife to Yaroslavl USSR the day after his wedding as "a very strange honeymoon." His wife Jane referred to it the same way by saying the day after their wedding they went to Yaroslavl for the sister city project. Admittedly the sister city project between Burlington VT and Yaroslavl was planned months in advance, so its co-incidence with the Sander's Wedding honeymoon might have rationale other than pure ideology, but given what we know about Mr. Sanders – it is reasonable to assume at least some of the reason for the trip as part of his honeymoon can be attributed to Marxist virtue signaling. And by the way, Politifact ruled that Mr. Will's reference to Sanders' 1988 Yaroslavl trip as a "honeymoon" was essentially true, if not the full and complete picture of the trip.

[231] Michael Kranish, *Inside Bernie Sanders's 1988 10-Day 'Honeymoon' in the Soviet Union,* (Washington Post, May 3, 2019).

[232] Ibid.

[233] Ian Schwartz, *Woman To Bernie Sanders: My Family Fled Soviet Russia, Socialism Has Failed IN Nearly Every Country,* (Real Clear Politics, April 22, 2019). The Real Clear Politics article includes a transcript of the CNN Town Hall exchange hosted by Chris Cuomo.

magazine in the league with *The Atlantic*, and *Harpers*. Win McCormack, its current Editor-in-Chief penned a well authored article entitled *Socialism in No Country*. In this article, Mr. McCormack nicely summarizes the autocratic nature of socialism when he writes:

> "There is now an organization in the United States called the Young Democratic Socialists of America (YDSA) – the youth wing of the older DSA. Unfortunately, ***no self-identified socialist regime in the world*** – all of which have been installed by professional revolutionaries in the Marxist-Leninist tradition – ***has ever been the least bit democratic. No democratically elected legislative body has ever voted to take control of the 'means of production,' except to the most modest extent***."[234] (Emphasis Supplied)

Precisely. Well said Mr. McCormack. Marxist economic regimes are nearly always installed by "professional revolutionaries" – violently. Not to gloat too much, but it is something to behold when a denizen of the left like the *New Republic* has to devote an entire issue on the "The Socialist Moment", and it's lead editor has to write a near polemic to convince himself and his readers that the risk of socialism in America is not as great as it seems. I respectfully disagree, as I believe there to be evidence that the threat of Marxism coming to America is the highest it has ever been. The only caveat I would add to the supposition quoted above, is that technically, as I previously noted, Chavez was democratically elected multiple times, so Venezuela must be viewed as a modest exception to the general notion that socialism/Marxism is never democratically embraced. And as already stated in connection with Venezuela, as soon as Chavez achieved power, he moved over time to despotism that was fully in place for his successor Nicolas Maduro.

The near complete absence of democracy in a socialist civilization means that it is a safe bet to assume any attempt to collectivize or "nationalize" industries in America, as both Sanders and Warren have previously advocated for, would result in massive resistance that would have to be countered by government suppression – an American form of dekulakization if you will. The real question is what would modern dekulakization look like if my hypothesis – that America may end up a socialist country - turns out to be correct? That indeed is the subject of the next chapter.

---

[234] Win McCormack, *Socialism in No Country: Why the revolutionary left has always been bad news for democracy,* (New Republic, May 21, 2019).

CHAPTER V

AMERICAN "DELULAKIZATION"

Nowhere to run, baby, nowhere to hide
Got nowhere to run to, baby, nowhere to hide
It's not the love I'm running from
It's the heartbreak, I know will come…

- Martha Reeves and the Vandellas, *Nowhere to Run*

The epigraph above brings to mind a passage from a book published in 1996 by Robert Bork, an American Legal Scholar who once served as a Circuit Judge on the U.S. Court of Appeals for the DC Circuit. The book was entitled *Slouching Towards Gomorrah*, and it was a conservative classic. In the final chapter, entitled *Can America Avoid Gomorrah*, Bork references a moment that had occurred a few years earlier, in the middle of the Clarence Thomas Supreme Court Senate Judiciary Committee Hearings where a horrified Bork goes to a colleague's office and says "Television is showing the end of Western civilization in living color."[235] Apparently, the colleague responds by saying: "Of course it's coming to an end. But don't worry. It takes a long time, and in the meantime it is possible to live well."[236] Bork is quick to ascribe this sentiment to what he refers to as the "Ausonian philosophy," which is the notion of finding refuge somewhere and living comfortably with your existing traditions all the while the civilization around you is crumbling towards ruin, just as Roman administrators and poets did in the second half of the fifth century when Rome's end was seen as inevitable.[237] Bork then promptly points out that the Ausonian philosophy may or may not be all that viable; and notes that there is nothing preventing a civilizations collapse from occurring relatively quickly.[238] More importantly, he challenges the notion that taking asylum in a protected sanctuary somewhere would even be available in the current era. As an example, he recalls the fact that the survival of Christianity and learning during

---

[235] Robert Bork, *Slouching Towards Gomorrah; Modern Liberalism and American Decline* (Regan Books, A Division of Harper Collins Publishers 1996)., 335.

[236] Ibid.

[237] Ibid.

[238] Ibid.

76

the Medieval period was made possible by the fact that there were monasteries such as the one on Ireland's Skellig Michael, which were spared invasion by the Germanic tribes during the Anglo-Saxon Conquest.[239] In other words, basically as a matter of dumb luck. Bork is most correct with the inference that the West may not be so lucky the next time.

It is this notion of safe harbor in a crumbling world that I wish to address in much more detail, because I share the same skepticism as Mr. Bork. There is simply no assurance whatsoever that those of us who value a free enterprise market-based system, as well as other Western traditions will find a place to run and hide if Bolshevik-minded progressives are allowed to seize the institutional corridors of power of the American Federal super-state. The prospect of the long and deep reach of the state is the supposition for this chapter, and the contours of what dekulakization will take is the subject matter for it. The increasing potential and consequence of a Bolshevik take-over will be the focus of chapter 6. In the event the Marxist Progressives are successful in seizing power like Hugo Chaves did in Venezuela in the late 1990's, my position is that there will be no place for retreat. There will be no hideaway in anything like a monastery or its equivalent where free enterprise can flourish all the while American Civilization is reduced to ashes over the ensuing decades – just as has happened in Venezuela over the past 20 years. Modern technology will not allow anyone to ever live in anonymity again. We will all be tracked down and accounted for. We will all be made to conform to whatever collectivist urge beguiles the new Marxist government. We will pay whatever absurd level of taxation will be required of us, or the IRS will send SWAT teams retrofitted with the latest battlefield weaponry to adjust our attitude. There will be no tax revolts, at least not ones that have a peaceful conclusion. It is a safe bet that government will win any potential violent standoff or resistance to excessive taxation if it ever comes to that.

The structure of this chapter will be to outline the initial steps a newly created American Bolshevik government will take towards wealth re-distribution. Some of the tactics are already in place, such as a payroll tax for example, which will be expanded rapidly and ferociously. Then there will be the outright tax increases on the marginal rates, first on the top brackets, then more gradually on the lower ones. In the beginning, the increases will be stealth like - quiet and lethal. Then they will increasingly be much bolder and aggressive. Subsequent steps will include crushing taxation on activities out of favor with the Marxist ideology. Religious entities will lose their tax exemptions. This chapter will also survey a litany of ways taxation will be used to obliterate purchasing power of the top half of income earners and the very wealthy. Capital Gains tax increases, wealth taxes, taxes on the sale of any capital asset will all be massively increased. Then when the long bemoaned "wealth gap", the gap in income and assets between the rich and the rest of us is effectively nullified, the temptation for outright nationalization of industries will be at its highest.

None of this will occur without massive resistance from a significant portion of the population. First will come backlash at the polls, but as socialism is increasing in allure among large segments of the young, electoral success by Marxists may increase materially with time. An American Bolshevik minded regime will surely move quickly to de-fang the threat posed by a large cache of firearms in the hands of private citizens. The first step to achieving this end will be to begin to curtail the Constitution's guarantee of the right to bear arms. Guns and ammunition, to the extent

---

[239] Ibid.

not formally outlawed will be taxed to the point that the cost of a purchase is not feasible for 90% of the population, ammunition will be taxed at levels that make it the province of only the rich and connected, and then ultimately all non-government issued firearms will be banned from private use altogether, and confiscation initiatives will be crafted to begin impounding the 300 million guns in private hands. The cost of obtaining a licenses for hunting and fishing will skyrocket.

As noted in the Introduction, as the older generations die off, and the current crop of Americans 40 and under ascent to real institutional power, the prospect of electoral success for socialism will exceed any point in US history. While this may seem outlandish, the prospect of "mainstreaming" socialism in ways no one could have imagined even 10 years ago is now being written about with all due seriousness by well-known Ivy League professors who are pointing out the potential generational transformation underway. A recent article by Niall Ferguson and Eyck Freymann in *The Atlantic*, speaks of a political realignment in the Democratic party where Millennials (age 23-38) and Generation Z (age 22 and under) will take control over the next 10 years.[240] As the Millennials and Generation Z are decidedly more left leaning than older generations, when they assume an increasingly larger and eventually dominant voting block within the Democratic party, we can expect that its' nominees will lean much farther to the left than ever before.[241] I posited the question in the preface to this book that the reader consider the prospect that Alexandrea Ocasio-Cortez, Elizabeth Warren and Bernie Sanders may one day constitute moderates – well within the political mainstream of American politics, something unthinkable even 10 years ago. Ferguson and Freymann point out that as the 2020's progress, the oldest generation – the "silent generation" (those over age 74) will begin to retreat and in their place will be Generation Z, today's most left leaning voting block.[242] Together with Millennials, they will comprise a key electoral cohort and may well be in a position to drive the U.S. political agenda much farther to the left than ever before contemplated. The main thrust of the article is the political dynamics of Democrats riding this demographic windfall and Republicans countering with a full-scale attempt at getting ever more Boomers and X'rs to join them – making for a potentially combustible generational war.

I have stated the view often throughout this book that I believe the likely result is that the overall political center of gravity will shift sharply to the left in American politics as it already has since 2008. In a two-party system, Democrats will elect their fair share of Presidents and Congressional majorities, and when they do win, their candidates will be increasingly left leaning in the extreme. So much so that we cannot rule out the potential that America may one day elect a full-on Marxist President with Congressional majorities of the same mind set. In what historians eons from now will no doubt view with the cruelest irony; what Vladimir Lenin, Josef Stalin, Nikita Khrushchev, Leonide Brezhnev, Konstantin Chernenko, Yuri Andropov and Mikhail Gorbachev could not achieve in 70 plus years of nuclear armed confrontation, the US is about to deliver unto itself democratically by a generation of Americans utterly ignorant of the horrors of Marxist rule.

In the Venezuelan model, more resistance came from the courts than from the electorate. After being reelected, Chaves was able to stack the courts with judges sympathetic to his views and agenda. Once the courts bought into his programs, he began to nationalize entire industries and over about a decade, transformed one of Latin America's most productive economies into a

---

[240] Niall Ferguson and Eyck Freymann, *The Coming Generational War* (The Atlantic, May 6, 2019).

[241] Ibid.

[242] Ibid.

Marxist civilization. It has not ended well. A similar strategy will be taken by American Bolsheviks if they win the Presidency and a majority of seats in Congress. A Marxist US President will also increase the militarization of federal law enforcement agencies and the newly minted jurists sympathetic to Marxism will approve a massive increase in the use of these agencies. Civil liberties will be radically curtailed. Resisters of the coming collectivization will face the harsh hand of the state. All of the above will be enumerated in much greater detail throughout this chapter and the next. The discussion that follows is an attempt to articulate what a 21st Century American form of "dekulakization" might look like.

The New Collectivization: Annihilation Via Taxation:

As we saw in chapters two and three, a key method of dekulakization was the use of absurdly high individual tax rates as a means of economic annihilation, which preceded the Kulak's actual physical one. In the event there is one day an American Bolshevik socialist government in full control of the American federal government, extreme increases in all levels of taxation will be the initial step towards wealth re-distribution. Indeed, self-described socialist candidates already routinely proclaim their intention to raise taxes on the "rich" and "well off" in our society. As long time self-avowed socialist Senator Bernie Sanders formally declared his 2020 Presidential Candidacy in February of 2019, he was most honest and forthright in his affirmation to raise taxes on the wealthiest American citizens under the guise of campaigning for "creating a government based on the principles of economic, social, racial and environmental justice."[243] In his 2016 presidential campaign against Hillary Clinton, Sanders routinely and regularly called for large tax increases on the "wealthy." Sanders believes his views and policy objectives are becoming mainstream within the Democratic Party.[244] Indeed as the 2020 presidential campaign got underway, candidates fell all over themselves to embrace increases in the top marginal rate to 70 or even 90%. Even more ominously, large majorities of voters appear to be very much, perhaps even overwhelmingly on board with such proposals.[245]

As history shows, taxes won't just go up for the top earners, they will go up for everyone. As we have repeatedly noted, the agenda wish list for the extreme American socialist measures in the hundreds of trillions;[246] it is so massive that gouging only the rich will in no way be enough. Let's proceed with some analysis of those taxes that will go up for everyone.

---

[243] Juana Summers, *Senator Bernie Sanders Says He's Running for President in 2020,* (Associated Press, February 19, 2019).

[244] Ibid.

[245] Louis Casiano, *Most Voters Back Ocasio-Cortez Plan to Tax Richest Americans Up To 70%: Poll* (Fox news, January 16, 2019). According to a Hill-HarrisX survey, which was conducted Jan. 12-13, approximately 59% of respondents support this idea. This is not the only poll supporting the notion that the public likes the idea of massive new increases in taxation for the wealthy. *See,* Ben White, *Soak the Rich? Americans Say Go For It: Surveys are showing overwhelming support for raising taxes on top earners.* (Politico, February 4, 2019). In this article Mr. White cites a POLITICO/Morning Consult poll released in early February 2019 suggesting Americans are increasingly on board with raising taxes on top income earners. The poll shows that 70% of the American Public favors increasing taxes on those earning $10 million per year or more. Furthermore, this poll, conducted Feb. 1-2, found that 61 percent favor a proposal like the "wealth tax" recently laid out by Sen. Elizabeth Warren (D-Mass.) that would levy a 2 percent tax on those with a net worth over $50 million and 3 percent on those worth over $1 billion. Just 20 percent opposed the idea. The poll surveyed 1,993 registered voters and carries a margin of error of plus or minus 2 percent.

[246] Charles Fain Lehman and David Rutz, *Analysis: Dem Candidates Call For More Than $200 Trillion in Spending*, (The Washington Free Beacon, July 31, 2019). This article does a nice job of categorizing and summarizing the estimated dollar cost of all proposals from 2020 Democratic Presidential Candidates during the first eight months of 2019 alone.

1) <u>The Stealth Taxes: The Tax Man's Neutron Bomb</u>:

When I was in the sixth grade in the late 1970's, the neutron bomb had been in the news a great deal. I asked my homeroom teacher what kind of device that was and she told me it was a terrible weapon that, when exploded, it released a radioactive plume that killed everyone and everything within a calculated radius without doing much physical damage, at least not like the damage that would come from a nuclear explosion. She left it that the neutron bomb would explode, leaving the buildings basically standing but obliterating the population inhabiting them. The buildings stay but the people go, is what I took from that conversation so many decades ago. Stealth taxes that we will discuss in this portion of the argument work much the same way. They won't kill you physically, but they can and often do annihilate people economically and financially.

Regarding the use of the term "stealth" in connection with a form of taxation, remember that there are a vast number of ways a governmental authority can levy taxes. The ones with the highest visibility are the taxes we pay based on our income, followed by those taxes we pay when we purchase goods or services (sales taxes). Property taxes rank right up there too. There is; however, a significant tax burden on businesses and individual income earners that gets far less attention. But don't let their surreptitious nature fool you, for affluent income earners, the payroll tax is so large it would dwarf the average total tax liability for the typical tax filer. Yet few people really understand that much about it. The payroll taxes (Social Security, Medicare and Medicaid) just show up on a few lines on the paystub of everyday earners, but most people do not really even know that the tax labeled "FICA" or "OASDI" (standing for old age and survivors disability insurance) is actually their social security tax. There are many other furtive taxes that we pay, but we will begin with the analysis of the Payroll Tax, as I believe this will be the most damaging to the affluent earner. The net effect is a form of "dekulakization" that is already underway.

    a. The Payroll Tax

        i. Current State and Historical Perspective

The term payroll tax comes from the fact that it is subject to Internal Revenue Service (IRS) back-up withholding rules and MUST be deducted from your paycheck, and your employer pays the same 6.2% in taxes on your wage and salary income to the IRS – hence the reference to "payroll". Failure to properly adhere to these backup withholding requirements and you and your employer would be in a good deal of trouble with the IRS, a battle you both would surely lose. There is a facet about this tax, at least as it pertains to the Social Security portion, that most taxpayers are not fully aware of, which is that this tax phases out after a certain dollar level of income is reached. In other words, the tax does not apply to 100% of one's income. For 2019 the wage cap for OASDI is $132,900, meaning that the 6.2% OASDI tax on wages will cease on dollars earned above the $132,900 threshold.[247] Stated differently, OASDI does not apply on those dollars earned over and above the $132,900 limit for 2019.[248] Each dollar earned above this limit is earned free of the payroll tax. A final way of looking at it is that the maximum Social Security

---

[247] Social Security Administration, Office of Retirement and Disability Policy, *OASDI and SSI Program Rates and Limits* (2019).
[248] Ibid.

tax one can pay in 2019 is $8,239.80 (132,900 x .062 = $8,239.80). Your employer pays an equal amount.

    To ensure proper perspective on this level of taxation, you will recall in chapter 4 we demonstrated that median family income in the United States was $61,372. According to Pew Research Center, the average effective federal tax rate for Adjust Gross Income of between $50,000 and $100,000 in annual income is 9.2%.[249] So for a family with median income filing a federal return, the tax liability would be approximately $5,646.22. As you can see, for an affluent income earner making $132,900, the Social Security Income Tax liability of $8,239.88 is materially higher than the average ***total income tax liability*** for a family with median income – higher by 45.9% actually. In other words, the payroll tax liability for an affluent fax filer with income at the 2019 social security benefit base will be 45.9% higher than the actual federal tax liability for a family with median income. Remember that – the payroll tax alone is significantly larger by 45.9% than the amount of federal income tax the average family owes. And if your income is above the $132,900, you can look forward to the Social Security Administration raising the cap next year, and the year after that and on and on. This last point cannot be overstated. To illustrate, I offer the table below as Figure 5.

---

[249] Drew DeSilver, *A Closer Look at Who Does (and Doesn't) Pay U.S. Income Tax.* (Pew Research Center, 2017). *See.,* http://www.pewresearch.org/fact-tank/2017/10/06/a-closer-look-at-who-does-and-doesnt-pay-u-s-income-tax/. It is worth mentioning that the median family income number of $61,372 is for 2017 and the average effective federal tax rate cited in the PEW Research article is for 2015. As the median family income for 2017 would not be materially different than for 2015, I allowed the effective rate to be used on 2017 median family income.

FIGURE 5.

Contribution and benefit bases, 1937-2019

Year	Amount	Year	Amount	Year	Amount
1937-50	$3,000	1986	$42,000	2006	$94,200
1951-54	3,600	1987	43,800	2007	97,500
1955-58	4,200	1988	45,000	2008	102,000
1959-65	4,800	1989	48,000	2009	106,800
1966-67	6,600	1990	51,300	2010	106,800
1968-71	7,800	1991	53,400	2011	106,800
1972	9,000	1992	55,500	2012	110,100
1973	10,800	1993	57,600	2013	113,700
1974	13,200	1994	60,600	2014	117,000
1975	14,100	1995	61,200	2015	118,500
1976	15,300	1996	62,700	2016	118,500
1977	16,500	1997	65,400	2017	127,200
1978	17,700	1998	68,400	2018	128,400
1979	22,900	1999	72,600	2019	132,900
1980	25,900	2000	76,200		
1981	29,700	2001	80,400		
1982	32,400	2002	84,900		
1983	35,700	2003	87,000		
1984	37,800	2004	87,900		
1985	39,600	2005	90,000		

Note: Amounts for 1937-74 and for 1979-81 were set by statute; all other amounts were determined under automatic adjustment provisions of the Social Security Act.

The Social Security Administration has been continuously raising this contribution and benefit base for OASDI since 1937. It will continue to do so for the foreseeable future. The chart noted in Figure 5 is taken directly from the Social Security Administration web site.[250] The impact of the constant increasing of the payroll tax, likely to the point of include literally all income, is going to be devastating for upper bracket affluent income filers in the years to come. As I will demonstrate below, no one will feel the impact of these increases than the American affluent professional – or "American Kulak". In that sense, the continuing increases in this tax has and will continue to have the "dekulakization" effect for the foreseeable future. To further elucidate the point, when I got into the workforce out of law school in 1993 the benefit base noted in Figure 5 was $57,600. In the quarter century since, the benefit base has more than doubled to the $132,900. Analysis of this table allows us to conclude that the benefit base has increased by $26,100 from 2009 to 2019 alone. At this rate, another increase of $26K over the next decade will mean that families with incomes of up to $159,000 will pay the 6.2% payroll tax on literally all of their income. Simple arithmetic applied to these figures (159,000 x .062) results in an annual payroll tax liability of $9,858. This will be owed on top of the state and federal income taxes, in just 10 short years.

---

[250] *See.,* https://www.ssa.gov/oact/cola/cbb.html.

To give you an idea of the hit, consider a newly minted Generation Z dentist in the year 2029 with an income of $160,000, who has none of the typical deductions older filers would have. She does not yet own a home, so no property taxes are paid. Assume he lives in San Francisco or LA. After the effects of the 2017 tax legislation, she can expect a federal tax liability in the neighborhood of $29,800. Then assume these federal rates hold for 10 years (a purely hypothetical assumption) and by then, the payroll tax is in full effect for the entire $160,000. The result is hideous. On $160,000 in income a typical filer will be faced with $39,650+ in federal and payroll tax liability. Then add the Medicare tax of approximately $2,300, then add a state tax, which in a state like California would be approximately $11,700+. Now we're up to $53,650 federal, payroll, Medicare and state income taxes. At this level, we will be talking about roughly 34% tax liability for all income taxes owed, which will bite the professional class very hard if they live in cities like Boston, New York, LA, San Francisco or Chicago. The net pay on $160,000 in gross income in the scenario above would be $106,350. Remember that in this hypothetical, she lives in San Francisco or Los Angeles. That may sound affluent when you are living in Lawrence Kansas or Lincoln Nebraska, but when you try and live on it in these high cost metropolitan areas, good luck with that. Remember the median house price in San Francisco is now over $900,000. So this newly minted dentist can look forward to a median house price that is almost ten times her take home pay. Again, absolutely absurd. And Dentists, like other medical professionals, often have high levels of student debt. All these factors combined will render a $106,000 take home income witheringly uncomfortable.

If by this point the reader considers my points to be an exaggeration or an unorthodox perspective, I submit to you that it is not. I will call your attention to a 2019 posting by a retired Bay-Area investment banker posting a blog under the name *Financial Samurai*. Remember we heard from him in the last chapter regarding what is "mass affluent". Four our purposes here, he performed an in-depth analysis of the living standards for a putative Bay Area resident earning household income of $300,000.[251] The blog post analyzes in detail, all the tax implications of income at this level and the typical expenses the average San Francisco resident could reasonably be expected to incur. The conclusion of the blog is contained at the outset when he writes:

> "Let me tell you a sad story. In order to live comfortably raise a family in an
> expensive coastal city like San Francisco or New York, You've got to make
> at least $300,000 a year. You can certainly raise a family earning less as
> many do, but it won't be easy if your goal is to save for retirement, save for
> your child's education, own your own home instead of rent, and actually
> retire by a reasonable age"[252]

In short the blog makes a very compelling fact based assertion that in major metropolitan areas on both coasts, even $300,000 in annual income is basically middle class, while in the eyes of most American's it is handsomely affluent. For the record, $300,000 in annual income is a smidge under 5 times the median family annual income in the U.S. If $300,000 is middle class in terms of actual living standards, first, it is taxed at a rate much higher than the median family income nd second, if $300,000 in gross annual income is what is required to be "comfortable" in major coastal

---

[251] Financial Samurai, *Why Households Need to Earn $300,000 A Year to Live A Middle Class Lifestyle Today.* Post as of June 2, 2019.

[252] Ibid.

cities – then what does that imply for our hypothetical dentist at $160,000? I think what it implies is that a $160K in annual income is not really even middle class in major cities anymore, and to continue raising the payroll tax on them is basically an immorality.

This last point calls for more discussion. I picked the hypothetical at $160,000 in income in the Bay Area for several reasons. First, it is still comfortably affluent on a nationwide basis in other cities and locations. When I was growing up in the 1970s there were so few income earners in this range that it was outright wealthy. As we have seen, it now arguably does not even qualify for middle class in San Francisco. A recent article by CNBC, citing data from *Unison*, a home co-investment company, demonstrated that the minimum salary level to buy a home in San Francisco in 2019 would be $202,094.[253] This assumes that the payment is calculated with the monthly payment of principal, interest, taxes and insurance that does not exceed 30% of gross monthly income; and further assumes a 20% down payment on a median home price in San Francisco of $1,031,732; and a 4.5% interest mortgage with a 30 year term.[254] And now for the real shocker. According to this analysis, it will take an estimated ***40 years*** to save the $206,346 down payment to do the 80% financing assumed in this example!!!!![255] Clearly, even $200,000 a year in San Francisco would struggle to have a Better Homes and Gardens style middle class living standard.

So, the hypothetical with the dentist earning an annual income of $160,000 is relevant for additional reasons than the ones mentioned above. I noted earlier in this chapter that if the current OASDI income thresholds continue to rise at the same rate as I have demonstrated for the past 10 years, then the entire $160,000 will be subject to the social security tax. As we can see from the foregoing analysis, this income level is already quite insufficient to support middle class life in San Francisco, to continue to raise the Social Security Tax on 100% of income up to that point is, as a matter of fact, raising taxes on an income amount that consigns its earners to a renters living standard.

In fact, payroll tax on income at these levels would have been unthinkable a generation ago. For a historical perspective, if we go back to 1990 for example, the wage base cap was $51,300. So the OASDI liability on $160,000 in 1990 would have been $3,180.60 ($51,300 x 6.2%). By 2029, it will be a tad more than *three times* that amount on the *same income*. And of course the purchasing power of $160,000 in 1990 would have been drastically more than it will be in 2029. In 1990 the median house price in San Francisco County would have been under $300,000.[256] By 2029 it will be comfortably over its current level of $1 million (its peak was $1,270,492 in 2017)[257]. For anyone who has relatives in the Bay Area or who has lived there themselves, living on less than $300,000 in such places requires people to start to forego attributes in life that have come to be hallmarks of middle class living. *Financial Samurai* depicts this in very stark terms. Hence, the net effect of these stealth tax increases is that of a "pincer action" where the purchasing power of this income level continues to be significantly degraded on one end, while the whole time the

---

[253] Emmie Martin, *The Salary You Need to Earn to be Able to Afford a Home In 15 Major US Cities,* (CNBC.com, June 11, 2019).

[254] Ibid.

[255] Ibid. To view the entire article, see, https://www.cnbc.com/2019/06/11/salary-needed-to-buy-a-home-in-major-us-cities.html.

[256] Compass, A California Real Estate Blog (June 2016). *See.* https://blog.pacificunion.com/what-bay-area-home-prices-looked-like-25-years-ago/.

[257] Ibid.

federal government will be raising the payroll tax at the other end. Think of a pincer with two opposing sides coming together to grip, crush or tear whatever it grabs. Another analogy is being caught between the proverbial rock and hard place. The affluent standard of living is being burned at both ends by the interplay of inflation and taxes.

If this isn't the first stage in "dekulakization" I'd love to know what is. To reiterate an earlier point, when I was in college, annual income of $160,000 would have been more than mass affluent. It would have been upper class, pure and simple. One would have had their kids in very posh private schools on this income – even in San Francisco. They would have had a condominium in Maui. They would have driven a brand-new luxury automobile like a high end Mercedes or BMW. I can assure you that someone in their 30s reading this now will attest to the fact that $160,000 in San Francisco has been very much relegated to a lower middle-class living standard, if that. To continue to raise the payroll tax to include all income is simply a surreptitious method of gouging the American Taxpayer. That Republicans go along with it is pure cowardice and appeasement. Truth be known, author Michael Lind made the point 20 years ago that the Republicans played a key role in shifting the tax burden from the top marginal rate for the rich to the payroll tax for the middle class.[258] That Undeniably then, was the first phase of the "dekulakization" (annihilation via taxation) of the affluent, and has been underway for a while. The upper middle and upper class affluent are the targets, and both political parties are to blame. All of this will escalate massively under any Marxist government that evolves in the U.S. in the coming decades.

The practical implications of this will be that the professional affluent class we surveyed in chapter 4 will continue to see it's after tax income lowered systematically, consistently and relentlessly. There will be no political debate, as the law is already in place and has been for decades. Republicans are unable to mount an effective fight on any principle they have ever held dear. They are utterly useless unless you are part of the super-rich donner class. Only for wealthy donor will they be willing to "fall on a sword" for the interests of their constituents. Nor will there be much of a protest from the left because the impact will be disproportionately borne on the affluent. An occupant of any of the job categories we surveyed in the chapter 4 will one day wake up to find they sacrificed years and years of youth to acquire skills that will no longer yield any discernable financial advantage. For those professionals who are astute, the day will come when they begin to perceive that an electrician or plumber with a fraction of the education and student debt has a roughly equal net after tax income because the tradesman does not get scorched with the neutron bomb effect of the payroll tax simultaneously accompanied by a much higher federal tax bracket. Maybe then the progressive professional so eager to champion higher taxes will see the fallacy of it all. Then again, with an agenda measuring in the hundreds of trillions, perhaps not.

In any event, the payroll tax escalation will only be one leg of a multi-legged stool in terms of taxes that will hit the high-income earners especially hard. For radical progressives with Marxist tendencies, this is music to the ears. For unwitting Republicans who have gone along with one of

---

[258] Michael Lind, *The Next American Nation: The New Nationalism & the Fourth American Revolution,* (Free Press, 1995), 192. In a section of the book entitled "Regressive Taxation", Mr. Lind does an excellent job of articulating just how acutely Congress and the Reagan Administration shifted the tax burden that underwrites the growth of government from the rich to the middle class via the payroll tax increases. It is worth noting that increasing the payroll tax burden was signed off on by a Republican President, and a Republican controlled Senate, the Democrats still controlled the House of Representatives at that time, so this obscenity was brought to the American People through bipartisan action. Both parties have a hand in this.

the most malignant forms of tax increases for decades under the guise of preserving Social Security, it is an embarrassment. Conservative attempts at "Entitlement Reform" have been so impotent as to be laughable. Progressives have achieved everything they ever wanted in connection with the payroll tax. They are slowly bleeding the affluent under the radar without even so much as a whimper. Indeed, as I have said many times before in this book, the American Affluent Kulak no longer has any natural allies. They will be bled to death financially with the steady increases in the payroll tax leading the way. And the best news of all for radical progressives, this is only the beginning.

ii) Payroll Tax: Future State and Proposed Legislation

If you are fearful that the steady expansion or the payroll tax likely to be an incentive crushing obligation for future generations, you have good reason. Radical progressives, now becoming mainstream thanks to the ignorance of the millennial generation and Generation Z, have escalated their calls for massive increases in taxation associated with Social Security. In the 115th Congress (2017 – 2018), Representative John B. Larson (D-Conn-1) introduced H.R. 1902 on April 17, 2017, [259] which was entitled the Social Security 2100 Act. This proposal would raise the Social Security (OASDI) tax to 14.8% from the 12.4% it is now by 2043. [260] So the employee portion of the tax would rise by from 6.2% to 7.4% by that date.[261] Here is an even more ominous prospect to consider, as if the mere proposal of such a large increase wasn't already bad enough, there appears to be growing support for this bill in the 116th Congress, such that Rep. Larson re-introduced it.[262] According to Sarah O'Brien of CNBC, more than 200 Democratic lawmakers in Congress have already signed onto this bill.[263] The bill was under review by the House Ways and Means Committee in the spring of 2019, where four separate hearings were held to discuss Social Security Reform.[264] A full Committee vote and ultimately a full floor vote by the summer recess in 2019 is the expected timeline for this bill.[265] Whether the bill can pass the Senate, and garner President Trump's signature is very doubtful. Nevertheless, the bill shows where the Democratic Party is ideologically. As presented in the 116th Congress, the legislation would apply the higher aforementioned rates to incomes over $400,000 per year,[266] the tax for earners below that threshold would gradually rise from the current rate of 6.2% to 7.4%. Moreover, beginning in 2020, income above the $400,000 mark would gradually start paying this tax with the 7.4% tax rate becoming in full effect by 2043. So, under this proposal, those whose sin in life was to earn more than $400,000 in a year would simply pay this tax for ALL income above that level.

Let's examine the net effect of this proposal. First, the example we discussed earlier regarding the newly licensed Generation Z , would be unaffected by this legislation, as Representative Larson

---

[259] Library of Congress at Congress.gov. *See*., https://www.congress.gov/bill/115th-congress/house-bill/1902.

[260] Representative Larson's official website contained much detail on the particulars of the proposal. For further reference, *see generally*, https://larson.house.gov/social-security-2100.

[261] Ibid.

[262] Sarah, O'Brien, *Social Security Expansion Bill Poised to Gain Traction in Congress,* (CNBC.com, February 23,2019).

[263] Ibid. *See generally, https://www.cnbc.com/2019/02/22/social-security-expansion-bill-poised-to-gain-traction-in-congress.html*.

[264] Lorie Konish, *This Bill Could Extend Social Security Solvency For The Rest of This Century. Here's What Stands in The Way,* (CNBC.com June 1, 2019)

[265] Ibid.

[266] *See* Representative Larson's website at: https://larson.house.gov/social-security-2100.

is careful to exclude incomes under $400,000. But, as we have noted, current rules and trajectories remain in effect for incomes between $132,900 and $400,000 threshold identified in the Social Security 2100 Act. That means that the current trajectory is for the OASDI wage base to continue to relentlessly increase each year, so the gap between the OASDI max and $400,000 is ultimately going to close. The bill attempts to address this with what proponents are referring to a "doughnut hole" cap, which would render income between $132,900 and $400,000 as not being subject to the tax. The provisions of the bill around this cap are not especially clear or well written, so it remains to be seen whether any final bill would even include such a provision. Furthermore, if this legislation passes, then ***all income*** over $400,000 is subject to this rule. If your income is less than $400,000 you do not have to be concerned with this proposal as much, but as previously noted, your social security tax will continue to increase under existing law. That said, it may well get much worse for those apparently irredeemable pariah's with incomes over $400K.

Just how bad with the hit be on them should the Social Security 2100 legislation ever be signed into law? In a word – horrible. After reading the text of the proposed legislation (sections 201 and 202), there is no limiting provision on incomes over $400,000. That means that as the bill is currently written, ***all*** income over $400,000 will be subject to the 7.4% tax by 2043.[267] To illustrate the perverse impact this legislation will have on this category of wage earner, let's do an exercise that demonstrates the magnitude of this proposal. We'll take a sample of five income groups of the $400,000 and above wage earner category. For illustrative purposes let's examine the impact of the 2043 rate of 7.4% for incomes at the following intervals:

- $450,000
- $500,000
- $750,000
- $1,000,000
- $10,000,000

---

[267] Ibid. Citing Sections 201 and 202 of the text of the bill. Representative Larson's website admonishes us that those making over $400,000 comprise 0.4% of all wage earners, as if that is supposed to mollify skeptics. In the eyes of the radical progressive, your reward for achieving economic success by earning more than all but 0.4% of your fellow wage earners is a massive tax increase on all income over that amount. We can plainly see that Representative Larson learned absolutely nothing from the sickening and desperate poverty in former eastern-block countries that was revealed by the fall of the Berlin Wall a generation ago.

FIGURE 6.

OASDI Taxes Under Current Law v. Social Security 2100

Annual Wages	Current OASDI Rate	Estimated Contribution and Benefit Base in 2043 $207,656	Proposed Rate Fully Effective By 2043	New Tax Liability Owed on Income Over $400K in $$	**Total OASDI Tax Estimated in the Year 2043**
$450,000	6.2%	$15,366.54	7.4%	$3,700	**$19,066.54**
$500,000	6.2%	$15,366.54	7.4%	$7,400	**$22,766.54**
$750.000	6.2%	$15,366.54	7.4%	$25,900	**$41,266.54**
$1,000,000	6.2%	$15,366.54	7.4%	$44,400	**$59,766.54**
$10,000,000	6.2%	$15,366.54	7.4%	$710,400	**$725,766.54**

As can clearly be seen, the application of: (1) a small increase in the percentage tax rate, (2) coupled with the absence of any limit on the income subject to the tax in excess of $400,000 and a relentless increase in the OASDI contribution and benefit base for incomes under $400,000; the amount of new money that can be generated on a relatively small block of income earners is nothing short of staggering. It must be remembered that this payroll tax is over and above the federal and state income taxes and Medicare taxes these earners will pay. Effectively, the radical progressives will be taking one component of what we all pay in taxes on our wages and literally "jack it to the moon". You hear a lot from the hard left about the well off needing to pay "their fair share" of taxes, the above table puts what is considered "fair" by neo-Marxists in the starkest possible terms.

I have included a category for wage earners who earn $10MM or more each year because this seems to be the line of demarcation on proposals for radical progressives such as Alexandria Ocasio Cortez when they propose things like a 70% top marginal rate on incomes. As we noted in the Introduction to this book, she has limited that proposal to incomes of $10,000,000 a year or more. So, it should be exceedingly clear right now, that if the radical progressive Marxist agenda comes to fruition, those earning $10MM per year or more will face astounding levels of increased taxation. We are not talking about the relatively modest levels of tax increase on the affluent and wealthy under Clinton and Obama, here we are talking about almost unprecedented increases.

Anyone making over $400,000 per year will be slammed with a colossal increase in the payroll tax, and then for those who make a million a year or more, the increase in payroll taxation borders on the absurd. An increase of nearly $60,000 per year in payroll taxes on an individual, as we have seen from prior chapters, is just shy of median family income in America at the time this manuscript is written. Then to cap it all off, those making $10MM a year or more will be paying nearly three-quarters of a million in additional OASDI taxes each year, which is plainly outlandish. That this would be imposed on top of a massive hike in the top marginal rates for these high-income earners will simply dissuade people from high achievement. In cities like NY, income earners making these levels of income already pay nearly 60% of their income to some taxing authority – these would approach or even exceed European levels of taxation, which of course is

88

exactly the point. Radical progressives have always envied the European model for social democracy, and that is what they intend to bring to America. These ludicrous proposed taxation levels are so ridiculous they cannot be taken seriously, except that we must take them very seriously. Radical leftists do not even hide their ambitions any longer. They are here to "dekulak" the earners making over $150,000 a year, and to do the same to the bourgeoisie making over $1M a year. Pure and simple. If you resist, you will be brought to submission. The violence shown almost daily by left leaning thugs on college campuses against anyone who does not agree with them will be replaced with a heavily armed SWAT team using similar tactics, just like in Stalin's Russia, just like in Mao's China, just like the Khmer Rouge, just like Castro's Cuba, just like modern Venezuela. We will talk more about the authoritarian militarization that will come with an American Bolshevik Marxist government in the next chapter.

> b. Loss of Deductions (which effectively increases taxable income)

As we noted in the introduction, the Tax Cuts and Jobs Act of 2017[268] has capped the deduction for state and local income and property taxes to $10,000. These are commonly referred to as the SALT deduction in tax jargon. Furthermore, this Act has eliminated for the time being, the Personal Exemption, which for a family of five, means an increase in taxable income of about $20,250 starting in 2019, as the personal exemption in 2017 was $4,050 per person. Hence the loss of these deductions will add to the blood bath for affluent tax filers in high cost, high tax states like Massachusetts, California New Jersey and New York. We just spent considerable time discussing the pernicious effect of the steady payroll tax increases over time, and on top of that we have literally thousands of dollars' worth of taxable income being added to the tax liability for affluent borrowers in high tax states.

Let's boil this down. For those affluent filers who itemize their returns, the loss of the personal exemption basically means a family of five will have an additional $20,250 in extra income that will either be off-set some other way, or they simply pay tax on it at their effective tax rate for ordinary income. The SALT limitation works the same way. If you paid $40,000 in state, local and real property property taxes (very easy to do in places like New York and New Jersey), but you only get to deduct $10,000, you have $30,000 in extra income that will, again, need to be off-set some other way or it will be taxed at your effective rate for ordinary income. So the net effect of both hits is literally thousands upon thousands or extra taxable income that would not have been taxed before, resulting in thousands of dollars of added income tax liability. Not to belabor the point, but in the discussion so far, if you have additional taxable income of $20,250 due to the loss of the personal exemption and it cannot be off-set; and you have additional taxable income of $30,000 due to the cap on the SALT deduction and you cannot off-set it elsewhere, then you have additional taxable income of $50,250 for which you will owe taxes to the IRS. If your effective tax rate is 15%, this amounts to an extra $7,575 in income tax you will be required to pay the IRS. If your effective rate is 20%, you will owe the IRS an extra $10,100.

While the cap on the SALT deduction made headlines during the debates surrounding this legislation, the discontinuance of the personal exemption made almost no headlines at all. Talk

---

[268] Pub.L 115-97.

about stealth. This particular change to the law was furtive, pure and simple, which makes it an unctuous act due to the lethality of the impact of the tax.

If this were the only change to the law, it would bite, but it wouldn't be devastating. Couple this with the steady and unremitting increase to the payroll tax that will absolutely continue in perpetuity, you get the makings of an acute degradation of after-tax income for affluent professionals over time. And it is occurring with little or no resistance because there is little or no awareness it is even happening. The frog in the hot water jumps out. The frog in the warm water gradually turned to a boil is much more at risk. That is the essence of these early stages of the "dekulakization" of the American affluent professional, the American Kulak.

One thing that got a great deal of attention in early 2019 were the results of these changes on people's tax liability. Nothing like sitting down with your accountant and figuring out the return when it counts – i.e., when you file it under penalty if there are inaccuracies and omissions. Nothing focuses the mind better than the prospect of an IRS audit because of a faulty return. The news coverage was not favorable. CBS reported that there were unwelcome surprises for many early filers in 2019, with refunds being down and some filers even having to pay when they were expecting a refund.[269] The authors were quick to point out that what really matters is the effective rate that one pays, and that indeed went down for many individuals who got smaller returns or actually had to write a check to the IRS.[270] They explained the reason for this as being due to the change in the backup withholding requirements under the law, which meant that employers withheld less during the year, resulting in a smaller amount of taxes paid during the year, which corresponded to a reduction in the refund or even owing money on the return.[271] This problem related to backup withholding was predicted by the General Accounting Office and reported on by Forbes in early August of 2018, where Americans were warned that failing to make changes to the amount withheld each month would result in about 30 million taxpayers owing money when they file their returns in early 2019.[272] In short, the impact of these modifications is confusing to taxpayers to the point of obfuscation. The fact that a dozen Republican Congressmen from high tax blue states voted against the Act suggests they knew full well the impact this would have on many upscale taxpayers. Dekulaization is going to be a dirty business.

      c. Loss of Tax Exemptions (religious entities and other tax-exempt entities linked to conservative causes)

Another clandestine way the American Bolshevik Progressives will attack the well-off is to quietly undermine their charitable contributions, which can have a large effect on their income tax liability. Once a radical Marxist American government takes hold, this will surely be one of their targets, as it has been for nearly all other socialist/Marxist countries. In chapter 3 we recall Solzhenitsyn reminding us that religious practitioners and lay people active in the church were

---

[269] Aimee Picchi, Irina Ivanova, *Are You Winning or Losing Under the New Tax Law? Here's How To Tell:* (CBS News, February 21, 2019). *See also., https://www.cbsnews.com/news/federal-tax-refund-2019-are-you-winning-or-losing-under-the-new-tax-law-heres-how-to-tell/.*

[270] Ibid.

[271] Ibid.

[272] Kelly Phillips, *Report Suggests More Taxpayers Will Owe Tax in 2019due to Insufficient Withholding,* (Forbes, August 4, 2018). *See also., https://www.forbes.com/sites/kellyphillipserb/2018/08/04/report-suggests-more-taxpayers-will-owe-tax-in-2019-due-to-withholding/#60699aa35f0f.* The GAO report cited in this article is GAO–18–548, issued July 2018.

rounded up and sent to the gulags almost immediately after the Bolsheviks took power. An American Marxist regime might be more circumspect and discrete in their persecution, at least at the outset. I believe one of their primary methods of intimidation will be to increase the tax liability on the wealthy and affluent by targeting the charitable contribution as step number one, followed by a formal attack on the tax-exempt status of the charitable entity – including and especially the Church. There is precedent for this in American History.

If you the reader believe me to be exaggerating the point, please try this exercise. Type in the following phrase in any internet search engine you prefer: "challenges to the tax-exempt status of churches in America". I tried this on both Google (46,500 results) and Yahoo (29,500 results), and found page after page of details ranging from actual court challenges by atheists challenging the tax exempt status of churches, to articles and treatises on the subject. This alone suggests there is much for churches to be concerned with. Admittedly, there are links that came from this search which do not pertain to content that challenges the practice of allowing churches to maintain tax exempt status. These accommodative sites range from church start up guides to IRS links for tax filers. But there were none too few adversarial ones where the whole concept of tax exemptions for churches was being questioned. This exercise alone is prima facie evidence that this issue is one of controversy. I make no representation where this controversy will end up as a matter of tax policy, I just remember the history well enough to know that radical Marxists have enormous disdain for religion. It is well documented that the Soviets systematically murdered religious people and lay people associated with the Church. Watching the American left assault religious freedom for Christians in the media, on campuses, and in the Entertainment Industry leads me to believe that in the event we have a Marxist American government, the first phase of the persecution will be to attack its tax exempt status.

d. The Dreaded Alternative Minimum Tax

Most Americans are not aware of the Alternative Minimum Tax, an alternate tax structure designed and implemented in the late 1960's when Congress became aware of a handful of income earners making over $200,000 in reportable income, yet paying nothing in federal income tax. This taxation edifice was designed to limit deductions available to the highest income earners by phasing out the deductions at certain income intervals. The Alternative Minimum Tax (AMT) became a problem several decades later as inflationary effects on wages and salaries resulted in an increasing number of Americans earning income at a level triggering the AMT when the purchasing power of that income had been eroded by decades of inflation. While an annual income of $200,000 was extraordinary in 1969, it was merely "affluent" by 2007 in high cost metropolitan areas. The failure to index the applicability of the Alternative Minimum Tax to inflation for the first four decades of its existence resulted in increasing numbers of American's falling under its purview, with the result being a loss of deductions and a stark increase in the tax liability for filers who were decidedly not wealthy. Your author had that exact effect in 2007, with the result being many thousands of dollars of additional tax liability when I thought a refund was on the way.

The AMT has been adjusted in the years since and has been revised to lessen the impact on middle and upper middle-class income earners. Finally, it was last amended by the 2017 Tax Cuts and Jobs Act. Remember, AMT a separate tax system with the primary difference being that it levies tax on specific types of income that would otherwise not be taxed under the standard federal income tax system.[273] As I also noted, there are certain tax breaks in the form of deductions permitted in the regular income tax system, which are disallowed under AMT.[274] For 2018, the first year of filing under the effects of the Tax Cuts and Jobs Act, the rates for the AMT applicability are as follows. The 28% AMT rate is triggered with AMT income exceeding:

- $191,500 for married couples filing a joint return;
- $95,750 for other filers;[275]

There are many more nuances to this tax system, and there is no need to delve into the arcane minutiae as our mission is not an exercise in tax theory. What is worth mentioning is the ease with which this alternative tax system can be revised and adjusted over time. In the last 20 years it has been "patched" on multiple occasions to limit the impact on middle and upper middle-income filers. It is perhaps the "stealthiest" tax of all as it impacts comparatively few "high dollar" filers, and that is precisely the point. It can, and most likely will be massively expanded in the event the American government ever becomes formally Marxist. We have said may times in this this book that taxation has an identifiable history of being used as a political weapon of mass destruction, with the Soviet Kulaks a prime example.

Ask yourself the following questions regarding this tax. If politicians have no qualms whatsoever about asserting high income earners need to pay a 70% or even 90% top marginal tax rate, what on earth would cause them not to proceed with quietly adjusting AMT so that it snags even the merely "Affluent"? Given that the effects of inflation eventually brought the AMT to the middle-class income filer, won't that repeat after 2025 when the freeze on the income triggers under current law expires? Doesn't all a future Bolshevik American government need to do is just remain idle and let the freeze expire? Won't the affluent again be subject to this tax by doing nothing? Isn't there precedent for that already with other forms of income tax? Isn't that exactly what President Obama did in 2013 when the Bush Tax Cuts expired (hint: that is exactly what he did) the result of which was a sharp increase in income taxes among the affluent and wealthy?

If you, the reader, honestly believes that a Marxist American Government in the mold of Bernie Sanders or Elizabeth Warren will not use every lever available to raise your taxes, including lesser known taxes, as high as possible to pay for their ambitious agenda, then you may as well believe in trolls under the bridge. When an increasing number of Democrats are jumping on board with the "Green New Deal" as proposed by (you guessed it) Bernie Sanders Protégé Alexandria Ocasio Cortez, that tells you all you need to know. Her "Medicare For All" proposal is estimated to cost $33 Trillion in the first 10 years as we noted in chapter 1. We now have estimates on the cost of her Green New Deal. One Study pegs the cost at $93 *Trillion*, or $600,000 per U.S. Household.[276] Howard Gleckman, writing for Forbes, would not put a cost estimate on this proposal, but simply

---

[273] Bill Bischoff, *Meet the New, Friendlier Alternative Minimum Tax,* (MarketWatch 2/26/2018).

[274] Ibid.

[275] Ibid.

[276] Greg Re, *Green New Deal Would Cost Up to $93 Trillion, or $600,000 per Household Study Says,* (Foxnews.com 2/25/2019) *citing* a study by the <u>American Action Forum</u>, whose president Douglas Holtz-Eakin, was at one time the Director of the non-partisan Congressional Budget Office.

said that the cost of implementing it would be "staggering".[277] In point of fact, the cost of this proposal is so colossal that even some well know liberals are disavowing it as unworkable and an effort in political suicide. An article in New York Magazine ripped the plan as unattainable and more importantly, that the plan and its' sponsor are radical outliers within the Democratic Party, let alone the mainstream of the American political spectrum.[278]

So we make the point once again that a progressive socialist agenda measured in the trillions stacked on top of trillions, stacked on top of even more trillions will require more than just a nominal increase in taxation. There isn't enough available investment capital in the entire world economy to borrow to pay for a combination of programs where the sum-total of estimates is already at $126 *TRILLION!!!* Keep in mind the entire global economy is $87 Trillion world-wide in a single year. These proposals dwarf the entire world annual economic output. And remember this about new programs. The initial cost estimates surrounding them are usually wildly off the mark and massively understated. For example, when Medicaid was signed into law in 1965, it comprised approximately 2% of all federal budget outlays.[279] By 1992, that had risen to almost 9% of federal outlays.[280] For any skeptical reader hearing this, go check the Office of Management Budge or Congressional Budget Office records on the matter. You will see the same results. The cost as a percent of all federal spending escalated by a factor of four in the first 27 years of the program's history. You think that might be a possibility with all these "Marxism in Wonderland" proposals flying around by a freshman Congresswoman who has never had a professional position in her career prior to getting herself elected to Congress? Is it entirely possible that the cost of these programs could actually be *underestimated,* as opposed to exaggerated? History is replete with examples where the programs initial cost grows geometrically over time – as we just demonstrated with Medicaid. We can conclude this section with the familiar admonishment that will be made throughout this book: An American Marxist government in the mold of Bernie Sanders and Elizabeth Warren will have a wish list measuring in the hundreds of trillions. In order to pay for it, all taxes will be going up for all of us. Period.

2) <u>The Wealth Taxes</u>:

We cannot conclude the "Taxes as Weapons of Mass Destruction" section of this book without spending some time talking about taxes that are and always have been targeted for the affluent and rich. Ever since the federal income tax was introduced in the early 20th Century, Congress has sought to capture revenue from those rich enough live off of investments versus any form of "employment," and it has sought to attain any sort of a "windfall" on the gains made when an asset appreciates over time and is sold for a much higher value than when it was initially purchased. These are, therefore, age old methods to derive revenue from the "idle holders of wealth." We'll talk a bit more about this in the discussion that follows, as I believe it will be an integral method

---

[277] Howard Gleckman, *The Green New Deal Would Cost a Lot of Green,* (Forbes, February 7, 2019). Gleckman also noted that the cost of this initiative might be larger than anything the US has undertaken since the second world war. Ibid.

[278] Jonathan Chait, *The Green New Deal is a Bad Idea, Not Just a Botched Roll Out*, (New York Magazine, February 12. 2019). *See,* http://nymag.com/intelligencer/2019/02/green-new-deal-aoc-bad-idea.html.

[279] Jagadeesh Gokhale, *Medicaid's Soaring Costs, Time to Step on the Brakes,* (Cato Institute, July 19, 2007) at P. 4.

[280] Ibid.

for any new Marxist American regime to plunder tax dollars out of the affluent, the rich and the super-rich.

a. Capital gains

An excellent summary of the capital gains tax for the non-tax professional can be found in an article authored by Sean Williams writing for the Motley Fool LLC. Before we jump into details, some background is warranted. To have a capital gain, you need a capital asset as defined by Congress in the Internal Revenue Code (hereafter the "Code"). The Treasury Department issues implementing regulations for this Code. A capital asset is a legally defined term, a creature of these tax laws if you will. Real property with improvements such as a single-family residence, commercial structures or other structures facilitating "use" of the land, are capital assets under the Code. Stocks and bonds are also examples of capital assets as defined under the Code. There are two basic categories of capital gains. There is a tax on the gain on the sale of a capital asset held for less than one year, in which case it will typically be taxed as ordinary income, and there is a tax on the gain of a capital asset held for more than one year, which will be taxed at a specially determined rate schedule that is often less than the tax on a filers ordinary income. Hence the distinction between long-term and short-term capital gains.

After that itty bitty bit of background, we'll talk a little about the history. A federal tax on capital gains has been around since 1922.[281] The maximum tax rate for long term capital gains has varied over its 97 year history with a low of 13% from 1922-34, to a high of 35% from 1972-79.[282] The current maximum rate for long term capital gains is 20% for single filers with incomes of $434,551 or more; married filing jointly filers with incomes of $488,851 or more; and, heads of household with incomes of $461,701 or more.[283] In order to "trigger" the capital gains tax, the gain has to be realized, which typically occurs upon the sale of the capital asset.

This highly condensed overview of the capital gains tax is offered for the purpose of illustrating the point that capital gains taxes are relatively low at the present time when viewed through the lens of its 97-year existence. If the maximum rate were instantly raised to 35% tomorrow, we would only merely tie a historic peak in the 1970s. What do you the reader think a newly minted Marxist American government will do with the capital gains rate if hard core radical progressives already talking about a top marginal income tax rate of 70%, and in some cases 90%? If your instinct tells you that the maximum tax rate on capital gains could go up massively in very short order, your instinct would have a factual basis in the history of this tax. And there is absolutely nothing that would stop a radical progressive American regime from going much higher than 35%. There is no magic in that number other than it was the highest rate Congress ever imposed for that tax. Going higher than that would absolutely be 100% constitutional for Congress and the President to so decide.

What is the likely impact of an abrupt and massive capital gains tax increase? The effect will be felt squarely on the shoulders of the affluent, the wealthy and the super-rich. For the affluent,

---

[281] Sean Williams, *A 95 Year History of Maximum Capital Gains Tax Rates in 1 Chart.*(The Motley Fool, February 11, 2017)

[282] Ibid.

[283] Jeff Rose, *The New 2019 Federal Income Tax Brackets and Rates,* (Forbes, December 5, 2018).

the sale of a rental house, summer home or a primary residence will trigger the tax and if the rate is massively increased, it is merely a method for the government to confiscate a bigger piece of the assets' equity when it is realized on the sale. For all you corporate senior managers reading this who are not in the upper echelons of the corporate ruling class but still get stock options as part of your compensation – you too will face the sting of a far higher capital gains tax should a Marxist regime come to pass in America. Whether you get Incentive Stock Options (ISOs) or restricted shares, either way, you will have a cost basis determined for you on the shares by your compensation program, and when you sell those shares – you got it, it will be the sale of a capital asset, triggering a taxable capital gain – assuming you sold shares above the cost basis. And if there is a massive tax increase delivered to you by a Marxist American regime, you can thank them for lowering your after-tax income on those shares. I'm sure that will make you feel especially good if those shares are issued in lieu of cash as part of your compensation package. Be careful what you vote for, you just may get it. If the affluent suburban voters continue to elect radical progressive candidates to Congress and the Presidency, they will be front and center for this aspect of American dekulakization.

If you are a top tier executive for an S&P 500 company, or inherited a significant amount of wealth, you will have a larger portion of your compensation effected by massive increases in a capital gains tax. But then again, your compensation is so high relative to those non-management employees working for you, the impact will likely be bearable. I will be transparent at this juncture as to my disposition regarding your future plight. I did not write this book for you, or the billionaire shareholders you work for. I write this book as a warning to those who work for you but do not share your bloated salary, or massively overvalued compensation packages. You get paid a literal fortune to do your job. You get paid a literal fortune when you fail and are shown the door with severance packages often measuring in the hundreds of millions. Failure in your class is often handsomely rewarded. More importantly, you have been funding left wing progressivism for decades with your charitable donations to left wing organizations, donations to liberal Democratic candidates, and general appeasement of the progressive left social justice agenda.

If Starbuck's Howard Shultz' trial balloon Presidential candidacy was any indication, you the corporate elite, are only now starting to realize you may have fed a Marxist beast that is about to break out of the cage and bite your head off. While you richly deserve your plight, many of your direct reports and those managers a couple of layers down from you most certainly do not. I pray they will survive this coming onslaught that you yourself will warrant so handsomely. Regarding the centa-millionaire and billionaire class (with centa-millionaire meaning one with a net worth in the hundreds of millions); because many of these individuals are already on record advocating for massive tax increases on their colossal fortunes, I have no issue with a prospective Bolshevik plunder of their wealth whatsoever. Warren Buffet has been championing tax increases on his class for decades. If current trends continue he will get his wish. The new Bolsheviks will happily oblige. They problem is they will annihilate the rest of us along with the billionaires, but at least the they will have a clean conscience on their way to the gulag. I'm certain that won't be of much comfort for the rest of us getting hauled off to the camps with them. So I really don't have much to say to the mega rich. It is with the merely affluent who bought into the American dream only to have the prospect of the Marxist plunder of their life's work that I believe will be the makings of tragedy.

b. Wealth tax outright:

The idea of a Wealth Tax was referenced in the introduction as there are politicians such as Massachusetts Senator and 2020 Presidential Candidate Elizabeth Warren actively issuing proposals. At the present time there is no tax on idle wealth in America. As we just discussed, in order to be taxed on the equity in a capital asset, one must "realize" the gain on the sale of that asset. Hence there need be a triggering event such as a sale. A wealth tax takes the idea of taxing the equity of capital assets or a trust corpus and taxes the dollar value of that corpus at a given rate – just by virtue of its existence. There does not have to be a triggering event in the case of a wealth tax. For now, the tax is being proposed on deca-millionaires, people with tens of millions in net worth or higher.

And let's not forget the retirement program millionaires. Those who have invested well and effectively utilized company defined contribution plans such as 401(k) programs with employer matching funds, or who have done well with Individual Retirement Accounts (IRAs) will not be immune from a Marxist plunder in the form of a wealth tax. I will remind the reader that these programs have come under the microscope many times before. Their beneficial tax treatment has been a target for elimination in the past because only about 20% of those employees eligible to use them actually do, so they become targets for budget cuts do to the fact that utilizing them reduces taxable income. Get rid of the 401(k) or IRA, and taxable income for the individual who used such accounts goes up and she pays more taxes. These accounts have also caught the eyes of tax hounds in Congress because the dollar amounts invested in them now measures over $25 trillion.[284] That is simply too big a number to ignore for those who would wish to raise government revenue by going after accumulated wealth. Remember that these programs are designed to legally allow your investments within the account to grow *tax free.* You have your 401k allocated to a stock portfolio that grows by 25% in a single year – you do not pay any taxes on that until you actually start withdrawing money from the account – many years down the road. A Marxist American government could change these rules over-night. They could do away with the programs altogether; they could do an annual surcharge on the account balance; or they could drastically cut back on what you can contribute. With a stated agenda measuring in the hundreds of trillions, there is no telling what a hard-left progressive Marxist regime will due to retirement funds.

As for the very rich? Many who are part of the super-rich in America publicly say they want higher taxes for themselves, ostensibly as a sort of "Noblesse Oblige," or noble obligation.[285] It is well known that such wealthy stalwarts as Warrant Buffet, Jamie Dimon, Ray Dalio, Howard Schultz, and Bill Gates have all recently advocated higher taxation on both their incomes and wealth.[286] Actually, as I have alluded to before, regarding this mega rich class, I couldn't agree more. In any event they won't have to worry for much longer, as they are quite likely to get the far higher taxes they seek to have imposed on themselves, but rest assured it won't dent their living standards much. Remember we are talking about Centi-millionairs and billionaires who could never earn another dollar in their lives and would still be lavishly wealthy. Tears should not be shed for them. It is when these sharply higher taxes work their way down to the small business or

---

[284] Nick Thornton, *Total Retirement Assets Near the $25 Trillion Mark* (Benefits Pro, June 30, 2015).

[285] Kate Rooney, *American Billionaires Call for Upgrades to Capitalism, Starting With Hire Taxes on Themselves,* (CNBC.com, April 8 2019).

[286] Ibid.

the family farm that the notion of "dekulakization" becomes pertinent. For wealth corpuses under $5 or $10 million, you start to bite into the wealth created by successful everyday Americans – and that will be not only a tragedy, it will be a travesty.

       c.   Taxing transactions that move capital:

There is nothing stopping the federal government from placing a surcharge on all transactions the result of which is capital changing hands. A sort of wealth "sales" tax if you will. Remember that Congresses power to levy taxes is broad and deep. And there are indeed proposals on the table to do impose taxes on every financial trade that takes place. A Financial Trading Tax has been proposed by Brian Schatz, a Democrat Senator from Hawaii, where there were effectively be a federal levy on all Wall Street trades.[287] Apparently, such a tax has a base of support in public opinion,[288] and such proposals appear to be gaining steam. In March of 2019, Representative Peter DeFazio (D – Ore.) is spearheading the drive to re-introduce a bill that will be called *The Wall Street Tax Act of 2019*, and will be co-sponsored by none other than Alexandria Ocasio-Cortez.[289] The bill would, if signed into law, impose a transaction tax on all stock, bond and derivative deals.[290] The bill is focused on high frequency trading, and if enacted the Joint Committee on Taxation estimates this legislation could result in $777 billion in added revenues over 10 years.[291]

So with the Schatz bill proposed in the Senate and the DeFazio bill proposed in the House of Representatives, the foundation has been set to move the process along. DeFazio proposed a similar bill in 2017, but it went nowhere in a Republican controlled House at that time.[292] Even if President Trump's veto of such legislation turns out to be the last line of defense, and even if he wins a second term, it is my view that it is only a matter of time before the stars line up for the American Marxists pushing strangulation level tax increases on every facet of American life. A newly and duly elected American Marxist regime would be certain to endlessly test the bounds of taxation. When Governor Newsom of California submits a formal plan to create a tax on drinking water (no joke) to fund a safe drinking water program at a time when the state enjoyed a record setting budget surplus,[293] you have empirical evidence that radical progressives will tax just about

---

[287] Marie Patino and Laura Davison, *How Democrats Want to Tax the Rich,* (Bloomberg, LP, March 4, 2019).

[288] Ibid., citing a spring 2018 survey conducted by Lake Research Partner, which showed that 42% of American's polled would support a financial transaction tax, while 36% would oppose. Twenty-two percent were unsure. *See,* https://www.bloomberg.com/graphics/2019-candidate-tax-proposals/?srnd=premium.

[289] Brian Schwartz, Peter DeFazio and House Democrats Are Reintroducing a Financial Services Tax with Alexandria Ocasio Cortez as a co-sponsor (CNBC.com, March 4, 2019).

[290] Ibid.

[291] Ibid.

[292] Ibid.

[293] Jeff Daniels, *California Governor's Plan to Create New Drinking Water Tax Faces Resistance,* (CNBC, March 29, 2019). Apparently some one Million Californians live without adequate clean fresh water for household use, so the Governor planned to charge all but the bottom 10% of households $10 per month to pay for clean-up efforts to mitigate contamination coming from agriculture and industrial activities. *Ibid.* You'd think a state that is the world's fifth largest standalone economy and running billions in surplus would already be taxed enough to pay for legitimate expenditures like this without having to resort so the idiocy of using after tax income from consumers to pay more taxes to cover what a general budget should already have covered with the taxes that were collected in the first place. Alas, that is not the world of the Marxist, who apparently sees no irony in taxing water. A tax on air is surely next.

anything and everything. In light of the current nonsense being proposed, a financial transaction tax almost appears quite reasonable.

    d.   Taxing Everything Else:

For readers who think I am exaggerating, consider some recent reporting by one of my favorite *Los Angeles Times* writers, George Skelton, who published an excellent recapitulation of the multitude of ways the California government in Sacramento intends to raise revenue. He writes:

> "But in California under Democrats, it's tax, tax, tax — a drip and a drop, nickel and a dime — all the time. That's not a political statement. It's a fact.
>
> Not all taxes are evil. Some are justified. But many are unwarranted. And others are eye-rollers.
>
> One of the more controversial and annoying taxes currently being proposed is a state levy on sugary soft drinks. More on that later.
>
> Here's an eye-roller: A bill that would authorize San Francisco to turn its crooked Lombard Street — a tourist attraction after so many movie appearances — into a toll road, maybe even requiring reservations. Think they have a traffic jam now on weekends? Wait until cars are lined up behind a tollgate.
>
> There are a whole bunch of taxing ideas in the Capitol: on new tires, firearms, water, prescription painkillers, lawyers, car batteries, corporations based on their CEO pay, estates worth more than $3.5 million, oil and gas extraction. The list goes on.[294]

Skelton goes on to cite the California Tax Foundation in noting the cumulative total of all tax increases currently proposed as of April 2019 was $6.2 billion, which the foundation expects to grow materially as part of the amendment process in connection with these proposals.[295] If you want an idea of what one party Marxist politics looks like, California and New York offer a hideous glimpse. Imagine a federal government with a Bernie Sanders style socialist and Alexandria Ocasio Cortez and Elizabeth Warren and their ilk in key leadership committees in Congress. If that doesn't scare the shit out of you, you'd have to be so hopelessly backed up you need emergency gastroenterological assistance immediately. I do not believe myself to be exaggerating in the least when I assert that these Marxists will attempt to tax the air you breathe, the water you drink, the rain drops that fall on your head and so on. As you can plainly see, a Marxist progressive minded government will tax everything under the sun, and would tax the sunshine if they could.

Indeed, as we have repeatedly noted, when the cost of the leftist wish list is measured in the hundreds of trillions, there is no telling where a Marxist regime would go or stop regarding

---

[294] George Skelton, *Sacramento Wants to Tax Soda, Tires, Guns, Water, Pain Pills, Lawyers and Car Batteries,* (Lost Angeles Times, April 8, 2019).

[295] Ibid.

taxation. There is no end to lengths leftist Bolsheviks will go to slurp revenue from wherever it might be. Consider yet another example. In March of 2019, the New York state legislature approved a budget that included a brand spanking new "mansion tax" on the sale of multi-million dollar homes, adding to the already considerable tax burden presently endured by New Yorkers.[296] This is not a joke, the state of New York is so starved for revenues that a mansion tax is needed, over and above capital gains a seller might incur from the sale, and over and above the massive real estate tax burden he or she withstood while owning the property. This "mansion tax" is essentially a levy or surcharge on the sale of luxury apartments and is triggered on units selling in excess of $1 million.[297] At that sales point, the tax is 1% and typically paid by the buyer. The levy increases as the sales price increases and tops out at 4.15% for the sale of a unit in excess of $25 Million.[298] And not to be outdone, neighboring Connecticut followed suit some months later enacted a brand spanking new "mansion tax" in the form of a 2.25% levy or "conveyance fee" on home sales above $2.5 million.[299] To Connecticut's credit, this levy only applies of the seller is moving out of state; those moving within the state would get some of the money back in the form of an income tax credit at a later date.[300]

As we saw with the Soviet Kulak experience in chapters 2 and 3, taxation was used militantly and maliciously by the Soviet government as one of the initial steps to extinguishing a defined class of people. I submit to the reader, should a full-on Marxist regime come to America, there would be nothing to prevent history from repetition. There is no "natural law" of some kind that will magically or mystically protect America from the horrible fate of the Kulaks. I submit to the reader, even something that remotely resembles "dekulakization", even without physical genocide, would be unbearable for Americans who have become very comfortable economically, even if incomes have been stagnant. They have stagnated at a very high level when viewed through the lens of history, and when compared to less developed countries. Americans still enjoy relative affluence when contrasted to the poor in other parts of the world. For example, Americans can go to a food bank if necessary to avoid hunger. Nearly all Americans have access to indoor plumbing and electricity.   Americans simply are not accustomed to intense deprivation, and any "dekulakization" that materially reduces after tax income and, therefore, their living standards, will cause significant and immediate discomfort and relative hardship.

The risk as I see it is when, to use a sports analogy, a "full court press" is made by American Marxists to massively raise taxes to pay for an absurdly expensive agenda, two things will happen. First the resistance to the loss of freedom coming from a massive leftist intrusion into our private lives will be acute, and perhaps very violent. The possibility that the use of extreme taxation as "dekulakization" transforms into a violent suppression of individual rights cannot be ruled out. Second, the damage done to the America economy will be at levels not seen in a century, and will

---

[296] Robert Frank, *Manhattan Real Estate Sales Fall for Sixth Straight Quarter – Longest Losing Streak in 30 Years,* (CNBC April 2, 2019)

[297] Henry Goldman and Keisha Clukey, *New York Budget Includes Plastic Bag Ban, Mansion Tax and Manhattan Toll,* (Bloomberg, April 1, 2019).

[298] Ibid.

[299] Brittany De Lea, *Connecticut Approves New 'Mansion Tax' With a Twist*, (FoxBusinessNews, June 22, 2019).

[300] Ibid.

by itself result in violent upheaval. We will explore the likelihood these events transpire in the next chapter.

CHAPTER VI

DO WE END UP 21ST CENTURY "AMERIKA" OR REMAIN THE LAND OF THE FREE?

———————

You and I have a rendezvous with destiny.
We'll preserve for our children, this last great hope of man on earth,
or we'll sentence them to take the last step into a thousand years of darkness

- Ronald Reagan, *A time for Choosing*, 1964

When Ronald Reagan gave his famous speech endorsing Barry Goldwater in 1964, he closed it with a stark warning that is the epigraph for this chapter. As in 1964, the height of the Cold War, in modern day America there will be no room for straddling the fence. Ambiguity will only result in a continued relentless advance towards Marxism in a country with no history of it. Reagan's genius was to recognize there is no compromising with someone who is a Marxist at heart. There is no placating hard core leftist progressivism. Appeasement will only result in changing the speed of the Marxist evolution. Regan was often harshly criticized for his lack of conciliatory benevolence towards the Soviets, but it turns out with the hindsight of history, he had good reason. His instinct that the USSR was an evil empire is now known to be true with empirical certainty.

I do not believe it to be an exaggeration to say that we find ourselves at a similar juncture as we enter the third decade of the 21st Century. Unfortunately, the lessons of history have not been properly taught to an entire generation of young Americans, who increasingly exalt socialism and view capitalism with disdain.[301] American youth are largely ignorant of the crimes against humanity that have been committed by communist regimes over the past century. There are many reasons for this. In my view, first and foremost is the faculty of nearly all institutions of higher education in our country have been infiltrated with tenured professors who are anti-American, and sympathetic to the Marxist economic mirage. While this may not be as acute a problem for technical majors on campuses; the social sciences and the humanities, which graduate a very large

---

[301] Tim Hains, *Frank Luntz: Sanders Most Likely to Win the Democratic Nomination, Capitalism Has Become a Dirty Word For the Left,* (RealClearPolitics, May 12, 2019). Veteran Republican Pollster Frank Luntz discussed a recent survey he conducted on Fox News Network's *Media Buzz* hosted by Howard Kurtz. The results of his survey indicate large portions of the public now associate the word "capitalism" with Wall Street, profits over people and layoffs.

number of our students, have become so radicalized as to render the modern university a virtual indoctrination factory for militant progressivism versus institutions that teach the history of intellectual thought. I will not belabor this point here, but it is my position that this educational dereliction has resulted in an increasingly large block of the largest generation in American history being historically illiterate with respect to the events of the century that directly precedes the one they are living in.

For the Millennial generation, numbering 86 million strong, to embrace socialism the way that is being reflected in public opinion polls and recent voting patterns, and doing so in light of the atrocities committed under so many Marxist regimes, is nothing short of despicable – a tragedy on an epic scale. If the rest of the population acquiesces to this trend, remains placid, and is unwilling to actively counterbalance this horrifying movement, then Mr. Reagan's fears as expressed so eloquently a generation ago may well come to pass. There is no supernatural force other than your prayers, hard work and devotion to our constitutional republic that will save America's free enterprise heritage. We now face political undercurrents that could well overtake 245 years of free enterprise democracy that we have apparently come to take for granted, and push us into the dystopian dungeon of progressive Marxist extremism. The unthinkable may become more than an aberration. When the Soviet Union was collapsing in the early 1990s, Washington Post columnist George Will would observe on the widely watched Sunday morning show *This Week With David Brinkley*, to the effect: if recent events had taught us anything it is that what seems impossible one day is reality the next. I will echo that sentiment. It may seem impossible that America would ever fall to the Bolshevik minded barbarians, but the adults in the room are well aware that nothing is impossible. I take it as a "given' that America falling to the 21st Century Bolsheviks is more than just a possibility, it is already a trend. I have already discussed what "dekulakization" might look like in previous chapters. What follows is an examination of the wherewithal that currently exists for the American federal super-state to be turned into a totalitarian Marxist nightmare. For the analysis below, I suppose that at some point in the future a radical Marxist in the mold of Bernie Sanders or Elizabeth Warren becomes a newly elected President with substantial majorities in both houses of Congress. I further Assume this happens sometime over the next dozen or so years (within the next three election cycles). What follows is a description of their likely agenda and what tools would be at their disposal to execute on that agenda.

Government Enforcement of the New Collectivization:

We start with the generally accepted notion that the predominant essential elements of Marxism are collectivization and the nationalization of industries. The means of producing economic output are to be put in the hands of the people as embodied by government. Hence, as in most Marxist societies over the past century, the first order of business is to move wealth out of private hands and into government ownership and control. In a land like the United States of America, with no history of hard left progressivism as a formal governing philosophy, this process will surely be ridden with violent uprisings and aggressive resistance. A civilization that has been based on the notion of free enterprise from its' inception, where capitalism and free market economic principles form the essential political and commercial fabric of our society, a radical reversal in the opposite direction towards Marxist style collectivism will not happen peacefully in my opinion. As I have noted before, those who have accumulated wealth, at any level, will not willingly forego it all for utopian notions of "fairness" or altruism. As has been noted, one does not give up a life's work for an abstract notion of the greater good. One does not willingly risk the pain of privation or deprivation. I challenge anyone reading this who has hard left progressive political proclivities to please tell us which pure socialist or outright communist country willingly and democratically agreed to nationalize industries and private wealth. When I ask this question of willful submission to Marxism to those who espouse such views, they invariably point to Europe as the modern beacon of the 21st Century socialist.

Point number one, it is technically debatable whether the Eurozone is even "socialist" at all. Have they nationalized private industry? No. Only the former east-block countries living under the Warsaw Pact had to endure communism. Have they ever forced collectivization? No. Only the Former east-block countries felt the sting of collectivism. Have they ever exacted 100% wealth confiscation through taxation or other means? No. Only the former Warsaw Pact countries living under the Iron Curtain experienced this. It is my assertion and contention that European countries are more properly considered capitalist nations who happen to have among the world's most generous welfare benefits for their citizens. They achieve this through very high rates of taxation on the affluent and wealthy and because they are not burdened with defense spending beyond 1 or 2% of their GDP – and many European nations do not even pay that. No – Europe is not "socialist" in the sense of being Marxist states, they are just very VERY liberal. The problem for America is that we have no history with that level of social welfare infrastructure. We never implemented a single payer national health care system. We never promised a university education for all at no expense to them. The risk is that when a hard core progressive American government of the near future attempts to bring the body politic down that path, and has to raise taxes massively in order to fund its' ambitious agenda, the revolt reflex will be triggered and things will likely get out of control quite quickly. I fear this is precisely what may occur, and so we move the discussion to a detailed explanation of the mechanics of how nationalization might occur.

1) <u>The Militarization of Federal Law Enforcement</u>:

Given the scenario that I outlined at the outset of the discussion, where a militant Marxist is elected President and has a Democrat Congress to support the radical agenda, a Congress filled with scores and scores of Marxists in the mold of Alexandria Ocasio Cortez, assume they will move quickly on something like the Green New Deal and Medicare for All. Remember that the Green New Deal proposal calls for the abolishment of entire industries and the use of all fossil fuels. The tax increases required for such an agenda will be stifling. Owners of the productive assets in industries basically outlawed will find those assets rendered immediately worthless, resulting in multiple billions in lost value. Equity markets will react with massive sell offs. Companies will respond to the plunge in their market capitalization with massive layoffs to conserve cash as the company shares they hold as "treasury stock" – company shares purchased on the open market via stock buybacks CFOs have splurged on for decades – are rendered virtually worthless. The whole initiative will be one of the great wealth destruction episodes in the history of all of mankind. Only an imbecile would believe all of this goes down without massive and violent civil unrest. In such a scenario unemployment could easily see levels not seen since the Great Depression of the 20th Century.

If violent social unrest results from such an economic calamity – and it would, the US Government is more than capable of ensuring the beast of the federal super-state remains well fed with all the tax revenue needed, and that the newly outlawed industries follow any prescribed legislation curtailing their business activity. The federal government is so well-armed, it is like its' own internal military force. While Governors of the 50 states regularly bring in National Guard troops to control for unrest, the feds can deploy a commando style paramilitary force to ensure laws, including tax laws are enforced before unrest even manifests itself. This "militarization" of law enforcement is already well underway, rendering American internal security at the federal, state and local levels one of the most powerful ever assembled. Imagine the kind of tool this will be were the US to fall to Marxist rule.

Our analysis now turns to the existing state of militarized law enforcement at the federal level, as it will be the federal agencies that will be deployed to enforce the wide-spread tax evasion that I believe will result from unfathomably large tax increases imposed quickly on the American taxpayer. And it will be the federal agencies that enforce national legislation curtailing the use of fossil fuels and other measures of a Green New Deal. As I have noted in earlier chapters, any material resistance to Kulak level tax increases will result in highly armed law enforcement units paying a visit to the disgruntled American Kulak taxpayer to enforce communist level taxation. The American peasant will be forced to pay what the Marxist demands, and the result will be to strip him of his comfortable standard of living. The U.S. Military will not be necessary to enforce the Marxist 21st Century collectivization. The federal agencies, will work in concert with state and local law enforcement – who are equally militarized, to force the Marxist agenda. The feds will have all the guns they need to drive compliance. Here are the facts.

    a) <u>Current State of Federal Agency Armament</u>:

In late 2018, CBS News reported that the General Accountability Office (GAO) had issued a report revealing that the Internal Revenue Service (IRS) had a supply of weapons to the tune of 4,487 guns and 5,062,006 rounds of ammunition.[302] Moreover, included in that total, were 15 fully automatic firearms accompanied by 56,000 rounds for those automatic weapons.[303] This might seem like overkill for a revenue/treasury function, but I will caution that the IRS is America's tax collector. Throughout history tax collectors have never been well-liked, and tax collection has always required a means of coercion to enforce payment of what is owed to the government. In that sense it is not surprising that the IRS would have to be armed. For any reasonable person, that is to be expected. The magnitude is a bit surprising, with nearly 5,000 firearms, and as we shall see, other heavy gear as well.

This report exists because the 115th Congress asked GAO to conduct the review of federal law enforcement agencies procurement practices pertaining to firearms and tactical gear. The GAO report notes there are 120,000 federal law enforcement officers (FLEOs) in non-military agencies with authority to make arrests and carry firearms within the U.S.[304] The IRS alone has 2,159 Federal Law Enforcement Officers who conduct investigations of criminal violations of the

---

[302] Terrence P. Jeffrey, *GAO:IRS Had 4,487 Guns; 5,062,006 Rounds of Ammunition,* (CBSnews.com, December 28, 2018).

[303] Ibid.

[304] Government Accountability Office (GAO), *FEDERAL LAWENFORCEMENT: Purchases and Inventory Controls of Firearms, Ammunition, and Tactical Equipment.* (GAO – 19-175, December 2018), P. 1.

Internal Revenue Code.[305] By way of comparison, when I resided in a large west coast U.S. city in the early 2,000's the entire police force for a city of 600,000 was 2,500 active officers. From that perspective, the IRS has literally a large city size police force, of course nothing like the 40,000+ officers in NY City, but certainly the size police force for a top 25 US city by population. And that is a number that should be taken with a grain of salt. In the event a Bolshevik Marxist American regime were to take a firm grip on power, they almost certainly would increase the size of the IRS FLEO force to cover for any serious tax revolt. In the event there becomes a full-fledged tax rebellion, the IRS could be doubled or tripled in size very quickly. The stroke of a pen so to speak.

And since we are talking about a hypothetical implementation of the actually proposed Green New Deal, the Environmental Protection Agency (EPA) is sure to play a massive role in implementation as this proposal calls for the abolishment of the use of all fossil fuels within the next decade. You will be pleased to know that according to this GAO report, the EPA has 205 Federal Law Enforcement Officials (FLEOs), with – get this – 608 pistols; 315,994 rounds for those pistols; and 243 shotguns with 177, 220 rounds for those shotguns.[306] The EPA also has 6 rifles with 5,278 rounds for those rifles on hand.[307] A couple of things to consider with these facts. First, you can safely assume the hundreds of long guns in the EPA's possession are not for the purpose of bird hunting or deer hunting, and the hundreds more pistols are not just for target practice. These weapons are for the prospective use of deadly force in the event environmental laws are not adhered to and the suspects require force for apprehension. You can also assume that if something as radical as a Green New Deal were ever actually enacted, the enforcement authority would be massively increased. There would hundreds more additional law enforcement officials working for the agency; and given the impact on the private sector economy, and the probable violence that would be in play with the literal destruction of wealth, there would likely be paramilitary capability added to the EPA arsenal.

Assume any Green New Deal would provide for all of this in the enabling legislation. To enforce something as mind numbing as the curtailment of the use of fossil fuels in a decade, the EPA would have to be armed to the teeth to carry it out. Imagine the social unrest when Midwesterners are told they cannot use fossil fuels to heat their homes during a polar vortex cold snap where the average temperature for a week or two might be 10 degrees below zero. Imagine the Southwest in the heat of summer where average temperatures are in the triple digits, and 40+ million residents who live there are told it is unlawful to use air conditioners running on electricity generated by coal or natural gas. The state and local police will have to quell the riots – probably with assistance from the National Guard, and the newly militarized EPA would have to raid and inspect power companies and distributors to enforce compliance – to ensure no fossil fuels are being used. A newly militarized EPA would have to use force to shut down oil and gas production and distribution. Welcome to the world of Bernie Sanders, Elizabeth Warren and Ocasio-Cortez.

If a rapid build-up in armaments of the federal agencies seems far-fetched to the reader, consider that the GAO report shows the US taxpayer spent $1.5 billion from fiscal 2010 – 2017

---

[305] Ibid., 11.

[306] Ibid., 28.

[307] Ibid.

on firearms procurement for the 20 agencies encompassed in the Report.[308] In the event the federal government got spooked by a bigger than anticipated tax revolt, or has to content with uprisings as a result of something like Green New Deal enforcement, Congress and a Marxist president could easily decide to increase the firearms procurement budget for these 20 agencies to $1.5 billion *annually*, and come up with another $1.5 billion annually to hire more FLEOs. This $3 billion increase in federal expenditure would add an amount equal to 0.0007% of the $4.5 trillion U.S. annual budget. It is sufficient to say that the U.S. federal super-state would have no financial difficulty whatsoever in massively increasing the firepower of the IRS or EPA to enforce the Internal Revenue Code or Green New Deal regulations should the public balk.

And this doesn't even begin to touch on the capabilities of the Department of Justice, which is the situs of the Federal Bureau of Investigation. The GAO report notes that there are 13,790 FBI FLEOs as of the issuance of the Report.[309] To the extent tax evasion were to take the form of any kind of money laundering or racketeering activity involving an instrumentality of interstate commerce like the internet, a telephone or the US mail, the FBI would have jurisdiction. The 13,790 FBI FLEOs would bring a vast array of fire power. They possess a wide range of equipment from armored vehicles to automatic weapons to drones for aerial surveillance.[310] While the FBI did not report specific data regarding the number of each type of firearm or piece of equipment or of the rounds of ammunition, it is well known that the FBI has very robust capacity to deploy Special Weapons and Tactics (SWAT) capability wherever and whenever necessary.

And we do have strong anecdotal evidence of the type of firearms in the FBI arsenal. We've known for decades that the FBI possess paramilitary weaponry. How do we know? We know because there is a well recorded instance where an FBI owned van used by an assault team from Little Rock, Arkansas was stolen from a motel parking lot.[311] The van was full of 13 high-powered weapons,[312] (12 of which would be recovered shortly thereafter). The type of weapons discussed in the FBIs statement to the press was more than revealing with respect to the type and nature of the recovered firearms. The FBI indicated to the media that there "were seven M-16 rifles, three MP-5 submachine guns, a 12-gauge shot gun, and two M-79 grenade launchers as well as thousands of rounds of ammunition and other assault gear."[313] The incident provided an illuminating view into the firepower the Bureau can bring to bear whenever it is deemed necessary. Most of us already suspected the FBI had such hardware, but it is nevertheless useful to get a glimpse into the actual reality instead of having to surmise. The short of it is that we have a reasonable basis assume the FBI has an abundance of commando style, battlefield weapons at its' disposal.

Now consider this, the FBI has over five times the number of FLEOs than does the IRS. In the event there was a large and sustained tax revolt from a miffed electorate rebelling against obscene, Elizabeth Warren levels of taxation, what is the likelihood or probability A Marxist President and a complicit Congress would allocate enough money to make the IRS FLEO population 80% of the

---

[308] Ibid., 1, 15.

[309] Ibid., 10.

[310] Ibid., 22.

[311] The New York Times, *F.B.I Finds Most of Arsenal,* (June 6, 1997).

[312] Ibid.

[313] Ibid.

FBI's? What if they did that plus expand the definition of activity triggering racketeering charges so that the FBI can get more involved in income tax evasion cases, and then turn around and add 30% to the Bureau's FLEO staff – and of course, arm them to the teeth. Hopefully the reader is getting the picture that the epigraph to the last chapter (Nowhere to Run and Nowhere to Hide) is more than pertinent. As asserted in the last chapter – there will be no refuge in some kind of Skellig Michael monastery where the monks of free enterprise can preserve the time-honored tradition "underground" for a thousand years while the rest of what's left of civilization lives under brutal Marxist rule. Once the radical progressive darkness devolves into the midnight of Marxism, only blood, sweat, toil and treasure will ever revive free market economics.

b) <u>Escalating Use of Militarized Policing</u>:

An additional basis for asserting there will be a massive increase in the use of paramilitary force in ordinary law enforcement under a Marxist American government is the fact that such developments have already been underway for years. The proliferation of SWAT teams across the country and the rapid increase in their use by state and local governments is surely one of the most ominous law enforcement trends in the United States today. Nobody minds a governmental heavy hand when there are real and deadly perpetrators on the other end. However, everybody should be unsettled when SWAT units are used for ordinary policing of non-violent offenses. As this book has focused on the prospect of massive increases in taxation and regulation as a sort of 21st Century dekulakization, it is noteworthy that the IRS has a factually demonstrable history of using paramilitary force. Imagine how easy it would be to re-institute and re-authorize such tactics in connection with tax collection efforts. To get an idea of how easily conceivable such an escalation would be in a totalitarian Marxist American regime, let's look at some history.

i) <u>Increasing Use of Commando Tactics in State and Local Policing</u>:

It has been widely reported that as the twin wars in Afghanistan and Iraq wound down in the late 2000's, surplus hardware in terms of armored vehicles and other battlefield weapons such as machine guns, grenade launchers and suppressers (silencers) were sold to state and local governments in an accelerating rate.[314] The volume of merchandise involved around the country is eye-popping, with machine guns sold in the scores of thousands, hundreds of thousands of ammunition magazines, night vision equipment, camouflage gear, gun silencers by the hundreds, and don't forget the armored vehicles and aircraft.[315] An equally unnerving aspect of it all is the increasingly routine use of such equipment and the urban warfare tactics that go with them for offences that do not involve any aspect of violence or even the threat of violence.[316] These *de facto* combat units are now deployed literally thousands of times per year throughout the United States, for such ridiculously banal purposes as a liquor inspection or to enforce a barber's license. Perhaps the most aggravating facet of all this is that larger cities are getting federal grant money under a transfer program that began in the early 1990s to make these purchases.[317] I'm all for law

---

[314] Matt Apuzzo, *War Gear Flows to Police Departments*, (New York Times, June 8, 2014). See, https://www.nytimes.com/2014/06/09/us/war-gear-flows-to-police-departments.html?action=click&module=RelatedCoverage&pgtype=Article®ion=Footer.

[315] Ibid.

[316] Ibid.

[317] Ibid.

and order, and I am unequivocally a booster for law enforcement, but that does not in any way mean I desire to live in a heavily armed police state where commonplace law enforcement functions are performed by someone resembling a combat troop. Regarding the procurement assistance by the federal government for this gear, more must be said.

The formal federal assistance to state and local law enforcement entities is known as "The 1033 Program," which gets its nick-name from the provision of the National Defense Authorization Act enabling it.[318] Under this program the federal government has transferred vast amounts of military equipment we noted above to local police departments. The use of these military grade law enforcement units has led to horrific and avoidable tragedies. A wrenching example is documented by the New York Times, and involved a 19-month-old boy who was critically injured in May of 2014 when a SWAT team in Georgia fired a stun grenade into a house that was the object of a drug raid. The officers were unwittingly searching for their suspect in the wrong place. Their grenade settled in the infant's crib.[319]

This astonishing proliferation of military hardware and tactics in standard police work across the country is not just catching the attention and ire of the left leaning print press; conservatives have also taken notice, and are equally appalled at the havoc being wrought on non-violent citizens. Conservative writer John Fund, writing for the *National Review,* called out the proliferation within the federal government by questioning the purpose of full on SWAT teams allocated to the following agencies:

- The Department of Agriculture
- The Railroad Retirement Board
- The Tennessee Valley Authority
- The Office of Personnel Management
- The Consumer Product Safety Commission
- The U.S. Fish and Wildlife Service.[320]

You are not misreading this. The Department of Agriculture has fully equipped paramilitary SWAT teams, as does the U.S. Fish and Wildlife Service. We all get it that the FBI, the Secret Service or the Bureau of Prisons would have such teams. But the ones noted above? Not so much. Fund goes on to bemoan the whole idea of a blurred line between police officer and soldier – or the "warrior cop" as he alluded to.[321]

Fund's analysis and conclusions are completely corroborated by what we noted from the GAO Report, which is that firearms procurement for some 20 agencies in the federal government depict an astoundingly well-armed federal bureaucracy. While the GAO report did include SWAT team procurement in its analysis, the most surprising amount of weaponry is just the ordinary side arm or pistol. The migration towards full blown paramilitary units is a whole other level. With respect

---

[318] Clyde Haberman, *The Rise of SWAT Team in American Policing,* (NY Times, September 7, 2014). See, https://www.nytimes.com/2014/09/08/us/the-rise-of-the-swat-team-in-american-policing.html.

[319] Ibid.

[320] John Fund, *The United States of SWAT,* (National Review, April 18, 2014).

[321] Ibid.

to how these arms are actually being used, Fund chronicles the same abuses as did the NY Times regarding the use of harsh militaristic tactics and weaponry against non-violent unarmed ordinary citizens who are accused of only non-violent civil or administrative transgressions.[322] Fund summarizes a list of SWAT team uses in cases so absurd as to border on the comical. He cites cases where SWAT teams were brought in to execute a search warrant for potential financial aid fraud of a spouse who no longer even lived in the house; he recalls another incident where a Food and Drug Administration SWAT team was brought in to raid a farm allegedly selling unpasteurized milk across state lines.[323] We can all agree that breaking the law requires law enforcement, which means arrests, searches and seizures. But a SWAT team for this kind of thing? Really? Of course not. Such use of battlefield equipment and tactics under these circumstances is ludicrous and every reasonable person knows it.

Fund concludes his article by identifying law enforcement professionals who themselves are as uneasy about the proliferation of SWAT teams and tactics as everyone else; and that SWAT teams should be used where there is a credible threat of violence.[324] His article reminds us that one of the triggers for the American Revolution in the 1770s was the routine use of British soldiers conducting basic police work. Nothing like having a search or arrest warrant being served on you by a fully armed combat soldier to stir up the passions.

On top of the excellent reporting by Mr. Fund, the most comprehensive analysis of the militarization of policing in the US came from a report issued in 2014 by the American Civil Liberties Union ("ACLU") (hereafter the "Report"). The ACLU study was summarized at length by the Washington Post shortly after it was issued and given much coverage throughout the press. From the Executive Summary, the ACLU writes:

> "Across the country, heavily armed Special Weapons and Tactics (SWAT) teams are forcing their way into people's homes in the middle of the night, often deploying explosive devices such as flashbang grenades to temporarily blind and deafen residents, ***simply to serve a search warrant on the suspicion that someone may be in possession of a small amount of drugs***. Neighborhoods are not war zones, and our police officers should not be treating us like wartime enemies. However, the ACLU encountered this type of story over and over when studying the militarization of state and local law enforcement agencies.
>
> This investigation gave us data to corroborate a trend we have been noticing nationwide: ***American policing has become unnecessarily and dangerously militarized, in large part through federal programs that have armed state and local law enforcement agencies with the weapons and tactics of war, with almost no public discussion or oversight.*** Using these federal funds, state and local law enforcement agencies have amassed military arsenals purportedly to wage the failed War on Drugs, the battlegrounds of which have

---

[322] Ibid.

[323] Ibid.

[324] Ibid.

disproportionately been in communities of color. But these arsenals are by no means free of cost for communities. Instead, the use of hyper-aggressive tools and tactics results in tragedy for civilians and police officers, escalates the risk of needless violence, destroys property, and undermines individual liberties."[325] (Emphasis added).

As a short caveat is in order in light of this quote. I am a law and order stalwart. I wholeheartedly support the use of SWAT tactics and militarized policing with respect to violent and dangerous criminals. I NEVER want to see the police outgunned where there is probable cause to believe the assailant or perpetrator is armed and dangerous. I rely on the public policing system at the state, federal and local level to keep me and my family safe at all times from violent criminals. However, notwithstanding my complete dependence on the "system" for safety and order, I DO NOT condone the use of military police tactics for non-violent offenders. If the law is not clear on when low level police supervisors can order the use of a SWAT team, then it needs to be. There is no basis for massive use of militarized equipment and tactics where there is no armed or dangerous, out of control suspect at large. Using SWAT teams for minor drug possession charges or other offenses not involving violent criminals is what a police state does, and is therefore wholly unacceptable. Yet, that is exactly what the ACLU study determined – that SWAT teams are now regularly being used for ordinary law enforcement activities a standard Peace Officer is more than capable of doing without a paramilitary "team".

The mechanics of the ACLU study was to: (1) issue public records requests for 26 states including the District of Columbia asking for all incident reports where a SWAT team was deployed between 2011 and 2012;[326] (2) take the information on the incident reports and any follow up documentation obtained with it and run it through an analytic filter considering some 13 factors such as the subjects race, whether children were present, and the number of deaths or injuries if any. Here are some startling statistics the ACLU noted in its survey/study:

- Fully 62% of the SWAT deployments analyzed by the ACLU were for drug searches;[327]

- An astonishing 79% of SWAT deployments from 2011-2012 were to execute a search warrant, primarily in drug related cases.[328]

- A piddling 7% of SWAT usage involved an active shooter, or someone barricading themselves in a structure, or a hostage situation.

As a licensed attorney of over 25 years myself, I understand that at the point in time police are executing a search warrant, the perpetrator is literally only suspected of committing a crime (remember the presumption of innocence?). The "crime" is still very much in the investigative stage, where wrongdoing is "alleged", but not yet proven. To bring in a SWAT team, and use SWAT tactics to carry out a search warrant for a non-violent offender is simply excessive. SWAT

---

[325] American Civil Liberties Union Foundation, *War Comes Home: The Excessive Militarization of American Policing*, 2014.

[326] Ibid., 8.

[327] Ibid., 33.

[328] Ibid.

policing was created in the 1970s for the purpose of providing overwhelming force in situations where traditional peace officer teams had been stretched too thin in large urban areas. Those scenarios now comprise less than 10% of modern-day SWAT team situations.

The ACLU Report goes on to note that the increased militarization of American policing has resulted in a "warrior cop" disposition among the SWAT officers, who often see the perpetrators as "enemy combatants," an attitude befitting a violent felon who has just taken an innocent bystander hostage, not so much for administering a garden variety search warrant. The Report cited the most common rationale for the militarization of police work is for the purpose of protecting life: "A warrior cop's mission is to protect every life possible and to only use force when it's necessary to accomplish that mission."[329] As the ACLU study revealed, this is most certainly not what is occurring in live situations involving SWAT teams and tactics. One of the key conclusions of the Report is as follows:

> "SWAT deployments often and unnecessarily entailed the use of violent tactics and equipment, including armored personnel carriers; use of violent tactics and equipment was shown to increase the risk of bodily harm and property damage. ***Of the incidents studied in which SWAT was deployed to search for drugs in a person's home, the SWAT teams either forced or probably forced entry into a person's home using a battering ram or other breaching device 65 percent of the time.*** For drug investigations, the SWAT teams studied were almost twice as likely to force entry into a person's home than not, and they were more than twice as likely to use forced entry in drug investigations than in other cases. ***In some instances, the use of violent tactics and equipment caused property damage, injury, and/or death***."[330]
> (Emphasis supplied)

So we know from the ACLU analysis that over two-thirds of the time the SWAT teams are either being called in to search for drugs, or to otherwise execute a search warrant, and the drug amounts in question are often miniscule amounts as opposed to a large drug raid. To use a battering ram or other breaching device for forced entry in nearly every one of those instances is pure agitation. This supports another conclusion the ACLU reached as part of this study when they wrote: "…it is important to take into consideration the fact that use of a SWAT team can escalate rather than ameliorate potential violence;…". While it is certainly true that in some U.S. jurisdictions, servicing a search warrant for drugs or other contraband is often a dangerous affair as the suspects are known to come to the door with a loaded firearm and start shooting. Where these risks are present and documented, then of course showing up with a SWAT team is not only warranted but outright advisable. For everywhere else, the use of SWAT and military tactics for a search warrant is purely antagonistic.

---

[329] Ibid., 18, *citing*, Jack E. Hoban and Bruce J. Gourlie, "The Ethical Warrior," PoliceOne , Aug. 12, 2013, http://www.policeone.com/Officer-Safety/articles/6383533-Police-militarization-and-the-Ethical-Warrior/. (last visited March 19, 2014).

[330] Ibid., 6.

Indeed, the increasing reliance of state and local governments, as well as federal law enforcement agencies on the use battlefield weapons, technology and tactics is *per se* evidence that the basic framework for an American police state is already in place. The GAO report taken together with the ACLU report and the myriad of reporting on the matter, provide a graphic picture of one of the most immense accumulations of law enforcement firepower ever assembled.

We should also be mindful of what additional tools of oppression may be on the horizon if not already here. For example, the pending roll out of fifth generation cellular technology (commonly referred to as "5G") is thought to possess the necessary technical components to allow for advanced surveillance and facial recognition capabilities.[331] In fact, we are seeing such practices put into place at this very moment with the Chinese having already installed a significant 5G infrastructure and are using its capabilities for an extensive network of surveillance cameras, coupled with advanced facial recognition technology to track whereabouts of targeted individuals at all times.[332] The threat posed by this technology for a totalitarian state is that the state will possess the electronic means to track everything you do and do so all of the time.[333] To be clear, such a surveillance apparatus does not yet exist in the United States and may be a ways off, and our current constitutional arrangement has protections for the American citizen that are unavailable to the Chinese. But the risk remains that 5G technology is rapidly expanding and being quickly deployed throughout the industrialized world, and will exacerbate the threat to American democracy over time.

At present, most Americans are not feeling threatened by the accretion of military force in our law enforcement apparatus. What must be considered is the prospective use of such force in the aftermath of a Bolshevik style Marxist regime actually taking hold of the levers of federal power. The assumption made in this book is that such a regime would most certainly use this awesome array of force to implement and enforce its collectivist goals. Were such a regime to ever come to power, they would need only rely on three federal departments to effectuate the world's most lethal internal security apparatus. Control over the Department of Homeland Security, the Department of Justice, and the Treasury Department (which controls the Secret Service and IRS), and you have most of what you need right there for the basic components of an internal police state. A Marxist regime could easily amend federal law to require state and local police forces to report up through Homeland Security. A Venezuelan style court stacking might be required to get the Judiciary to support such a move, but that is most certainly in the realm of the possible. Once such steps were to be implemented, America's internal security force would be so overwhelming it would make even the Chinese government blush.

Furthermore, if a massive internal security arrangement were somehow not sufficient, the President, with the blessing of a complicit Congress, can suspend *habeas corpus*, as Lincoln did in the Civil War. Moreover, the President can use actual military force for domestic policing if he ultimately determined it is necessary under the circumstances, and not violate the Posse Comitatus Act of 1878 so long as Congress consents to such action. Then there is the availability of Martial Law as an option for the president, which is well established in American constitutional governance. If a duly elected Marxist regime, facing wide spread violent tax revolts, decided to

---

[331] Sue Halpern, *The Terrifying Potential of the 5G Network,* (The New Yorker, April 26, 2019).

[332] Ibid.

[333] Ibid.

invoke such action, and had the consent of Congress and the freshly packed federal court system, why would anyone think a Marxist oligarchy wouldn't take the final step as other despots have in the past and dispense with the constitutional arrangement as we now know it? This notion of the prospect of widespread tax revolt escalating to violence and a subsequent chain reaction ultimately leading to the imposition of martial law is what I will explore next. Warning: it is not as far-fetched as the reader may think.

The political back-drop to all this is that we already have far left political office holders championing a Marxist wish list that we have demonstrated will have costs that run in the hundreds of trillions. As we have already explored, a "Green New Deal", or "Medicare for All", if ever fully executed upon would most certainly require the use of coercive force as entire industries are either nationalized (like health care) or forced out of business (like the airline industry). The taxes required to pay for these colossal collectivist ventures would be nothing short of staggering. Indeed, we have already shown that many leftist politicians in America as of the writing of this manuscript are proposing Olympian sized tax increases of 70% - 90% top marginal rates on the wealthy. We have also demonstrated that with an agenda measured in the hundreds of trillions, these beastly tax increases will work their way down to just about all of us. You can take every billionaire fortune in the US, add it all up and you do not have even five trillion dollars. There is no way tax increases on the rich alone will cover the gargantuan revenue appetite of an Elizabeth Warren or Alexandria Ocasio Cortez.

As the American upper and middle classes are hit with crippling taxes they thought would only be applied to millionaires and billionaires, the discontent will begin to build. As after-tax income is forcibly reduced by obnoxious levels of taxation coupled with inflation caused by shortages of goods, open rebellion cannot be ruled out. When tax revolts get large enough to impact the treasury, the IRS will be on the front line to correct the situation. Like US Marines or Army Rangers hitting the beach on an amphibious landing invasion, the IRS will be re-weaponized with full paramilitary fittings and be given the authority to make examples of willful tax evaders. This is the aspect we will analyze next.

ii)   <u>The IRS Paramilitary Tactics of the Past</u>:

By the late 1990's the IRS had engaged in the use of SWAT tactics often enough to catch the eye of its congressional overseers. In the spring of 1998, the Senate Finance Committee, chaired by Delaware Republican William V. Roth Jr., held a week-long hearing on alleged I.R.S. abuses. The testimony given at the hearings was eye-opening, and revealed a federal agency that had stepped up the use of violent armed paramilitary force against non-violent taxpayers to a level that warranted Congressional review.[334] These hearings were held because the Senate was set to vote on legislation to overhaul the agency. The Committee heard sworn statements depicting dramatic instances of IRS agents using commando style raids on taxpayers who were not suspected of violence or involved in material fraud.[335] Chairman Roth was quoted as saying that aggressive militaristic tactics were unheard of 10-15 years prior.[336]

---

[334] David C. Johnston, *Senate Committee Is Told of a Vast Range of Abuses by IRS*, (New York Times, April 29, 1998).

[335] Ibid.

[336] Ibid.

While the reported instances of armed raids by the IRS has declined over the past two decades, we saw in the GAO report discussed previously in this chapter, the IRS still has plenty of firepower with approximately 2,500 armed Federal Law Enforcement Officers (FLEOs), nearly 5,000 handguns with five million rounds of ammunition for those guns, and also has automatic weapons accompanied by over 50,000 rounds of ammunition. The point is that even though the IRS has been tamed of late, it still has the personnel and firepower the size of a large metropolitan police force. And we all know that Bolshevik progressive Marxist leaders in Congress and the White House – should that day ever come, would with the stroke of a pen, massively upgrade the IRS paramilitary capability, or pull in other federal agencies such as the Department of Justice or Homeland Security to assist the IRS with apprehending material tax evaders.

To reiterate the theme from this chapter, there will be nowhere to run or hide. The American citizen will acquiesce to whatever obnoxious level of taxation a Bolshevik style Marxist government crams down their throats, or face potentially brutal coercion into doing so. When one sees the neighbor hauled off by a SWAT team even for a seemingly petty tax evasion, compliance will be assured. We won't be a free country anymore, but freedom and democracy are rarely the concern of a rabid Marxist. Even when they are democratically elected as in the case of Venezuela, they regularly devolve to a militarized police state. Some readers may at this point be questioning whether red-blooded American patriots would ever allow themselves to work for a federal agency that got turned into a fascistic or Stalinist type of "secret police". These same readers will express skepticism that career law enforcement officers would allow themselves to become politicized, and would not carry out the politically tinted tax collection or other law enforcement of a Marxist nation state. First, that is not the lesson of history, as Stalin's Russia, Mao's China, or the Khmer Rouge in Cambodia have taught us, and secondly, that is not the lesson of American history. I will offer two examples below.

2) <u>Politicization of the Federal Law Enforcement and other Agencies:</u>

The first and foremost example of the politicization of high-ranking bureaucrats will be the recent history of the IRS itself. The second will be with the recent history of the Department of Justice, and in particular, the FBI. Finally, I will conclude this section with a brief statement on J. Edgar Hoover, the famously tyrannical head of the FBI for decades ending with the Nixon Presidency. At that juncture , the reader will see that there is no reasonable person who can, with a straight face, assert that powerful bureaucrats are beyond being politicized.

Beginning with the IRS, if the names Lois Learner and John Koskinan do not mean anything to you the reader, then you would appear to be mal-informed. You should recall that in 2013, then Acting Director of Exempt Organizations at IRS, Lois Lerner, during an American Bar Association (ABA) Meeting, responded to a question from the audience by admitting that organizations were targeted by beliefs [for denial of their request for tax-exempt status], and she further said: "They selected cases simply because the applications had [Tea Party or Patriots] in the title. That was wrong, that was absolutely incorrect, insensitive."[337] These comments would trigger a cascade of events that would lead to Congressional action that would slice IRS funds, result in firing of senior

---

[337] Kelly Phillips Erb, *IRS Targeting Scandal: Citizens United, Lois Lerner, and the $20 Million Saga That Won't Go Away,* (Forbes, June 24, 2016).

government officials, including Acting Director Steven Miller, and bring impeachment jeopardy to IRS Director John Koskinen for his role in the matter.[338] The resulting scandal would be one of the worst in the history of the IRS, and it was front page news for the years 2013 – 2015. In June of 2013, the IRS issued a report on the matter which admits fault and said:

> "… **_"inappropriate criteria" were used for review of organizations applying for tax-exempt status_**. It blames ineffective management for procedures that remained in place for more than 18 months, resulting in lengthy delays and burdensome requests for information. The IRS also stresses that there is no evidence of intentional wrongdoing, nor any "involvement in these matters by anyone outside of the IRS."[339]

The IRS effectively admitted to doofus level management snafus but no "enemy hunting" that would be the basis for the Department of Justice to file criminal charges. It was later learned that Lois Learner's e-mails from 2011 and prior were missing and never provided to the Inspector General. In the end Koskinan was censured by the House Oversight Committee, but not impeached and Lois Lerner was never charged with any crime.   Her admission at the ABA conference was not under oath. Hence all we are really left with is the IRS report that attributes the matter to incompetent management as opposed to sinister politics, but without the Lerner e-mails from 2011 and prior, we will never know the truth. It is an utterly amazing coincidence that ALL of the e-mails from the time period that would have been the most dispositive regarding what actually happened, remain missing to this day. A politicized IRS? – you decide. As for me, I absolutely refuse to give the benefit of the doubt to Ms. Learner and other IRS officials. Maybe her response at the ABA conference wasn't enough to convict in a court of law – where we want the highest standards of proof, but it is enough of an "admission against interest" for me to believe there is some "there" – there. It is not unreasonable to believe that Learner and her seniors got away with felonies because they splendidly hid their tracks.

Then there is the Department of Justice. Exhibit "A" for agency politicization would have to be the Russia Collusion Investigation.   As Special Counsel Robert Muller convened an investigative taskforce at the direction of Assistant Attorney General Rod Rosenstein to investigate potential collusion between the Trump Campaign and the Russian government during the 2016 presidential election, several e-mails had been discovered between high ranking FBI officials. The texts between Lisa Page, a senior FBI attorney, and Peter Strzok, a senior FBI investigator were most damning. Prior to being selected for the Mueller investigative team, both of these officials had previously participated the investigation by the FBI of e-mails from a secrete server candidate Hillary Clinton had while she was Secretary of State under President Obama. Ultimately classified e-mails were in fact found on this unauthorized non-government server as noted by former FBI Director James Comey in July of 2016, yet she was not charged with a crime and faced no serious legal jeopardy. The e-mail investigation, and subsequent Russia Collusion investigation wound up producing the now famous Strzok/Page texts. The two were secretly romantically involved (both were married) and exchanged a large number of texts between them that were ultimately discovered during the subsequent Mueller Investigation, which revealed their romantic relationship and, more importantly, were ripe with overt disdain for then Candidate Trump.

---

[338] Ibid.

[339] Ibid.

The relevance of the Page/Strzok texts is more than just their distaste for now President Trump; these texts showed rank political bias against Trump supporters as well as against the man himself. The texts referred to an "insurance policy" for preventing Trump from ever taking office or remaining in office. One e-mail text in August of 2016 had Strzok asserting that "we'll stop it", referring to Trump's election. The explicit nature of these now commonly known text exchanges establish conclusively that high ranking public servants who are supposed to be politically neutral, are often anything but. While the Democrat friendly media downplay these developments, us regular folk who have voted both sides of the aisle over the course of our lives know damn well how leftist progressive values and views have permeated the top echelons of our public bureaucracies. Telling us that this is an overblown fear simply insults the intelligence of those of us who live and work outside the D.C. Beltway.

One of the lasting legacies of the Department of Justice's actions in connection with the Mueller Investigation is a lingering legacy of the increased politicization of the U.S. justice system. For example, National Public Radio writes:

> "Members of Washington's elite legal community decried the "increasing politicization" of the justice system at a particularly sensitive time: as the special counsel probe of Russian election interference edges toward a conclusion.
>
> Abbe David Lowell, a veteran of high-profile cases who has defended members of Congress and Cabinet officials, ***lamented that public confidence in the FBI, the Justice Department and the rule of law itself has waned***, even as he offered praise for Robert Mueller, the man leading the Russia Investigation."[340] (Emphasis Supplied)

It is quite disconcerting that lawyers "on the ground" so to speak are getting the drift that the public is beginning to see through to the weaponization of the justice system, or use of the justice system to further a political agenda. Don't like the outcome of an election? – try and undue it with a special counsel and endless investigations. There is so much political infestation in our administrative agencies that an entire book can be written about it. In fact, books have indeed been written about it.

I won't belabor the point here, but I will refer the reader to some useful books that articulate the depth and breadth of the politicization of our administrative state. First, since we've talked about the Russian Collusion Investigation, I will refer the reader to *The Russia Hoax: The Illicit Scheme to Clear Hillary Clinton and Frame Donald Trump,* by Gregg Jarrett. The title of the book speaks for itself and it is a detailed enumeration of the rancid political nature of activities by top Justice Department officials in one of the most important investigations in FBI history. There is also *The Benghazi Scandal: Betrayal in Benghazi*, by Richard S. Parker. Here the politicization pertains to the State Department under Hillary Clinton in one of the most atrocious international relations scandals in my lifetime. A scandal that involved the deaths of four Americans including

---

[340] Carrie Johnson, *As End Nears To Mueller Era, D.C. Lawyers Fear Lasting Politicization of Justice*, (NPR, March 15, 2019).

an American Ambassador to Libya, the first death of an ambassador in decades. When the violence was first reported, the Obama Administration, including Secretary Clinton, blamed the outbreak on a video that had been released by an American that was very unfriendly to Islam. In reality, it has been conclusively determined that instead of being a spontaneous angry mob, the attack was a *bone fide* terrorist attack. Worse yet, there is evidence that Clinton and Obama knew it was a terrorist attack all the while they were blaming an angry mob extemporaneously reacting to a US made video mocking Islam. If this doesn't constitute one the most noxious instances of the politicization of a U.S. cabinet level agency, then please tell me what would. I could continue *ad nauseam*, but that is not the main thrust of this book. The point is that public administrative institutions are quite easily politicized with potentially devastating effects.

Then there is the infamous J. Edgar Hoover, the longest serving FBI Director in American History. That he was Tyrannical and a hyper political animal is so well known that there is no need to go into detail. He had secret files on politicians, he is known to have threatened some of the Presidents he served with going public on embarrassing details on their private lives that would likely have been their political undoing. With all of these foregoing examples readily available, there is ample basis for asserting that senior and executive level agency heads and directors have been and will likely continue to be political animals. In a newly minted American Marxist regime, this dynamic will be outright lethal.

In such a scenario, there is every likelihood that law enforcement and homeland security agency heads would be staffed with hyper partisan Marxist "true believers" and the immense power of America's federal agencies would be brought to bear on those poor souls who were brave enough, or foolish enough to resist. In Marxist Progressive America, the heavy hand of the state will be regularly used to crush any political opposition. Indeed as the manuscript for this book was being prepared, there were ample signs that the hard left has openly embraced authoritarian means to further their ends.[341] You can see the dark impulses of left leaning politicians almost daily by their obnoxious bullying tactics.[342] You don't like paying Kulak level taxes? In the prospective Marxist brave new world, be sure you don't express your views publicly, or the knock on your door at 2:30 in the morning might be in the form of a forced entry device that literally breaks your door down. When the flash bang grenades start going off, and police officers dressed up as military troops with battlefield weapons start swarming your house, you'll know you crossed the line. If you resist

---

[341] Philip Klein, *Democrats Celebrating New Zealand Gun Ban Exposed the Left's Authoritarian Impulses*, (Washington Examiner, March 21, 2019). In the aftermath of the Christchurch mass shooting in New Zealand, which targeted Muslims, the New Zealand Prime Minister Jacinda Arden announced a national gun ban rendering assault weapons illegal effective immediately. Alexandria Ocasio Cortez and Bernie Sanders immediately praised this executive level fascism and stated their approval of the notion of formal gun confiscation involving law abiding citizens not suspected of any crime without any debate, judicial proceeding or legislative action. The move by Prime Minister Arden is by definition 100% pure authoritarianism. Bernie Sanders was explicit in a "tweet" that the U.S. ***must*** follow New Zealand's lead. If this isn't *prima facie* evidence of Senator Sanders' totalitarian instinct then one wonders what would be.

[342] Salina Zito, *In Front of a Philadelphia Abortion Clinic, Democratic Lawmaker Shows Us the Darkness of the Cultural Divide,* (Townhall, may 14, 2019). In this article Ms. Zito carefully chronicles the actions taken by Democratic State Representative Brian Sims, an ex-football player, as he harasses a protester with whom he disagrees politically with some of the most belligerent and aggressive tactics ever recorded. He video taped the entire incident with his smart phone and was so proud of his efforts and its result that he posted it on Twitter for all the world to see, which sparked large scale counter protests and a national outcry. He derided her religion, her age and her race. Does this sound like a benign political participant? Or is this a sign of the malicious, malignant and very dangerous politics we can expect from the left in the future? Now imagine Mr. Sims as a mainstream moderate in an American Bolshevik run government and you will understand the basis for fearing what the left may have in store.

with a tax revolt, the American Marxist will get a complicit Congress to pass laws that will amend punishments for such behavior to include hard time in forced labor camps. Sound surreal? Exaggerated? Hyped up hyperbole? What do you want to bet that is what the Kulaks would have said in 1910 if you could go back in time and tell them what awaited them beginning a decade hence? The point is that we rarely see a calamity coming until it is immediately at hand.

The Ultimate Marxist Endgame - Nationalization of the Private Sector and the Venezuelan Experience:

Twenty-one years after the election of Hugo Chavez in December of 1998, Venezuela is an utterly failed state with starving citizens in the streets. It is readily documentable that the country cannot even reliably provide basics such as electricity and fresh drinking water.[343] The military is the only institution preventing a purest form of anarchy, though it remains to be seen how long that can hold. Soldiers need to eat and drink too. And we now know with concrete empirical evidence that its petroleum industry is now nearing total collapse following the electrical blackouts of 2019, with production falling to under one million barrels per day, (it was three times that when Hugo Chavez was elected in 1998).[344] In a land atop one of the world's great stores of petroleum, Venezuela has chronic shortages of gasoline, which has been subsidized by the government for years.[345]

Not to belabor this point, but you know things are horrid when even the left leaning New York Times piles on with observations of the calamity unfolding in Venezuela. In an editorial in early April 2019, the Times bemoaned the chaos in that country, and excoriated the meddling of Putin's Russia, along with the Cuba's, in propping up Nicolas Maduro. In their ostensible support for Maduro's opposition leader Juan Guaido, the Times wrote in part:

> "… and it certainly would be a great relief for Venezuela to be rid of the leader [Maduro] ***who inherited a broken country from his revolutionary mentor Hugo Chavez and has continued to push it to utter ruin, creating a humanitarian disaster atop the world's largest oil reserves***. But how long that 'transition' might last, and what horrors it may yet visit on people hovering on the edge of starvation are open questions."[346] (Emphasis supplied).

That the New York Times is forced to admit this catastrophe brought was about by the socialist reigns of Messers Chavez and Maduro, and does so in such stark terms, is also *per se* evidence of the ghastly results of Marxist based governance. Perhaps the Times remembers how affectionate

---

[343] Ben Kew, *Taps Run Dry in Socialist Venezuela as Blackout Chokes Water Supply,* (Breitbart News Network, April 2, 2019). The electrical blackouts that had begun in early March of 2019 continued and intensified, and by early April 2019, the electrical outages were so widespread that approximately 70% of Venezuela had no electricity for almost a week. *Ibid.* As the fresh water supply relies on electrical pumps, no electricity, no running water, causing acute daily hardships with the lack of clean fresh drinking water driving people to drink water from contaminated sources and exposing them to infectious diseases. *Ibid.*

[344] Ben Kew, *Venezuela's Oil Industry Close to Total Collapse Following Nationwide Blackout,* (Breitbart News Network, March 18, 2019), citing the International Energy Agency (IEA).

[345] Ibid.

[346] Editorial Board, *As the Crisis in Venezuela Grows, the Options Narrow,* (New York Times, April 3, 2019).

the American left was towards Mr. Chavez early on. Perhaps not. In any event, that not even the New York Times can avoid acknowledging the socialist fiasco heaped upon the people of Venezuela has to be one of the great indictments of the Marxist economic track record as ever there was.

And if the reader is still not convinced of the carnage that socialism has wrought on the good people of Venezuela, after all this, then I call your attention to a shocking report from the British Broadcasting Corporation (BBC) published in April 2019. If you still need to be persuaded, then heed this astounding report. According to the BBC, as reported by Will Grant, desperate Venezuelans have now resorted to grave robbing in search of jewelry and other valuables for resale.[347] Things like gold fillings in teeth, or even skeletal bones used in religious rituals are being heisted from graves.[348] The litany of appalling living conditions evidencing the ghastly state of affairs in Venezuela seems to get more shocking with each passing day. So much so that the American public runs the risk of becoming numb to what they are seeing in the news. Not so much for the average Venezuelan stuck in that hell hole. For them, near starvation, the humiliation of having to find fresh water in putrid rivers or sewage effluent, and the degradation of seeing the graves of loved ones desecrated and looted for what amounts to literal pocket change are all now part of routine life in the aftermath of a failed socialist experiment.

The failure in Venezuela is so acute that it is even affecting the governing class, normally part of the elite in any functioning civilization. Bloomberg recently reported that Juan Guaido, the man whom scores of countries recognize as the legitimate Venezuelan leader, has to periodically bathe with a bucket of water like he did when he was growing up in poverty because the taps don't work when there is no power.[349] Not even for the rich or for government officials. So, in light of the foregoing, we know what has, as a matter of empirical fact, happened to Venezuela, let's look at how it came to be, and what are the parallels with what American Marxists champion in the present day?

The short answer is that Chavez was not truthful when he campaigned on some phantom "third-way" malarkey; he was a socialist pure and simple. As soon as he got himself elected he went about three main objectives on the road to his clandestine socialist objective. First, he had the Venezuelan government radically altered with a reformed constitution immediately upon his getting elected. Then he went about stacking the courts, then he finished the job of nationalizing major industries. Once those steps were completed, he had succeeded in transforming Venezuela into a Marxist entity. Here are the details.

---

[347] Will Grant, *Where Not Even the Graves Are Safe,* (BBC News, April 7, 2019). To view the full segment, see., https://www.bbc.com/news/av/world-latin-america-47831569/venezuela-the-country-where-not-even-graves-are-safe.

[348] Ibid.

[349] Patricia Laya, Andrew Rosati and Daniel Cancel, *Forced to Bathe With a Bucket of Water, Juan Guaido Soldiers On,* (Bloomberg Business News, June 7, 2019).

1) <u>1998 – The Unlikely Victory for Chavez</u>

When Hugo Chavez won his improbable victory to the Venezuelan Presidency in December of 1998, Venezuela was a functioning civilization sitting atop one of the world's great reserves of crude oil, a vast mine of the coveted "black gold" producing over 3 million barrels per day for world markets. As was the case with so many countries in Latin America, even resource rich ones like Venezuela, wealth had concentrated and there was unrest in the lower economic echelons. Chavez main campaign promise was to find a sort of middle ground or "third way" between socialism and capitalism. But by early February of 1999, only just being sworn-in, and within less than 60 days of his election on December 6th, Chavez was already issuing a decree mandating a referendum to re-write the constitution.[350] By April of 1999, the people of Venezuela approved Chavez' proposal by wide margins, culminating in voters approving a new constitution radically modifying the existing government by eliminating the Senate and lengthening Chavez' term to six years among other things.[351] Chavez was then elected to a six year term in July of 2000.

In April of 2002 Chavez was deposed but quickly restored to power by loyal army officers.[352] Another two years of turbulence with the petroleum industry and dissent at home, Chavez manages to win re-election in 2006 for a six year term, and within days of re-election, pledges to transform Venezuela into a socialist state; then proceeds to announce plans to nationalize key industries.[353] So by the mid 2000's, he totally abandoned the pretense of being anything but a full-scope Marxist. From then on, until his death, in no way can Venezuela be considered anything but a communist country.

2) <u>Stacking the Courts:</u>

None of this would have been possible without the consent of the judiciary. It is well understood that Chavez successfully stacked his courts in 2004. When the Venezuelan Congress voted to increase the country's Supreme Court by more than half by adding 12 new justices, Human Rights Watch lambasted the move as a severe blow to judicial independence.[354] The law increased the number of members from 20 to 32.[355] Human Rights Watch described it this way:

> "The court-packing law signed in May also gave the governing coalition the power to remove judges from the Court without the two-thirds majority vote required under the constitution. In June, two justices retired after facing possible suspension from the Supreme Court as a result of these new provisions.
>
> ***The political takeover of the Supreme Court will compound the damage already done to judicial independence by policies pursued by the court itself.*** The Supreme Court, which has administrative control over the

---

[350] *See, Hugo Chavez: timeline* (The Telegraph, March 5, 2013).

[351] Ibid.

[352] Ibid.

[353] Ibid.

[354] *See, Venezuela; Chavez Allies Pack Supreme Court,* (Human Rights Watch, December 13, 2004).

[355] Ibid.

judiciary, has failed to provide security of tenure to 80 percent of the country's judges. ***In March, the court summarily fired three judges after they had decided politically controversial cases***.

Chávez supporters have justified the court-packing effort largely as a response to pro-opposition rulings in a deeply divided court, such as a highly questionable decision that absolved military officers who participated in the 2002 coup.

"President Chávez and his supporters should be taking steps to strengthen the judiciary," Vivanco said. ***"Instead, they are rigging the system to favor their own interests***.""[356] (Emphasis supplied)

It is widely believed that none of the formal moves toward nationalizing major industries in Venezuela would have been sanctioned by the country's Supreme Court as constituted at the outset of Chavez election in 2004.

This fact is highly relevant in present day U.S. politics because there are voices on the left openly advocating for the very kind of "court packing" that occurred in Venezuela in 2004. In March of 2019, Obama Attorney General Eric Holder open advocated that Democrats consider packing the U.S. Supreme Court with additional justices.[357] New York Senator Kristen Gillibrand, also a one-time 2020 Presidential Candidate, also lent support to the notion of adding justices to the Supreme Court if Democrats take power.[358] Other 2020 Presidential candidates began to embrace the idea as 2019 rolled on. Indiana Mayor and Presidential candidate Peter Buttigieg is now on record from a number of venues as openly calling for stacking the US Supreme Court as a means of dealing with its current conservative majority. He first broached the idea in response to a question he received in a CNN Townhall appearance in March of 2019. The court stacking position he took on the CNN Townhall appearance would be recapitulated in some detail in a *Boston Globe* profile on Buttigieg published in May of that year.[359] The *Globe* reports the mechanics of his court-stacking proposition would be to have the court expanded, and then nominate five new Supreme Court Justices, and each new justice would need to be unanimously approved by the existing justices.[360] Buttigieg has repeated this idea in other venues, such as an interview he gave with Mehdi Hasan on the *Deconstructed Podcast* published in *The Intercept* on March 21, 2019, where he also expressly advocated for the abolishment of the electoral college.[361]

By late June of 2019, according to the New York Times interview project where all 22 Democratic candidates were asked whether they would support expanding the Supreme Court (in

---

[356] Ibid.

[357] Peter Hasson, *Eric Holder: Democrats Should Consider Packing SCOTUS,* (Daily Caller, March 8, 2019).

[358] Ibid.

[359] Liz Goodwin, *Mayor Pete And the Order of the Kong: How Buttigieg's Harvard Pals Helped Spur his Rise in Politics,* (Boston Globe, May 18, 2019).

[360] Ibid.

[361] Mehdi Hasan, *Mayor Pete Buttigieg on Trump, Islamophobia, and his Presidential Bid,* (The Intercept, March 21, 2019). For the full text of the Podcast Interview, see, https://theintercept.com/2019/03/21/mayor-pete-buttigieg-on-trump-islamophobia-and-his-presidential-bid/.

additional to 17 other questions); 11 of the 22 Democratic candidates for President in the 2020 election cycle openly stated they would support such a measure to one degree or another.[362] The other 11 were not as open to the idea. That 50% of the candidates would respond in favor of such an unprecedented move renders it a safe assertion that an increasing number of left leaning policy makers are embracing this radical prescription for reforming the judiciary. In my estimation, the idea of stacking the US federal judiciary is rapidly becoming a mainstream and prevailing view within the Democratic Party.

The salience of this development is that it is widely known among Constitutional experts and scholars that the U.S. Constitution does not prescribe a fixed number of justices for the court, but leaves that to Congress and the President. So, if a given Administration does not like the Court's rulings, just persuade congress to add justices sympathetic to the Administration's views, and presto, you have the votes on the court to drive opinions in your favor. Of course the new justices would need to be confirmed, but if the Congress was willing to stack the courts in the first place, it nearly goes without saying that the Administration and the Congress would be able to agree on who would fill those new seats.

Were this scurrilous political behavior regarding the courts ever come to pass, the independence of the Court would most certainly be forever impaired and the Court's reputation for neutrality tarnished indefinitely. It is a widely known historical fact that Franklin D. Roosevelt formally considered such measures in the late 1930's and was rebuked by a majority of the D.C. establishment as well as voters. But that was a different breed of American back then, not the snow-flake America-haters of today's Millennial generation. It is entirely foreseeable and maybe even probable that another Roosevelt like court stacking attempt will be made within the next decade. God help the USA should this obscenity ever be seriously attempted much less actually be implemented.

Throughout this book, I have made repeated assertions about what a Bolshevik like Bernie Sanders might attempt were he to be elected President of the United States with convincing majorities in both houses of Congress. Much of what I have described in foregoing chapters would at the present time most certainly face a credible constitutional challenge in America's judiciary. A good court stacking would be a solution to that impediment. Do NOT put this past radical Marxists who may one day assume the mantle of all power in the United States federal government. And may the Lord be with us if that day ever arrives.

   3) <u>Nationalization</u>

The goal for any Marxist is ultimately to strip "the means of production" from private hands. This notion of state ownership of wealth is textbook Marxism, clearly enumerated in the *Communist Manifesto* since its first publication in 1848. As noted in the introduction, there is nothing "new" or "fresh" about Marxist based socialism or communism. The only reason young people under age 45 today view it as "hip" or "cool" is that they are utterly ignorant of its history, and of the savage atrocities that have been committed in furtherance of its principles. The Soviet

---

[362] Alexander Burns, Sydney Ember, Jonah M. Kessel, Haeyoun Park, *Meet the Candidates,* (New York Times, Spring 2019).
All 22 candidate responses to the 18 questions asked, including expanding the Supreme Court, can be seen at:
https://www.nytimes.com/interactive/2019/us/politics/2020-candidate-interviews.html.

Union was a full and complete attempt at Marxism in its absolute and purest form. All wealth was confiscated by the state, and as we saw with the collectivization of the peasantry, this confiscation was often performed in the most cruel and inhumane manner possible. In a purist Marxist society, there will ultimately be no room for private ownership of wealth or any of kind of property – period.

Back to the story of Venezuela. As Chavez' regime continued to consolidate and entrench its power, by the close of the 2000's nearly all of Venezuela's core industries were effectively nationalized and government run. "Power to the people" as the militant Progressives always chant, had become reality – and a decade after that – a stark reality indeed. By June of 2007, the Venezuelan government had expropriated physical assets from ExxonMobile and ConnocoPhillips, effectively "sealing the deal" on nationalizing the petroleum industry.[363] After the full nationalization of many other key industries by 2008, Venezuela gradually descended into economic malaise. By 2012, inflation had become a significant enough problem, as it often does in Marxist regimes, to require government imposed price controls on basic goods, and companies not adhering to these controls were threatened with expropriation.[364] Chavez passed away from cancer in April of 2013 at age 58, leaving effectively a busted country in his wake, and by 2016, Venezuela was regarded by most observers, to be in an economic crisis.[365]

The end-state for the reigns of Chavez and Maduro is a collapsing civilization where unlucky Venezuelans are scavenging landfills in Brazilian border towns for food and other necessaries, or facing actual starvation if they remain in-country.[366] Tens of thousands of Venezuelan nationals have fled the country to avoid the near death living standards in their home country.[367] The unmistakable history of Venezuela from 1998 to 2019 has been the tale of a decent from the social and economic penthouse of Latin America with a relatively high standard of living and the world's largest know petroleum reserves, to the economic and political outhouse where the once great society has become yet another ash heap of failed socialist policies.

4) <u>Conclusion</u>

As Americans flirt with the embrace of Marxist based economics, we must be mindful of the likely consequences of such policies, with Venezuela providing the most current example. As the Democratic Party moves decidedly to the left towards the Marxist ideal, Americans should take an honest and deep look at what is being sold by the likes of Senators Sanders and Warren, because it is my view that much of what they espouse would land us right in the middle of the Venezuelan experience in a matter of a couple of decades. And we can be sure Mr. Sanders is most certainly a committed Marxist. We now know for an empirical fact that Bernie Sanders has in the past adhered to a virulent form of Marxism that seeks to strip private ownership of property and nationalize industry. At the end of Chapter 4 we noted an excellent piece of investigative reporting from CNN that chronicled in explicit detail that exact American industries that back in the 1970s, Sanders had advocated be nationalized. Now that he is again in 2020, a top tier candidate for the Presidency

---

[363] *See, Venezuelan Profile – timeline* (BBC, February 25, 2019).

[364] Ibid.

[365] Ibid.

[366] Anthony Boadle, *Venezuelan Scavengers Vie With Vultures For Brazilian Trash,* (Reuters, April 16, 2019).

[367] Ibid.

of the United States, he is even doing us the favor of tearing off his moderate façade to show us his true intentions.

On August 22, 2019, in an interview with Chris Hayes of MSNBC, Senator Sanders openly discussed the particulars of his "Green Energy Plan" whose initial estimates ran to the tune of $16 trillion in cost to the American economy.[368] In this interview, Hayes asked if the plan would essentially be a federal takeover (i.e., nationalization) of power generation in the US along the lines of what the Tennessee Valley Authority ("TVA") has done for decades. Sanders answered in the affirmative – basically TVA for the whole country.[369] He continued by extolling the virtues he perceived in TVAs work over the years and made clear his intention would be that the federal government would aggressively force the nation toward the use of wind and solar in the process of power generation.[370] Rest assured, if he is open to the federalization of energy generation, he is open to the nationalization of all industries. It is hard to know whether the affluent suburban progressive supporting this kind of garbage actually understands the longer term implications of such coercive measures in public policy, and whether these actually support it; in either case, nationalizing the US energy industry is Bolshevik Marxism in the purest sense of the terms. We now know with absolute certainty that Sanders is an open and unapologetic Marxist, who makes no bones about the use of coercive federal power to facilitate policy goals. That he is a leading candidate for the Democratic Party nomination in 2020 is therefore somewhat horrifying.

It is breathtaking that Sanders continues to sell the American people on Marxist based progressive extremism in light of what has and continues to happen in Venezuela, a country with hyperinflation so out of control, the government has issued a new currency with denominations of 10,000, 20,000 and 50,000 bolivars.[371] Inflation is so bad that minimum wage is 40,000 bolivars an hour (translating to $8.13 per hour).[372] For the record, inflation in Venezuela peaked at 1.3 *million percent* in April of 2019.[373] Yet Sanders maintains a steadfast commitment to an ideology marked with failure and misery almost from inception. It is the hallmark of ignorance that his supporters embrace a man who himself embraces on of the deadliest, incompetent and infeasible ideologies if the past 100 years. Ditto for Elizabeth Warren, basically Bernie "Lite", with her embrace of Medicare for All and proposed ban on the use of fossil fuels. Talk about central planning – she embraces it as well as any Soviet aparachnik ever did.

And this ignorance is so pervasive that those Americans tempted by both Sanders and Warren - the ideological Marxist Pied Pipers – are impervious to the parallels between current day Venezuela and certain places in the United States at this very moment. In states like California and Washington, virtual one-party leftist denizens of trendy hard core progressivism, the homelessness epidemic has become so patently out of control that medieval diseases like typhus

---

[368] Tim Hains, *Sanders Announces $16 Trillion Green Energy Plan: "You Can't Nibble Around the Edges" on Climate Change,* (RealClearPolitics, August 23, 2019). You can find the full script of MSNBC interview provided in this post.

[369] Ibid.

[370] Ibid.

[371] Jeff Cox, *Hyperinflation Pushes Venezuela to Offer 50,000-Bolivar Bank Note,* (CNBC.com, June 13, 2019), citing a report in *The Guardian.*

[372] Ibid.

[373] Ibid.

are making a serious comeback in their homeless encampments.[374] Infectious diseases are hitting homeless "Hoovervilles" especially hard in Los Angeles, Seattle and San Francisco, as rodents and insects are drawn to raw urine and fecal matter routinely deposited in the open by these unfortunate residents.[375] In May of 2019, a local Los Angeles NBC television affiliate did an expose' on the mounting homeless driven sanitary crisis in the city. The report detailed numerous rat-infested piles of garbage left uncollected by the City of Los Angeles, which are the magnets for disease infested rats carrying typhus infected fleas which can easily carry this age old disease to humans; these rats and fleas even have the potential to carry the bubonic plague.[376] Finally, the NBC4 investigation noted that other large cities such as New York, Washington D.C. "have teams devoted to aggressive rat control."[377]

Topping off the coverage of the potential for infectious disease outbreaks in Los Angeles homeless encampments is the interview Dr. Drew Pinsky (yes – THE "Dr. Drew"), where he issued a stern warning to public officials in the City of Los Angeles that the putrid, rubbish ridden, rat infested homeless populations in the city of LA have a realistic probability of triggering the spread of the afore mentioned infectious diseases.[378] He lambasts the lackadaisical posture of L.A. City officials as being even worse than the famous Roman Caesar Nero who literally slept while Rome burned.[379]

A few hours north up the California Pacific Coast Highway, in San Francisco, the public sanitation issues associated with homelessness in have become so well- known and so well covered that the issue has moved to outright caricature. There are so many articles making fun of the public defecation problem in downtown San Francisco it's hard to know where to begin. Many of the articles feature "poop maps" that depict the known locations where the city has had to clean up human excrement and drug paraphernalia.[380] Other articles chronicle the yearly incidents of

---

[374] Anna Gormaan, *"Medieval" Diseases Flare as Unsanitary Living Conditions Proliferate: Typhus and Other Infectious Illnesses Hit Homeless Communities,* (Scientific American, March 15, 2019). See, https://www.scientificamerican.com/article/medieval-diseases-flare-as-unsanitary-living-conditions-proliferate/. *See also,* Eric Johnson. *Seattle is Dying,* (KOMO News 4 Special March 14th 2019). Mr. Johnson graphically depicts "degradation and filth all around us" in the form of heroin addiction and homelessness. To view the full special, see https://komonews.com/news/local/komo-news-special-seattle-is-dying?fbclid=IwAR3Po8-9xl4rqBnVNRORDvXNv5ubqRtG4tvmcWqG0Fh_-XOelV5Ku9LFNFQ. Finally, see also Barnini Chakrabiorty, *San Francisco Homeless Stats soar: City Blames Big Business, Residents Blame Officials,* (Fox News, August 20, 2019). This study chronicled the toll progressive policies have had on homelessness in the Bay Area, Los Angeles, Seattle and Portland, Oregon.

[375] Ibid.

[376] Joel Grover and Amy Corral, *Rotting Trash Piles Sky-High in LA, Attracting Rats and Raising Concerns of a New Epidemic,* (NBC Los Angeles Chanel 4, May 21, 2019). The broadcast showed heartbreaking images of homeless people literally living and sleeping in trash.

[377] Ibid. For the full article and video of the broadcast, see, https://www.nbclosangeles.com/investigations/Rats-Fleas-Los-Angeles-Garbage-Trash-Piles-Health-Mayor-Eric-Garcetti-510171121.html.

[378] Victor Garcia, *Dr. Drew Pinsky Warns Los Angeles Could Be At Risk of a Deadly Epidemic This Summer,* (Fox News, May 23, 2019). Dr. Drew made his comments in a radio/TV interview with Brian Kilmead. To view the interview in its entirety, see, https://www.foxnews.com/us/dr-drew-pinsky-major-epidemic-los-angeles-kill-thousands.

[379] *Ibid.*

[380] News Editors, *Disturbing Defecation Map Reveals Why San Francisco Is An Actual Shithole,* (Natural News, January 15, 2018). The article contained a virtual map entitled "Human Wasteland" that depicted with poop emoji's indicating all the physical locations where excrement had been cleaned up by city officials in downtown San Francisco. For the full article see, https://www.naturalnews.com/2018-01-15-defecation-map-reveals-why-san-francisco-is-an-actual-sthole.html.

human feces being located in the streets of San Francisco since 2011.[381] The numbers are staggering, with the instances where human excrement had to be ameliorated by city officials rising from 5,547 in 2011 to over 28,000 in 2018.[382] There is even now smartphone applications for dealing with excrement on San Francisco sidewalks.[383] The city itself has an official "SF311" app tied to the "San Francisco at your Service" program; and, then there is an app from a private web developer called the "Snapcrap," which allows users to upload pictures they take of the fecal matter on public sidewalks into this SF311 website.[384] This process apparently alerts the cities new "poop patrol" which entails five individuals tasked with ameliorating the offending specimens.[385] Drive still further up the Pacific Coast Highway and then over to I-5 and make your way to Seattle, and you will find a similar epidemic sanitation disaster among its' homeless population as well.

It is useful to consider the policy backdrop surrounding this hideousness, and recall that the State of Washington has not elected a Republican Governor since John Spellman concluded his term in January of 1985. Since 1999, California has had only 6 years of the hapless Arnold Schwarzenegger to carry a conservative flag, the rest has been card carrying progressive liberals. Los Angeles, San Francisco and Seattle regularly elect Bernie Sanders like progressives for their mayors. The legislatures in these states are regularly a rubber stamp for neo-socialist policy, and the results are loud and clear – third world living standards for their most unfortunate residents, and a public health crisis for everyone else. For a tourist to wander down certain districts in downtown San Francisco is a literal experience with the biohazard of human waste and spent hypodermic needles. And the only thing uber-liberal politicians have to say is that we need to do more – more government, more programs, more spending, after all, their efforts today have had such impressive results (that was intentionally sarcastic). Indeed, there are parts of the United States that are beginning to mirror parts of the undeveloped world. Funny how all of them are run by bluer than blue Democrats.

This point has become so obvious, that even the uber left-wing *New York Times* has had to concede the fact that cities led by Democrats, particularly in hard-left leaning California, have devolved into filth-ridden homeless ghettos. The article is found in the opinion section of the *Times*, penned by Farhad Manjoo, and attributes one of the primary causes of the homelessness related sanitation epidemic is the extremely high cost of housing in the state.[386] He astutely points out that in San Francisco alone, the annual household income now required to purchase a median priced home is $320,000.[387] He equates California's situation to a developing world nightmare.[388] He notes that a recent affordable housing measure was thwarted by wealthy business interests in the ultimate "Not In My Back Yard" and "Not At My Expense" fashion, lending credence to the

---

[381] Ben Gilbert, *People Are Pooping More Than Ever On The Streets of San Francisco,* (Business Insider, April 18, 2019). For the full article, see, https://www.businessinsider.com/san-francisco-human-poop-problem-2019-4.

[382] Ibid.

[383] Charles Kesler, *California's Biggest Cities Confront a 'Defecation Crisis',* (Wall Street Journal, August 16, 2019).

[384] Ibid.

[385] Ibid.

[386] Farhad Manjoo, *America's Cities Are Unlivable. Blame Wealthy Liberals.* (New York Times, May 22, 2019).

[387] Ibid.

[388] Ibid.

argument that wealthy progressives are sanctimoniously embracing measures that hurt people they claim to champion.[389]

That progressives who regularly vote for the likes of Sanders, Warren and their ilk cannot see the logical conclusion of hard left policy prescriptions is an indictment of their intelligence. That Senators Sanders and Warren, and politicians like them. have any sympathetic adherents in the media and the press given this obvious and readily apparent analogy between Venezuela and the likes of these cities is one of the great political travesties of our era. The media know exactly who Sanders and Warren really are, they know who their supporters are, but they still treat them as mainstream candidates, as well as avuncular personalities when in fact they embrace and adhere to an ideology that has never EVER won the hearts and minds of a majority of Americans. Yet either one could conceivably be our 46th President of the United States. Victory in 2020 by one of them cannot be ruled out. Even if Trump wins in 2020, it may be only a matter of time in my view before we wind up with a Marxist based federal government given the affection Millennials are demonstrating for socialism. Older Americans committed to our free enterprise past are dying off by the thousands each day, and the electorate is being replenished with younger voters not at all committed to our free market heritage. So, if not Bernie Sanders or Warren in 2020, then quite possibly someone else just like them within a decade.

Would a Sanders victory, or victory by another Marxist take us on the trajectory of Venezuela? At least you could say for Chavez, he had the pretense of seeking something in between socialism and capitalism, but turned out to be a good old fashion Marxist. Sanders makes no such pretentions of moderation, and now that socialism is apparently "cool again", neither will any future hard left progressive running for the Presidency. Regarding Sanders, his is a lifelong story of one form of Marxism or another, to one degree or another. To cast a vote for him knowing what is knowable is folly beyond comprehension. But that is how civilizations come to their end. It is often said the road to hell is paved with good intentions. True enough, but it is also paved with apathy, ignorance, self-absorption, sloth and envy. A vote for Sanders requires all of these.

As we have asserted many times, the precept for this book is that the younger generations are going to attempt to take us to a "socialist paradise" and risk destroying our economy in the process. If they are successful, and there is enough evidence to render their success a viable possibility, one of their first initiatives will be wealth confiscation on the largest scale in American history. Affluent professionals will be in a particularly precarious place because they are not wealthy enough to be indifferent to taxation like billionaires are, and they don't have the means to protect their interest the way the top 0.01% does. I believe these will be the most vulnerable citizens to a modern "dekulakization". As in the first decade of the Soviet Era, the initial attempts at collectivization will involve a ruthless levying of crippling taxation on the affluent as discussed in detail in Chapter 5.

Resistance to these efforts will likely be met with harsh governmental reactions. A militarized IRS is easily foreseeable as an enforcement mechanism. We saw earlier in this chapter how militarized the agency is now, indeed how militarized the entire federal government is – even aside from the Armed Forces. Expanding this militarization would be nearly effortless. Spending an

---

[389] Ibid.

additional three billion to beef up tax collection would be a virtual blip on the US federal budget. Then there is the over militarization of state and local law enforcement, which we covered earlier in this chapter. Suffice it to say, in the event a Marxist regime takes power in America, and winds up with total control of all three branches of government, the basic infrastructure for a Soviet Style police state is in place and could be centralized under one a single agency headed by a single agency head – reporting directly to the President.

For reasons which I will touch on in the next and final chapter, Americans seem bent on proceeding in a most dangerous political direction. A course they may find extremely difficult to reverse should they wander too far down the path. Given the vast nature of the law enforcement network assembled in America today, should we ever find ourselves to have squandered our constitutional arrangement, and wind up living in a militarized police state, there will be no going back any time soon. We may well have consigned our children and grandchildren to Reagan's thousand-years of darkness if we are not able to muster sufficient will to defeat the leftward march younger generations seem intentionally to want to pursue.

If that happens, and a historian a millennium from now finds himself, somehow, someway reading this book, let it be said there was at least one private citizen frightened enough about the prospect of a high tech "dark ages", potentially lasting 10 centuries, that he wrote a book to scream at the top of his lungs to stop the madness. Let it be known there was at least one American quietly living his life that noticed the potential death trap we are flirting with and vowed not to remain silent as 240 plus years of America's successes are literally flushed down the toilet by a pugilistic, pugnacious and ignoramus generation who in no way possess the gumption or the guts to ever have built the country they live in, much less run it.

CHAPTER VII

WHAT IS TO BE DONE, AND HOW DID WE GET HERE ANYWAY?

—————————

Silence in the face of evil is itself evil:
God will not hold us guiltless.
Not to speak is to speak
Not to act is to act

- Dietrich Bonhoeffer

For most of my life there has been little debate or disagreement that the United States of America was a European nation steeped in the traditions of Western Civilization. Sure we were the world's great ethnic melting pot, but that diversity and heterogeneity was in the context of European cultural subsets, with Christianity, in its' various permutations, as the primary religion and Latin and Greek based languages and customs forming the building blocks of societal norms. There is a growing consensus among American intellectuals that at this point, at the end of the second decade of the 21st Century, America is morphing into something else entirely. It very much remains to be seen whether this metamorphosis occurs peacefully, or is plagued with violent conflagrations.

No one knows for sure what exactly the new American nation will look like, what its' dominant religion will be, or whether the current republic survives in its present form at all. While I am hopeful, I have many misgivings about the direction we are heading. As we have demonstrated in prior chapters, there is a growing acceptance and even admiration among young people for Marxist based economics. But there is very little institutional history in the United States with such an economic system. Sure we've had communist parties and various socialist parties politically, but they have little or no effect on American economic policy. What we face with Bernie Sanders and others like him amounts to a grand experiment, it could go well in the end, or it could be as bloody and violent as any previous regime that based its economic system on the principles of Marxism. We will be in uncharted territory during this transition.

The notion of American civilization as some kind of experiment is not new, in fact, it was quite prevalent in the writings of the forefathers during the founding period of the United States of

America. There is no better summation of this notion than the one given by Arthur M. Schlesinger, Jr. in *The Cycles of American History* published in 1986. Say what you will about the adequacy and precision of Mr. Schlesinger's conclusions regarding the actual cycles, his understanding and articulation of the notion of the "American Experiment" is authoritative. He writes:

> "This was a dominant theme of the early republic – the idea of America as an experiment, undertaken in the defiance of history, fraught with risk, problematic in outcome.[390]

Schlesinger weaves a compelling narrative loaded with quotations from American leaders who espoused this notion, with perhaps the best coming from Abraham Lincoln. Schlesinger writes:

> "…For the Presidents of the middle period must have known in their bones that the American experiment was confronting its fiercest internal trial. No one understood the risks more profoundly than the young man who spoke in 1838 on 'The Perpetuation of our Political Institutions' before the young Men's Lyceum of Springfield, Illinois. Over most the first half century, Abraham Lincoln said, America had been felt 'to be an undecided experiment; now, it is understood to be a successful one.' But success contained its own perils; 'with the catching, end the pleasures of the chase.' As the memory of the Revolution receded, the pillars of the temple of liberty were crumbling away. 'The temple must fall, unless we … supply their places with other pillars, hewn from the solid quarry of sober reason."[391]

For Lincoln, according to Schlesinger's account, keeping the experiment on a successful track requires a constant replenishment of the "pillars" of the temple of our civil society - of liberty. Without such replenishment, the temple falls. For the entirety of American history, the economic system that furthered the cause of liberty was that of free enterprise. As the above noted passage suggests, there is a tendency over time for the basic tenants of American society degrade, or evolve to something much less desirable. America in the early 21st Century appears to be in the middle of just such a regression. The overriding question of our era is whether we will rise to the occasion and replenish the pillars of our civil society with a refreshed and vibrant form of free enterprise, or will we devolve to rank socialism/communism, and thereby descend into the "thousand years of darkness" as Reagan had warned.

If this evolution does land in a place where America has formally adopted a Marxist based economic model, history suggests that pure economic equality comes with the staggering price of the loss of freedom. It is well known that communism has killed nearly 100 million people world-wide in the former USSR, China, Cambodia, Viet Nam, Cuba and now Venezuela. While it is true the vast majority of this carnage came from USSR and China in the early and mid-20th Century, the violent nature of a Marxist regime is well documented and pervasive. Juxtapose this with the fact that American history itself is riddled with violence, especially in the 18th and 19th Centuries. Mix Marxism with the American capacity for violence, and you get a very combustible situation. The position I assert in this book is that a pure form of Marxism is in fact evil, and the people who

---

[390] Arthur M. Schlesinger Jr., *The Cycles of American History,* (Houghton Mifflin, 1986), P. 12.

[391] Ibid.

would embrace such a system are either ignorant of its history or are evil themselves. To adopt a system that would forcefully and wantonly strip hard earned wealth from those who have worked a lifetime to earn it for the sake of collectivization is a form of larceny and is a governmental abomination. To use aggressive taxation as a back-door means to such a policy is no different than armed robbery. The rule in the Marxist jungle will be: Pay the absurd level of taxes, just like the soviets imposed on the Kulaks, or face an armed to the teeth SWAT team that will fire on sight at any resistance.

1) <u>What to Do – The Individual</u>:

There is only one thing an honorable person does in the face of evil. He stands up to it! She calls it what it is. He fights it, speaks out against it, and resists it, even if there is risk to life, limb or treasure. Our forefathers stared down the barrel of a tyrant King, and risked everything to stem his self-interested rule. They froze to death in the bitter cold of New England winters, often fighting without shoes or adequate clothing. They stood up to tyranny, and they won. What will history say of us at this darkening hour? The quote by Dietrich Bonhoeffer in the epigraph to this chapter offers a glimpse of what honorable men hundreds of years from now will have expected us to do. He should know. He stood up to Adolf Hitler and the Nazis, and is thought to have played a role in the assassination attempt on Hitler known as "the July 20 plot" (Operation Valkyrie), that nearly succeeded. Bonhoeffer payed the ultimate price for his gallantry, and was executed by hanging after being convicted by the People's Court of Nazi Germany. He lived by the inspirational words he spoke.

The primary thrust of Bonhoeffer's quote for purposes of this book is that there will be no place in history's good graces for those who do not stand up to the American political system's apparently relentless decent towards the abyss of Marxist ideology. Make no mistake, Marxism, whether in the form of socialism or communism outright, is evil. Advocating the nationalization of private industries and collectivization is a malevolent form of state sanctioned theft. Ripping away the accumulated wealth from the individual, acquired through life-long efforts is nothing short of politically driven pilfering. Any notion that such actions could be done peacefully does not stand up to historical analysis. Everywhere such actions are taken by Marxist based regimes, the action is either administered through authoritarian violence or results in an authoritarian rule. American civilization now faces an insidious threat from radical left leaning progressives who, if given the chance, will destroy America as you know it. We now regularly hear Presidential candidates espouse proposals that would purposefully pack the US Supreme Court, which would turn it into a rubber stamp for the leftist agenda. We have come to see proposals that would elevate taxation to Kulak levels of absurdity, dismember entire industries and vastly expand the regulatory state. Even reparations for slavery are now openly entertained by multiple Democratic Presidential hopefuls.

Regarding the reparations, I will digress for a moment to note that if you are Caucasian and emigrated to the U.S. any time after 1865, and whose ancestral lineage never owned a slave or otherwise participated in the American slave trade, you would nevertheless still be forced to pay reparations to a generation of African Americans several times removed from the atrocity being compensated. It has not been legal to own a slave in the US for over 155 years, the last known person to have ever been a slave died many decades ago – but we now have an unenlightened generation of belligerent young people who are hell bent on ripping the guts out of the American political and economic system. The Marxist playbook is front and center for them. There can be no other logical reason to advance the issue of reparations other than good old-fashioned wealth re-distribution. Suffocating Taxation, reparations, Green New Deal, Medicare for All – you name it – it is the same old Marxist rubbish.[392] Take money earned by someone working hard, confiscate it with one of the aforementioned theories – by force if necessary, and transfer it to another citizen who has not in any way "earned" it; "Robinhood Economics" in its purest form. The Democratic Party has become the 21st Century Visigoths at the gate ready to plunder the hard work of the generations before them for the purpose of "passing around the wealth" as President Obama once famously said.

In light of the increasingly obvious redistributive agenda of the radical progressive left, which now controls the Democratic Party, the only thing left to do is become a zealous advocate for the America we knew – for free enterprise, for the private ownership of wealth and property, for the notion that the individual should be the primary beneficiary of the fruits of his or her toil and tears. Apathy will ensure the left succeeds in its quest to remake America in the Marxist image. Not bothering to vote when people have died so that you have that right is dreadfully irresponsible. Informed citizens simply must rise-up and beat back these Marxist ignoramuses. If you can't do it for your own interest, then ponder the lives of your children and grandchildren. What kind of world will they inherit as a result of your inaction? In short, VOTE MAN VOTE! Stay informed, be engaged. Donate to candidates who support freedom, free enterprise and the American Constitution. Volunteer politically. There has never been a more appropriate time than now for activism on behalf of the free enterprise system and America's constitutional heritage.

   2) <u>What to do – All of Us</u>:

If we are to avoid a descent into Marxism (if that is even still possible), then we must embrace some compromises. The doctrinaire conservative laissez fair purist must acknowledge the fact that four decades of capitalist dogmatism has left more than half the workforce behind with no relief in sight under the current economic structure. If no reforms are embraced and implemented, then I believe the current system will collapse and we stand a very good chance of falling into a Marxist abyss. The compromises that need to be made will essentially be a Faustian Bargain where free enterprise types like myself make a deal with the Marxist devil in order to maintain the basic tenants of the market driven free enterprise system where there is private ownership of the means of production and the individual remains the primary beneficiary of fruits of his or her own labor. What we will have to do in exchange is what I enumerate in detail below. Basically, embrace an American populism or risk hell under Marxism. Allow me to explain.

I have taken some admittedly hard shots at both the Millennial generation and their younger counterparts in Generation Z for what I perceive to be their uninformed embrace of Marxist based ideals. To be objective and fair, I have attempted on several occasions to acknowledge the political and economic "ecology" in which these young people came of age, which I believe is driving their

---

[392] A point made very eloquently by Jadan Horyn, in an article entitled *Today's Greens Are Yesterday's Reds,* (RealClearPolitics, April 29, 2019), where he demonstrates the connection between today's environmental proposals for those such as Bernie Sanders, NYC Mayor Bill de Blazio and Alexandria Ocasio Cortez and yesterday's socialism. Another way of viewing the situation is that the most aggressive environmentalists of the present day are also socialists looking to shield their redistributionist ideology behind environmentalism. It's wealth confiscation no matter how you look at it.

radicalization. Like all people, America's Millennials and Generation Z are products of the environment in which they live. And they are living, in the prime of their youth, in the aftermath of a 40-year reign of purest free-market ideologues who drove economic policy by the plutocrats, of the corporations and for the shareholders. No other constituencies mattered, and it showed. America now embodies a malignant "winner take all" ethic where a comparatively small portion of the gifted and talented in our population walk away with virtually all wealth and income.

We document in this chapter and elsewhere, that the bottom half of the U.S. labor force is largely left out of our current prosperity and has been for decades now. Sure, employment is presently at record levels for all racial and ethnic groups. But what this ends up meaning is that the bottom 50% of the workforce are living a nose-hair away from abject poverty – even if they are employed. Even small disruptions can push people over the edge, as the bottom half of the workforce has no economic cushion and no savings. Many have 0 net worth, and as we will see, some even have negative net worth. All they can do is work their butts off to barely get by. And the problem is especially acute among the Millennials and Gen Z. There is now objective documentation that the Millennials are in the poorest financial shape of any other American cohort – save for Generation Z which is just entering the workforce. Specifically, a recent study reported by the *Wall Street Journal* demonstrates that the Millennials are now hitting the stride of their working years, lagging behind all other generations economically.[393] What's worse according to the *Journal* is that they may never recover.[394]

If I were running for office, I would propose a seven-point plan to inoculate America from the Marxist virus currently infecting our body politic. I suspect my plan may offend hard core conservatives and I know for a fact it will enrage the radical Marxist progressive. That is the primary reason I believe it will be a viable solution; the trick will be to get the vast middle of the American political spectrum to see the virtue in what I offer – or something similar in its place. To the free market purists, I would assert you will either find in your heart and mind where you can make rational compromises with those on the left, or you will find yourself living in a socialist country in a matter of a few short decades. To reiterate my view: The hard-right intransigence from so many in the conservative movement on economic and social matters is facilitating our current Marxist radicalization. We already know the hard left will not compromise, and that the Democratic Party is drifting ever further to the left. What we need to realize as conservatives and libertarians, is that some kind of government sponsored populist reform is critical to fending off the socialist barbarians at the gate. In a land where the top sliver of income earners and asset owners has enjoyed nearly all the benefits of productivity increases over the past 35 years, clinging to doctrinaire conservatism will ultimately be rejected by the American people. The risk is that they turn to hard core Marxistism by default, a possibility we explored in prior chapters. Think of it as our being tossed out of the current "frying pan" of political turmoil into the literal "fire" of Marxism where we will find ourselves right next to the hottest of burning coals.

Unfortunately, America has now become the land of entrenched interests, so much so we've lost our ability to view compromise as a virtue, when in fact it has been America's unique genius since inception. With that acknowledged, I believe the following seven proposals will ensure it

---

[393] Janet Adamy and Paul Overberg, *'Playing Catch-Up in the Game of Life." Millennials Approach Middle Age in Crisis,* (Wall Street Journal, May 19, 2019).
[394] Ibid.

prosperously endures for another century with widespread tranquility and mass happiness. The steps are as follows: (1) eliminate inheritance tax loopholes completely with an exemption from the tax on assets up to $10 million; (2) force Congress to adhere to its own laws without exception; (3) radically curtail public employee unions; (4) limit and restrict the degree to which college tuition is allowed to increase, and amend the bankruptcy code to allow all student loans to be fully dischargeable; (5) cap compensation for wage and salary earners and other non-entrepreneurial related income in any in all cases, except for the individuals who founded and run their own companies; (6) end the notion and practice of "at-will" employment in our country; and, (7) enact legislation that disallows off shore investments whose sole purpose is income tax avoidance. These elements are what I believe will form the basis of a populist reform that still adheres to free enterprise basics. We will discuss each proposal in detail below.

Before delving onto detail on each of these six proposals, it is worth mentioning that other than the inheritance tax, and closing the off-shore account loopholes, you will not find a call for higher taxation. There is a reason for that. I do not generally believe more taxes are the answer (other than to say that if the billionaire and decamillionaire classes wish to substantially increase their income or wealth related taxes we should assist them with all due haste). More taxes on the merely "affluent" will degrade their living standards to the point where they lose enough economic incentive to want to continue noble pursuits in the professional disciplines like, law, medicine, mid-level corporate management and the sciences. My belief is that American civilization is degenerating into a high-tech dark ages because capitalism, a very good and workable economic system, has been allowed to run amok, and metastasize into something that no longer benefits the average American working family. We therefore run the risk of falling for Marxism in our efforts to reform free enterprise. But informed people know that Marxism is bunk. It doesn't work because it is absurd. Perhaps the most succinct and articulate view and critique of the communist doctrine was once offered by the great British economist John Maynard Keynes when he said:

> "How can I accept the Communist doctrine, which sets up as its bible, above and beyond criticism, an obsolete textbook which I know not only to be scientifically erroneous but without interest or application to the modern world? How can I adopt a creed which, preferring the mud to the fish, exalts the boorish proletariat above the bourgeoisie and the intelligentsia, who with all their faults, are the quality of life and surely carry the seeds of all human achievement? Even if we need a religion, how can we find it in the turbid rubbish of the red bookshop? It is hard for an educated, decent, intelligent son of Western Europe to find his ideals here, unless he has first suffered some strange and horrid process of conversion which has changed all his values."

That about sums it up. I first read that quote as a college student in the 1980s and it has stuck with me for 35 years. Whatever capitalisms faults, reforming it is far, FAR preferable than rummaging the junk yard of Marxism for any kind of economic salvation. With that notion clearly stated, on with the details.

a) Increase Inheritance Taxation on the Mega Rich (Leave the Merely Affluent Alone):

One of the key drivers motivating the current generation of young people to embrace Marxist based economics is surely the perception that purist Laissez-Faire capitalism is resulting in absurd levels of income and wealth inequality. While there are those who find virtue in successive generations of Trust Fund Babies, I do not count myself among them. There is no reason a multi-billion-dollar fortune should be handed down to generations who had little or no hand in creating the wealth. The US faces a credible threat of a Marxist uprising internally because we have allowed our free enterprise system to degenerate to the "winner take all" ethic, where only the gold medalist is revered, and everyone else is forgotten. Even if the winning time difference between a Gold Medalist swimmer and the 4th place swimmer is only fractions of a second – or the length of a human body, the reward for the victor is a king's ransom, and for the 4th place finisher – virtually nothing. The silver and bronze medalist take home a prize, but it is nothing in comparison with the winner of gold. American civilization has taken an analogous ethic regarding the distribution of wealth and income. Some examples include a quarterback in the NFL making many times the average salary of the linemen protecting him, the same linemen who have many times the risk of brain injury as does the quarterback. In the entertainment industry, the "A" list actors and actresses, at best 2-3% of the Screen Actors Guild total, make a radically disproportionate share of the income from motion pictures. It is not uncommon for a lead actor's salary to comprise $25-35% of a motion pictures total budget. Ridiculous and obscene, especially when one considers that Hollywood is a notorious hive of rancid ultra-left politics. Nothing like a good dose of hypocrisy to go with the sanctimony.

Other examples include some of the big-name professions, say top law firms in any given city for example. A small band of partners making literally 10 or 20 times the average associate salary is not out of the realm of possibility. Then compare what these partners make versus their support staff (law clerks, paralegals, legal secretaries etc. etc.). Let's just summarize to say there is a vast gulf in terms of what the top of the house gets paid versus the rank and file attorney and the support personnel. American's are tired of it, and these kinds of differentials are not justifiable – at least not in their current magnitude. Then rub insult to the injury and watch as a large trust fund corpus is handed down to the children of these income oligarchs in almost every industry or profession, and you get the volatility we have today.

With the exception of corporate officers who are not also entrepreneurs, I generally take the position that one ought **_not_** to have any cap on income they earn in life or wealth they accumulate. We want people "reaching for the stars" when they start a business. This is foundational for American economic success. But what does this principle have to do with inheritance? While we all certainly want to leave our children better off than we were, what is the virtue in bequeathing multi-billion dollar estates to someone who had no real hand in accumulating it? The extreme concentrations of wealth and income in the U.S. are becoming so severe they are destabilizing the country politically.

A modest proposal would be to keep the current exemption at their 2017 levels of $5.49 Million for an individual and $10.98 Million for a married couple.[395] Then freeze the exemption level at

---

[395] Chye Ching Huang and Cloe Cho, *Ten Facts You Should Know About the Estate Tax,* (Center on Budget and Policy Priorities, October 10, 2017), citing The American Taxpayer Relief Act of 2013 set the estate tax exemption at $5.25 million for 2013 (effectively $10.5 million for a couple), and indexed that level for inflation in future years. It set the top rate at 40 percent. See Internal Revenue Bulletin 2013-5, *Revenue Procedure 2013-5*, January 2013, http://www.irs.gov/pub/irs-drop/rp-13-15.pdf. Congress could easily repeal the facet of these limits that indexes these levels to inflation in future years.

this amount and ***not*** index it to consumer price inflation. As incomes and wealth accumulation rise, mathematically there would be more taxable income subject to this tax with each passing year. At present, approximately 2 out of every 1,000 estates is actually subject to the federal estate tax; and, conversely, 99.8% of estates *are not* subject to this tax.[396]

If that isn't bad enough, there are beyond the pale loopholes readily available for ultra-wealthy estates to avoid taxation that have the appearance of pure avidity. The Center on Budget and Policy Priorities provides illustration of the magnitude of this gluttony when they write:

> "Many wealthy estates employ teams of lawyers and accountants to develop and exploit loopholes in the estate tax that allow them to pass on large portions of their estates tax-free*. **These strategies don't benefit the broader economy; they only allow the wealthiest estates to avoid taxes.***
>
> For example, some estates use grantor retained annuity trusts (GRATs) to pass along considerable assets tax-free. The estate owner puts money into a trust designed to repay the estate the initial amount plus interest at a rate set by the Treasury, typically over two years. If the investment — typically stock — rises in value any more than the Treasury rate, the gain goes to an heir tax-free. If the investment doesn't rise in value, the full amount still goes back to the estate. Such techniques have been described as a "heads I win, tails we tie" bet.
>
> The GRAT loophole enables wealthy estates to avoid extraordinary amounts of tax when stock or other assets rise in value quickly, as has happened frequently in recent years. ***The tax lawyer credited with discovering the loophole estimates that it has allowed wealthy estates to avoid as much as $100 billion in estate taxes since 2000, or close to one-third of the amount that the tax raised over the period.***
>
> A top estate tax priority for policymakers should be to eliminate loopholes such as these."[397] (Emphasis Supplied) (Citations Omitted).

The authors of the above quotation end this excerpt by asserting the urgent need for Congress to act and discontinue these absurd loopholes. I will echo that sentiment. These types of loopholes have little economic value for the economy at large, and mainly exist due to effective lobbying by the well-healed. Garbage such as this is exactly why America is headed for a Marxist style revolution in the next decade or two if nonsense like this is not reigned in.

Americans do not appear to be inclined to let this kind of farce stand indefinitely. The wealthy benefit immensely from doing business in the United States, with its highly literate population and first-rate infrastructure. After all, if these wealthy tax avoiders were so fabulously brilliant that

---

[396] Ibid.

[397] Ibid.

they could have become superbly rich doing business anywhere they so choose, then why aren't they creating fortunes places like El Salvador, Guatemala and Darfur? We all agree capitalism stimulates high levels of wealth creation, but there are capitalist states that don't create the magnitude of wealth the U.S. does per capita. Why isn't New Zealand minting centimillionaires and billionaires like the U.S. does? Probably because our national wherewithal to create wealth is facilitated by us little peons and "worker bees" too, and the U.S. has a fantastic workforce that aids wealth generation better than anywhere else in the world. The average American is so tired of hearing about what virtue there is with the rich while their incomes have stagnated for decades. Given the way the Washington establishment reacted to Trump's election, it is apparent that the ruling class basically doesn't get it, which is becoming increasingly dangerous.

The purist free chauvinist is well advised to begin thinking about ways to compromise with left of center interest groups before the rage builds to the point where the wealthy and affluent get crushed politically. What is at stake is our very civilization. As I've said, we all know that whatever ills and warts capitalism has, they are far preferable to the open boils and leprosy of Marxism. Make the compromises now so that America can get out of the political frying pan into something sustainable versus landing next to the hot coals of Marxism in base of the fire.

The affluent, who are comfortable but not going to benefit from protections against federal estate taxation are well advised to support estate tax reform. If this book has accomplished anything at all, hopefully it has driven home the point that the sting of dekulakization of the American Affluent class is going to hit the comfortable high earning professional waaaaay before the Marxists really do much damage to the very rich. America's Kulaks have a vested interest in compromising to avoid the hits they would take under a Marxist regime, where they will be economically gutted rather quickly. For the affluent to pretend their interests align with the billionaire class is a charade that has left them quite vulnerable.

   b) <u>Congress Must Live By Its' Own Laws – ALWAYS</u>:

Certainly, one of the most absurd and atrocious aspects of the American political system is that Congress has discretion as to whether to adhere to the laws it enacts. There isn't a whole lot more on this topic that warrants additional discussion. If you think it would ever, under any circumstances be permissible to allow a legislator to live by a different rule – any rule – than what you have to obey, then the status quo is fine for you and I have nothing to say except that I respectfully disagree. One of the core fundamentals of American civilization is the rigorous adherence to the "rule of law". Entire books have been written on the matter of the rule of law being an essential component of the success of Western civilization. This assumes a codification of a uniform set of requirements and standards that apply to all of us – not just to some of us. The minute we start exempting entire classes of people from a given standard, is the point at which we take the first step towards a caste system where ones' social status defines the rules they must follow. One set of rules for the privileged and another set for everyone else is a philosophy that will end America as we have ever known it.

If we continue down the road of allowing legislators to exempt themselves from the laws they pass – under any circumstances, then someone should remove the "Equal Justice Under Law" quote on the Supreme Court Building in Washington D. C. If we are not going to adhere to this principle or only selectively abide by it, then it is only a matter of time before the principle is rendered meaningless. For Congress to have any special dispensation on this point is simply unacceptable. Herein lies the quandary: Getting Congress to reform itself on this point will not likely happen absent some massive national trauma. Unfortunately for you and me, a Marxist takeover of the American government will certainly provide trauma, but I wouldn't expect much in the way of positive reform from it. Perhaps in the event the U.S. survives the forthcoming national distress, and an astute historian picks up on the dynamic of legislators exempting themselves from their own legislation as at least one contributing factor to the shock, future legislatures decades or centuries from now will have learned this lesson. There is much cause for concern in the short run.

    c) <u>Radically Curtail Public Employee Unions</u>:

Without question, one of the most insidious developments in modern American history is the astonishing proliferation of public sector unions at the state and federal level. The absurdity of government employees, both state or federal, ensuring themselves better pay and much better retirement security benefits than what the average taxpayer receives is nothing short of an abomination. The constant budgetary woes states regularly encounter is in no small part due to the high levels of compensation and benefits afforded to government workers. American Citizens are figuring out this sham and various states have been successful at calling it out and ensuring reforms. Wisconsin's former Governor Scott Walker is first to come to mind. When he enacted legislation that discarded mandatory union membership and compulsory union dues for state employees with the exception of policemen and firefighters, he caused a popular uproar among the bureaucratic class nationwide. Former New Jersey Governor Chris Christie built his political career on public sector compensation reform and took on the public unions as well. This trend started a decade ago and is likely to continue over time. It needs to escalate and is sure to be contentious. When Governor Walker drove through his reforms, he met with wide-spread civil disobedience, with sit-ins and massive protests at the Wisconsin State Capital building making national headlines for weeks.

One of the most urgent reform measures needed is to *radically* reign in these public employee unions. It is critical at the outset to understand that public sector unionization is a relatively new phenomenon, largely a creature of the mid-20th century, which means that their prevalence is less than three-quarters of a century old. One of the best summaries regarding the contemporary nature of these types of unions comes from an article written by Daniel DeSalvo for *National Affairs* in 2010. The article is entitled *The Trouble With Public Sector Unions*. She provides a succinct and compelling recapitulation of the notion that these types of unions were never preordained and have grown incessantly when she writes:

> "The emergence of powerful public-sector unions was by no means inevitable. Prior to the 1950s, as labor lawyer Ida Klaus remarked in 1965, "the subject of labor relations in public employment could not have meant less to more people, both in and out of government." ___*To the extent that people thought about it, most politicians, labor leaders, economists, and judges opposed collective bargaining in the public sector. Even President Franklin Roosevelt, a friend of private-sector unionism, drew a line when it came to*___

government workers: "Meticulous attention," the president insisted in 1937, "should be paid to the special relations and obligations of public servants to the public itself and to the Government....The process of collective bargaining, as usually understood, cannot be transplanted into the public service." The reason? F.D.R. believed that "[a] strike of public employees manifests nothing less than an intent on their part to obstruct the operations of government until their demands are satisfied. Such action looking toward the paralysis of government by those who have sworn to support it is unthinkable and intolerable." Roosevelt was hardly alone in holding these views, even among the champions of organized labor. Indeed, the first president of the AFL-CIO, George Meany, believed it was "impossible to bargain collectively with the government."[398] (Emphasis added).

It appears the instincts and inclinations of our past leaders on this matter – across many various disciplines – proved prescient and sagacious. They understood that there is no legitimate collective bargaining between the taxpayer and the government. If a government worker strikes, the taxpayer could lose essential and critical services. Roosevelt understood that the paralysis of government brought on by such strikes would be "unthinkable and intolerable". Yet here we are today with 7.2 million public sector employees belonging to a union as of 2018, with a union membership rate of 33.9%, which was five times the rate for private sector workers.[399]

Aside from the unfair nature of having a taxpayer fund a far more generous and secure income and retirement for unionized government workers than what is available to the average wage earner in the labor force,[400] there is also the problem of rank politicization within the union membership at hand. As an example, in 2014, Henry Enton, writing for the blog *FiveThirtyEight* noted that in 2012, Obama won union households with a margin of 18 percentage points, 58% for Obama, 40% for Romney, comprising 75% of Obama's margin of victory.[401] It is worth mentioning that Obama won the union vote over Senator John McCain in 2008 as well. Union bias for Democrats goes back a century, and while union membership has declined overall, that is attributed to the decline of private sector industrial unions, not public employee unions. Both remain a stalwart component of the Democratic Party coalition. And if you really want to understand the public sector union membership's commitment to Democrats, one only need to understand their political contribution trends. From 1990 through the 2018 election, fifteen electoral cycles (both mid-terms and Presidential) the public sector unions have donated on average 91% of all their donations to the Democratic Party candidate, versus 9% to the Republican.[402]

---

[398] Daniel DeSalvo, *The Trouble With Public Sector Unions*, (National Affairs, Fall 2010). For the full article, see, https://www.nationalaffairs.com/publications/detail/the-trouble-with-public-sector-unions.

[399] U.S. Department of Labor, Bureau of Labor Statistics, *Union Membership Summary,* (Economic News Release; January 18, 2019).

[400] Ibid. The BLS notes that "[a]mong full-time wage and salary workers, union members had **median usual weekly earnings** of $1,051 in 2018, while those who were not union members had median weekly earnings of $860." It does not take a math genius to figure out that this translates to a union member earns an additional 22.2% over and above what a private sector wage earner makes.

[401] Henry Enton, *How Much Do Democrats Depend on the Union Vote?* (FiveThirtyEight.com, July 1, 2014).

[402] OpenSecrets.org, Center for Responsive Politics, *Public Sector Unions: Long Term Contribution Trends*. See, https://www.opensecrets.org/industries/totals.php?cycle=2018&ind=P04.

To say that public sector unions are in bed with Democrats would be quite an understatement, and if you believe the only thing public sector unions get in return for their devotion is a back rub then you'd have to believe just about anything. The corruption involved in this relationship is notorious. Public sector unions have interjected themselves in state, local and federal politics wherever possible and the result has been an increasing leftward radicalization of our state and federal bureaucracies. There is no better illustration of this corruption than the spectacle of 100% of the Bureau of Consumer Financial Protection employees giving all of their donations to Hillary Clinton or Senator Bernie Sanders in 2016.[403] Additionally, 100% of their contributions went to Democrats overall, easily placing this agency as by far the most politicized federal bureaucracy.[404]

This political infestation of institutions that are presumed to be politically neutral is certainly one of the most urgent public policy issues of our time, and public sector unionization is a contributing cause of the problem. Therefore, the inoculation of these institutions from political bias by limiting the spread of public unions surely warrants immediate action. Fortunately, the U.S. Supreme Court has handed down several decisions over the past decade that are facilitating this re-balance, but more will have to be done. It is appropriate for any sitting U.S. President to school himself in the writings of Franklin Roosevelt on the issue of public unionization and follow the lead Ronald Reagan set with the Air Traffic Controllers strike in the early 1980s. The idea that federal employees can use the threat of denying vital public services to the taxpayer in order to collectively bargain for their own pecuniary interest is nothing short of outrageous. That these same employees got in bed with Democrats for no other reason than to preserve their monetary interests at the expense of state and federal taxpayers is both unsustainable and immoral. That the citizen being forced to pay for a guaranteed retirement for a public employee when that same taxpayer may well have no retirement benefits at all aside from Social Security is simply an injustice. Public employee union members have become a backbone of the socialist progressive left and used taxpayer dollars to get there. The time has come to put this absurdity to an end.

    d) <u>Limits on College Tuition Increases:</u>

An additional great tragedy of our time is that young college students are graduating from American institutions of higher learning with atrocious levels of student loan debt. Total outstanding student loan debt in the United States as of the first quarter of 2019 stood at $1.5 *trillion*, the highest cumulative balance ever.[405] As of 2017, the typical student borrower owes on average $28,650, and student loans as an asset class exceed the total outstanding balance of all other debt categories except mortgages, which means Americans owe more in student loans than for credit cards or autos.[406] This fact is one of the great blemishes on modern American Civilization. Other useful information surrounding student debt includes the fact that there are 44.7 million U.S. borrowers who owe student debt, and the rate of serious delinquency (90 days past due) is 11.4%,[407] a rate several times that of other types of debt.

---

[403] Bill McMorris, *100% of CFPB Donations Went to Democrats: Controversial Agency is Most Partisan*, (Washington Free Beacon, November 23, 2016).

[404] Ibid.

[405] Zach Friedman, *Student Loan Debt Statistics in 2019: A $1.5 Trillion Crisis,* (Forbs, February 25, 2019).

[406] Ibid.

[407] Ibid.

It is not uncommon for students to rack up undergraduate debt nearing $100K, and for professional students such as medical or dental school, debts regularly run well in to the six figures. American society has been quite willing to allow some of the smartest among us to incur a crushing burden of school debt as they start out their professional lives. Then there is the increasing phenomenon where students borrow large sums for dubious degrees in something with "-studies" affixed to it at little known institutions and then struggle to find work that even begins to pay down these absurd student loan balances. The Starbucks Barista making $12-15 and hour with a degree in general-studies who borrowed $70,000 to attend a small obscure liberal arts college will struggle for years, perhaps decades trying to pay that balance down.

How this has come to pass has widespread culpability. Colleges and Universities allowing their tuition to increase at rates that far exceed consumer price inflation have some serious explaining to do (hint, one primary answer is their increasingly bloated administrative overhead).[408] Students who do not fully understand the impact of borrowing such amounts for degrees for which they have not adequately ascertained the demand in the marketplace is certainly another factor. But then again, at age 18-20 when people start making these decisions, how financially astute were you and I? How do state governments allow for this? Where are the feds? No one is looking out for young people on these matters, with the result being that young Americans are winding up saddled with previously unfathomable levels of debt at a very tender age. That our society allows this borders on the criminal. I take the position that this is a societal-wide failure; one that gets nowhere near the attention it deserves and seldom have we heard viable solutions.

Furthermore, the facts pertaining to massive student debt levels are bad enough on their own, when you factor in changes made in the U.S. Bankruptcy Code since 1976, the situation becomes outright combustible.[409] Before 1976 all education debt was fully dischargeable in bankruptcy, then a series of reforms were enacted beginning that year and over time restrictions on the dischargeability applied to more and more types of student loans.[410] Then the Big Kahuna came with the Bankruptcy Abuse Prevention and Consumer Protection Act of 2005.[411] This Act significantly expanded the types of student loan debt that would not be dischargeable,[412] unless a debtor could show undue hardship – a notoriously difficult standard in a bankruptcy proceeding. The effect of this legislation is that ALL student loans are non-dischargeable in bankruptcy, or stated in the converse – no student loans of any kind can be discharged without the showing of undue hardship. If you are struggling with your payments, the court can discharge your credit card debt with the stroke of a pen, no matter how fecklessly and recklessly the debt was incurred. But your student loans – you'll figure it out or carry the debt to your grave. For many of today's Millennial generation and Generation Z to follow, this feels like being lost in the forest with no

---

[408] Trends in Higher Education, *Average Rates of Growth of Public Charges by Decade,* (Collegeboard.org as of May 16, 2019). For full article see., https://trends.collegeboard.org/college-pricing/figures-tables/average-rates-growth-published-charges-decade. The article summarizes as follows: "Between 2008-09 and 2018-19, published in-state tuition and fees at public four-year institutions increased at an average rate of 3/1% ***per year beyond inflation,***, compared with average annual increases of 4/1% and 4/2% over the prior decades".

[409] Kayla Webley, *Why Can't You Discharge Student Loans in Bankruptcy?,* (Time, February 9, 2012).

[410] Ibid.

[411] Pub. L. 109-8, 119 Stat. 23 (2005).

[412] 11 U.S.C. § 523(8)(a) (2005).

indication on how to get out. Bankruptcy experts agree that to meet the undue hardship threshold, one basically must demonstrate some form of disability.

So, the net effect is that 18-21 year-olds are borrowing large sums of money without fully understanding the repayment burden they are taking on (did you understand it at that age?). Most reasonable individuals just coming out of high school are not yet well versed in personal finance, which is becoming a complex discipline all its own. They are winding up over their heads at the prime of their youth with no apparent exit. The 2005 bankruptcy code revisions are so one-sided in favor of the financial institutions making and servicing student loans, it is almost embarrassing to say I worked in the industry. There is no question that high levels of student debt, coupled with stagnant income growth for two decades, coupled with no possibility of exiting the situation except to break both your legs, is a toxic brew that is turning vast numbers of American youth against capitalism. Many young people have permanently ruined their personal financial situation for their entire adult lives and there is no legal way out. Their only sin is they dared to believe that higher education still bought a ticket to prosperity in America's middle class.

As Millennials and Generation Z gain in their share of the electorate in the coming years, this will almost certainly be an issue that Congress will be forced to address. The obvious solution is to return the bankruptcy code to its pre-1976 posture and allow ALL student loans to be dischargeable once again. Alternatively, another option is to revise the standard for what is considered an undue hardship into something more reasonable under the circumstances so that someone who truly did "get ahead of their skiis" so to speak can get a fresh start. The current situation borders on the immoral. The financial services companies lending student loans will object to any of this of course, but that is to be expected. This is where conservatives and libertarians must drop the ideological posturing and get pragmatic with the facts as we find them, not how we would like them to be. Failure to solve this problem will result in the continued drift toward Marxism among Millennials and the upcoming Generation Z.

Bernie Sanders makes massive political "hay" every time he points out that in an era where higher education is required for American international competitiveness, we are punishing our students with infeasible levels of debt when we should be rewarding their educational achievements. If the Washington establishment cannot satisfactorily address this nauseating situation, then I put the odds of the U.S. descending into the socialist abyss at roughly a coin toss. I have said many times that the fundamental dynamic of present-day politics is that older, free market friendly Americans are dying off at an increasing rate, and their place in the electorate is being replenished by much more radically progressive young people. The inflection point – critical mass if you will, – is likely within the next two decades, possibly much sooner.

e) <u>Address and Seriously Mitigate Wealth Inequality</u>:

1) The Problem:

While the afore-referenced causes for the decent towards Marxism are indeed key drivers, if the reader wishes to fully understand the growing groundswell of antipathy for 21st Century capitalism in the United States today, I have called attention to establishment conservative elites who have for decades now championed a near purist form of free trade, lower taxes for the wealthy and minimalism regarding the power of government to regulate interstate commerce. This addiction to dogma has resulted in the implementation of a political agenda that has economically disenfranchised essentially half of the workforce. There is no better example and expression of such an ideologically perfectionist form of conservatism than the writings of the well-known and well-regarded opinion columnist George F. Will, who has been a member of the Washington Post Writers Group for many decades now. Furthermore, there is no better illustration of the kind of academic laissez fair orthodoxy than what he exhibited in a June 2019 column he wrote taking on the issue of wealth inequality. In making his points, he first extols the virtuous strictures of conservatism generally when he writes:

> "Warren and Obama asserted something unremarkable — that the individual depends on cooperative behavior by others. But they obscured this point: It is conservatism, not progressivism, that takes society seriously. Conservatism understands society not as a manifestation of government but as the spontaneous order of cooperating individuals in consensual, contractual market relations. Progressivism preaches confident social engineering by the regulatory state. Conservatism urges government humility in the face of society's extraordinary — and creative — complexity. American society, understood as hundreds of millions of people making billions of decisions daily, is a marvel of spontaneous cooperation. Sensible government facilitates this cooperative order by providing roads, schools, police, etc., and by getting out of the way of spontaneous creativity. This is a dynamic, prosperous society's 'underlying social contract.'"[413]

For anyone whose read Mr. Will's work over the decades, this excerpt reiterates the very familiar conservative talking point proclaiming genius in the "spontaneous order of cooperating individuals in consensual, contractual market relations", whereas progressivism is regarded as the summation of social engineering of preordained outcomes via the power of the state to regulate. While I surely agree that the kind of hard left progressive Marxism of which I warn the reader throughout this book will universally devolve to a command and control civilization, and a loss of the freedoms we have enjoyed for centuries now; the dogmatic form of conservatism of the kind espoused by Mr. Will has lost all credibility. I will explain why.

To begin, we'll start with what is perhaps the most incredulous passage in his essay, one immediately following the citation above. He writes:

> "**Many contemporary ethicists, however, believe that _inequalities of wealth_ that are produced by exceptional individual productivity rising from exceptional natural aptitudes _do not deserve society's deference or protection_.** The more that science establishes genetic bases for differences of aptitudes and even of attitudes and desires, the more pressure there will be for government actions to remedy the unfairness of life's lottery. Many of these pressures, however, will be opportunistic — old agendas seeking,

---

[413] George F. Will, *Is The Individual Obsolete?: Progressives Want To Dilute The Concept of Individualism, But That Is Antithetical To America's Premise* (Washington Post Opinion Essay, May 31, 2019).

through science, new momentum for respect. ***And it is not obvious why political power should be put in the service of ironing out differences that are, strictly speaking, natural.*** Nevertheless, the science of genetics is joining the social sciences in complicating our understanding of what equality of opportunity means."[414] (Emphasis Supplied).

The reader will never find a more bald-faced justification for America's current "winner take all" economic conditions than this one. After reading such excerpts as these, one could be forgiven for viewing Mr. Will as the great self-proclaimed arbiter of conservative virtue whose primary function in life is to provide the intellectual rationalization for the oligarchic status quo, which effectively makes him a stooge for the American Plutocracy. There is no American intellectual that has more stridently defended high octane free trade, lower taxes and deregulation over the decades than George Will. As Mr. Will is an exceptional scholar, he would no doubt be able to rattle off the names of the "ethicists" to whom he refers when justifying inaction in the area of wealth inequality. With that acknowledged, let's be clear, his unmistakable assertion is: That wealth inequality is a naturally occurring phenomenon driven in large part due to the uneven distribution of cognitive abilities; those on the losing end of the inequality spectrum "do not necessarily deserve any deference or protection;" and, any government role in ameliorating such disparities should be met with some degree of skepticism. This essay, like many others Mr. Will has written, provides the intellectual rationale for a notion that Nixon Era Republican Strategist Kevin Phillips would one day coin with the phrase "the triumph of Upper America." The remainder of Will's essay explores the concept that class has a measurable impact on wealth distribution. Those who are already educated and functioning well in the high-tech age pass those aptitudes and skills to their offspring while the underclass, trapped in the cycle of poverty, pass that on to their offspring as well (intergenerational poverty).

His points pertaining to the role of class are appropriate and well taken but they do not, and cannot form the basis for justifying or even explaining the natural dispersion of cognitive aptitudes that would defend or vindicate the extraordinary mal-distribution of wealth in our society at this point in history. It is reasonable to argue that doctors will attempt to breed doctors, lawyers will breed lawyers and the highly educated will take extraordinary measures to ensure their offspring are well educated. However, we all know there are many marginally talented privileged and connected students who are accepted to elite universities via "legacy affirmative action" despite mediocre cognitive ability at best; and, there are countless examples of talented individuals who cannot escape their environment and receive no education at all. As education at prestigious institutions of higher learning has been repeatedly proven to be mathematically correlated to higher income and wealth accumulation, education is a key proxy for our class system. That students with, at best, average cognitive talent are routinely admitted to our finest institutions, either on the basis of legacy affirmative action to keep the donor class and alumni happy, or race based affirmative action to satisfy diversity goals, provides justification for the assertion that achievement is not always awarded on the basis of "merit" as understood by the average American. In other words, there are no small number of students in our best universities that got their slot by virtue of factors other than their cognitive aptitudes. If income and wealth are mathematically linked to education, and education is not fully meritorious, then how can there be a "natural" condition for wealth and income concentration?

---

[414] Ibid.

A large portion of the American populace is coming to view the current political and economic system as rigged against them. Hearing arguments that justify or attempt to provide reasoning defending vast wealth inequality as the natural order of things increasingly rings hallow for millions of our fellow countrymen. Mr. Will is acutely aware of this. He has preached ideas such as the ones quoted above since the early 1970s, and had been a staunch member of the Republican Party all of that time. Until the rank and file stopped listening. During the 2016 Presidential campaign, ideas like the ones cited in Mr. Will's afore refenced passages ceased to be compelling or effective for most Republican voters. Republican's turned to the populism of Donald Trump, much to the chagrin of Mr. Will, and half of the Democratic electorate went for Senator Sanders. Will would ultimately leave the Republican Party in disgust over the Nomination of Trump.

The newsflash for Mr. Will should be that there is no going back. While his views still resonate with the Washington elite, or as Missouri Senator Josh Hawley calls them – the "Cosmopolitan Elite," such views do not so with the electorate at large. George Will is likely to enjoy only a posthumous resurgence of his philosophy with the average American long after his death. The Democratic Party is going hard to the left, the Republican Party is 90% behind the populism of Mr. Trump, and will be for the foreseeable future. Comparatively few Americans will ever again buy the doctrinal conservativism of Mr. Will. When half the population is essentially hanging on by an economic thread, living a nose-hair away from financial depravity, people are not going to line up and vote for candidates who tell them that this is the natural order of things. Telling voters that those with "middling" IQs are naturally going to get left behind to wallow in subsistence living, and that such a phenomenon is a moral and just outcome will not be a winning political message. People will want a government role – not professorial diatribes on "limited government".

In fact, there is a now a significant and growing consensus in the American electorate that corporate power is becoming excessive, that there is more to our civilization than the interests of the shareholder, and that everyone who is working full time should have a respectful living standard. Former Reagan/Bush advisor James Pinkerton, now writing for *Beitbart* has called attention to developments pointing in the direction of a material block of voters gravitating towards economic liberalism – or economic "patriotism" and rejecting classical conservatism and outright socialism.[415] Pinkerton's essay draws heavily from a June 16, 2019 *Vanity Fair* Article by T.A. Frank, who observed that while the Washington establishment still clings to the ideas the free trade is the ticket to prosperity, corporate shareholders are rightfully the dominant interest group and social liberalism the prevailing domestic philosophy, this is not where a substantial portion of the American people are.[416] Pinkerton, citing Mr. Frank, points to polling data suggesting, much to the chagrin of the likes of Mr. Will, that American's do not feel corporations pay their fair share of the tax burden; there should be more spending on education; government should improve the floor on healthcare availability; more should be spent on environmental protection; and more should be spent on veterans benefits.[417] Pinkerton ends the essay by approvingly referencing what Mr. Frank refers to as "Deplorable New Dealers," those voters who would have fit right in with

---

[415] James Pinkerton, *Pinkerton: Mainstream Media Pundit Argues "Deplorable New Dealers" Will Be Decisive Voting Block in 2020:* (Breitbart, June 22, 2019).

[416] Ibid.

[417] Ibid.

FDRs New Deal coalition and who are pro family patriots skeptical of the woke social justice warrior agenda advocated by most present-day Democrats.

The ideological conservative that cannot recognize this will contribute to America's descent into the socialist abyss. The purist conservative who attempts to justify the large-scale economic pain being felt across the American economy, and tell us it really isn't all that bad, will be complicit in our political unwinding because the American People will naturally reject this; and, the risk will be that the voter ends up falling for the Marxist message because it offers at least of glimmer of hope. That Marxism will wind up killing America as we know it is unfortunately not readily apparent to the Millennials or to Generation Z. They will experiment with what Thomas Sowell referred to as that "wonderfully sounding rhetoric" because they are ill-informed of history's lessons that such policies lead to something more like Venezuela rather than utopia. So the conservative has a duty to compromise, and not act as though life is being lived on a college chalk board. With that acknowledged, we now turn to our attention to just how bad is the wealth inequality in our country. The discussion that follows is a quick summary of the facts.

It is widely known that a Chief Executive Officer of an S&P 500 corporation has total annual compensation (salary + bonus + various stock option awards + other "benefits") valued at several hundred times the compensation for the average employee working at their institution; 361 times than the average worker compensation to be exact.[418] Contrast this obscenity with the fact that in the 1950's, when the American economy undisputedly ruled the world, a CEO made on average about 20 times that of the average worker at his firm.[419] To put this vulgarity in the starkest possible terms, a CEO now earns, on average, $13,900,000 annually, versus an average yearly salary of $38,613 for the employees working at S&P 500 firms.

In contemporary America, a Chief Executive Officer of a major corporation (and a whole host of smaller ones as well) live a life that is flush with virtually endless resources. They go through life never having to seriously ask "how much", they pay no attention to the right-hand side of a menu as C. Wright Mills once said.[420] Their direct reports and other senior managers are in a similar boat – either lavish affluence or outright wealth. The rest of the American population is left to fend for the economic scraps left by the wealthiest. America has become government of the Ivy League bureaucrat or jurist; for the privileged elite, and by the plutocrat. An astonishing number of American's live paycheck to paycheck – 78% of workers to be exact.[421] A recent survey conducted by the Board of Governors of the Federal Reserve found that 40% of Americans do not have $400 to cover an emergency or other unexpected expense in their lives as they have essentially little or no cash on hand.[422] They would have to sell an asset of some kind or borrower the money.[423] To put this into perspective, while total American household net worth

---

[418] Diana Hembree, *CEO Pay to 361 Times That of the Average Worker,* (Forbes, May 22, 2018), citing an AFL-CIO Executive Paywatch news release.

[419] Ibid.

[420] C. Wright Mills, *The Power Elite*, (Oxford University Press, 1956).

[421] Zack Friedman, *78% of Workers Live Paycheck to Paycheck*, (Forbes, January 11, 2019), citing a 2017 survey by CareerBuilder, a leading job website.

[422] Board of Governors of the Federal Reserve System, *Report on the Economic Well-Being of U.S. Households in 2017,* (May 2018), at P. 2.

[423] Ibid.

was $108.6 _**Trillion**_ as of the First Quarter of 2019,[424] 40% of Americans cannot even come up with $400 for an emergency.

It is worth mentioning that this acute concentration of income and wealth is now a longstanding situation in America. In 1990, Nixon era political analyst Kevin Philips wrote a bombshell of a book entitled *The Politics of Rich and Poor: Wealth and the American Electorate in the Reagan Aftermath,* which was the talk of official Washington throughout the 1990-92 election cycle. The book offered a scathing depiction of wealth concentration during the 1980s, with the advertising tag on the back cover of the paperback edition of the book reading "The Rich got Richer. Everyone Else Got Squeezed. Even you." Philips essentially confirms, with encyclopedic recitation of statistics, that the 1980s paralleled two other eras in America, the great gilded age of the late 1800s with the rise of the "robber barons" and the Roaring 1920s.   Phillips entitles his first chapter: "Introduction: The Triumph of Upper America." The first paragraph starts off out of the gate with the following:

> "The 1980s were the triumph of Upper America – an ostentatious celebration of wealth, the political ascendancy of the richest third of the population and a glorification of capitalism, free markets and finance. But while money, greed and luxury had become the stuff of popular culture, hardly anyone asked why such great wealth had concentrated at the top, and whether this was the result of public policy. Despite armies of homeless sleeping on grates, political leaders – even those who professed to care about the homeless – had little to say about the Republican party's historical role, which has not been simply to revitalize capitalism but to tilt power, policy, wealth and income towards the richest portions of the population. ..."[425]

Mr. Phillips could have written this passage in 2016 or 2018 and it would be just as pertinent to the American economic condition as it was when he first wrote it thirty years ago. Clearly, we have not made significant progress in addressing the wealth and income concentration issue. Indeed, as this chapter demonstrates, this problem not only festered over the last 30 years, it has gotten noticeably worse. A recent study by the Federal Reserve demonstrated that the share of wealth for the top 1% of households increased from 23% in 1989 to 32% in 2018, and the top 10% of households owns 70% of all U.S. wealth.[426] This "Triumph of Upper America" as Phillips called it, has remained in effect, uninterrupted through to this day. Even the election on Donald Trump, who won largely because of the discontent among the working class resulting from decades of income stagnation, is itself a vindication of Mr. Philips' sentiments.

Furthermore, Kevin Phillips was not the only sage of his time warning of dire consequences in the event wealth inequality were to ferment indefinitely. A writer and one-time editor at The *New Republic* and *Harpers* by the name of Michael Lind wrote a book entitled *The Next American*

---

[424] Board of Governors of the Federal Reserve System, *Financial Accounts of the United States - Z.1* (Household Balance Sheet – Changes in Net Worth, as updated June 6, 2019).

[425] Kevin Phillips, *The Politics of Rich and Poor: Wealth and the American Electorate in the Reagan Aftermath,* (Random House, 1990), xvii.

[426] Federal Reserve Board, *Introducing The Distributional Financial Accounts of the United States,* (Finance and Economics Discussion Series of Research and Statistics and Monetary Affairs, March 2019), 41.

Nation: The New Nationalism & The Fourth American Revolution, which was first published in 1995. The book received a great deal of attention upon its release that year, even getting a cover page article in *Newsweek* summarizing its main points.[427]

In this book Lind warns that the US had by the mid 1990's evolved into a political and economic entity ruled by a very small subset of the white population that he referred to as the "Overclass", which was largely occupied by legacy money, the new business titans and the extremely highly paid professional class that provided their services.[428] In the introduction to his book he asserts that the overclass had systematically destroyed unions, reduced wages for the middle class cut benefits and replaced full time workers with temps, and shifted the tax burden from the rich to the middle class via the payroll tax increases of the era.[429] His book would provide a detailed history and data regarding how this "Third Republic" or "Multi-cultural America" as he referred to the 1995 status quo came into being. He insists throughout the book that Multicultural America is where a tiny white ruling class perpetuates itself with legacy quotas at elite universities for overclass children and rules a large transracial work force for the benefit of the overclass to the detriment of the working class. In his introduction, he offered a stern warning when he writes:

> "If Multicultural America endures for another generation or two, the future of the United States is a bleak one of sinking incomes for the transracial American majority and growing resentment against the affluent and politically dominant white oligarchy. The Balkanization of America, in the form of civil war along racial lines, is unlikely. American vernacular culture is so powerful in its appeal that it will break down even the strongest immigrant cultures, and interracial marriage is already undermining racial categories. ***The real threat is not the Balkanization of America but the Brazilianization of America, not fragmentation along racial lines, but fissioning along class lines. Brazilianization is symbolized by the increasing withdrawal of the white American overclass into its own barricaded nation-within-a-nation, a world of private neighborhoods, private schools, private police, private healthcare, and even private roads, walled off from the spreading squalor beyond. Like a Latin American oligarchy, the rich and well-connected members of the overclass can flourish in a decadent America with Third Worlds levels of inequality and crime.***"[430] (Emphasis supplied)

It has been a full quarter century since this book hit the shelves in 1995, and by all indications the reign of Multicultural America has indeed persisted for at least one full generation since he issued his warning. The returns are in and the verdict is that Mr. Lind was most prescient with his predictions. Wealth inequality has continued apace, uninterrupted for 40 years since the dawn of the Reagan Revolution, and has reached the extreme levels Lind predicted they would. The richest 1% of Americans live as Lind expected, in gated communities with either private security forces or in neighborhoods with the lowest crime rates in the metropolitan area in which they reside. The

---

[427] Jerry Adler, *The Rise of the Overclass,* (Newsweek, July 30, 1995).

[428] Michael Lind, *The Next American Nation: The new Nationalism & the Fourth American Revolution,* (Free Press, 1995).

[429] Ibid., 14.

[430] Ibid.

next 10% is very comfortable and the closer the members of that cohort get to the 1%, the more closely their living standards resemble the 1%. For the top 25% of earners, maybe even the top third, things are not bad, this cohort usually can save and has generally a comfortable life. For the bottom 70% of America, there is little or no net worth. For the bottom 60% life is paycheck to paycheck. For the bottom half – as we have noted many times in this book, they are essentially excluded from prosperity, unable to save, and zero cash reserves for emergencies. The bottom half of the workforce is patently uncomfortable economically – just as Lind warned they would be. Lind's world has arrived, with the result being the threat of Marxist rule in America has never been greater.

That Middle America had to be "rescued" by a billionaire political outsider – a traitor to his class - is quite telling. The Washington political establishment of both parties has essentially formed a sort of "cartel" as Texas Senator Ted Cruz has noted, and it rules for its own benefit and the benefit of what Phillips refers to as "Upper America," and what Lind refers to as the overclass. We previously noted that Missouri Senator Josh Hawley has taken to referring to this over class as the new "Cosmopolitan Elite", except that it is not new – it was first identified a quarter century ago by Michael Lind. The press and electronic media, for the most part, champion the current *status quo* and have done so since the early 1990s, through the Bush, Clinton, Bush, and Obama eras. As they are part of this Cosmopolitan Elite, the mainstream media resistance to Trump was epic. The reaction to Trump by the media is a key indicator of the entrenched nature of this establishment cartel. The current economic and political state of affairs in our nation can be summed up by saying Americans are living through another gilded age that took off in the 1980s and has continued unobstructed ever since with a complicit press and a political class that has written the law to ensure the perpetuity of this age. This Cosmopolitan Elite class has many factions – the media, government officials, faculty in academia, celebrities in entertainment and sports and so on. These factions work in concert with each other but not always formally. They hold the same point of view of cultural, political and economic matters, and their collective influence forms a sort of oligarchic consensus that drives public policy in countless ways, and is a key contributor to income inequality.

And people wonder what is causing the leftward radicalization of American civilization? There is no justification for the top income earners and the rich owning the vast lion's share of American wealth. If doctrinaire free market boosters keep insisting that there is, they will one day wake up and find themselves fending off the Bolshevik wolves in a communist society. Such boosters are not likely to fare very well in a Marxist state. It is time for those of us who have not only regularly advocated on behalf of free enterprise, but actually lived our working lives employed by private sector businesses, to realize something has gone terribly wrong. There is no legitimate excuse for the largest share of the productivity gains since 1973 going to top management and the top 1% of wealth holders and income earners in our society while the bottom 50% of earners in the workforce are left with barely enough to survive. It is a very safe bet that there is no long run political feasibility in the bottom half of the workforce being reduced to a sort of 21st Century serf, or modern day "rent seeker" having only minimal skills to sell in an open U.S. market.

This last point bears some additional discussion. We have already noted earlier in this chapter that we have evolved into a particularly virulent form of capitalism; a sort of "winner take all" system. I submit to the reader this will be a most destabilizing dynamic and one that will usher in a Marxist order in the relatively near term if it is not satisfactorily addressed. Even billionaire hedge fund maven Ray Dalio has gone on record advocating that capitalism is in serious need of reform and views education as a big part of the issue, noting that 20% of American children are poorly educated as one main factor in the spiraling wealth inequality.[431] He goes on to remind us that the bottom 60% of wage earners in the workforce have real incomes that have not risen since 1980 – 40 years.[432]

We have been told for generations by the High Priests of free market economics that this rabid wealth inequality is inevitable, and that the drivers are international competition from foreign countries with lower labor costs, and a skills gap in what the workforce is equipped with versus what a high tech economy actually demands; along with other failings of the educational system in the country. These capitalist purists point to hundreds of thousands of decent paying jobs that go unfilled each year due to a skills mismatch between the skills the workforce actually has versus what businesses actually need. I am certainly not worth $18 billion, so forgive my insolence as I criticize the notion that pouring more money into education will solve the income inequality problem, or even play a major role. Let me explain why. While education is certainly a massively important indicator of who will succeed economically and a good statistical predictor of poverty, it absolutely cannot explain the wealth gap in both income and wealth accumulation. Allow me to illustrate. Take the General Electric Company over the sixteen years that it was run by Jeffry Immelt as CEO (2001 – 2017). Mr. Immelt, an educated man with a Harvard MBA made millions upon millions in that role over the sixteen years he held that position, all the while the company lost hundreds of billions of dollars in market capitalization. Publicly filed Securities and Exchange Documents show his total compensation package in some years to have exceeded $20 million. His decades long tenure at GE has left him certainly a decamillionaire approaching $100 million perhaps more (and that is what can be gleaned through public documents).

Contrast that with one of the staff level engineers working on the advanced medical devices equipment, power generation turbines or jet engines. These engineers very often have advanced degrees in their fields, even doctorates, certainly as well educated as Jeff Immelt, certainly as smart as he is – or smarter. What do you want to bet there would be many of them who are not anywhere close to being a decamillionaire. Truth be known, there are probably thousands of highly educated employees at GE who are not even millionaires. It is highly likely that there are long tenured employees at GE with advanced degrees who have never made $200,000 in a single year in total compensation. The cosmic distance between the net worth of Jeff Immelt and thousands of other highly educated employees at that company simply cannot be explained by the education variable. I do not mean to downplay the importance of education in people's lives and the criticality of a good education for future economic success, but with that acknowledged, please do not insult my intelligence by suggesting that education is the reason we have a wealth gap. We have a wealth gap because our civilization has adopted – as I have already said, a malignant "winner take all" variant of capitalism that is as putrid and corrupt as any system there ever was. The problem before us is that trading in this now malignant capitalist system for plain old rotten to the core Marxism will accomplish nothing more than worsening the situation – from the frying pan to the fire so to speak.

---

[431] Aimee Picchi, *Billionaire Investor Ray Dalio: Capitalism Run Amok is Economically Stupid,* (CBS News/Moneywatch, April 5, 2019).
[432] Ibid.

Likewise, regarding the foreign trade argument discussed above, it too is inadequate by itself to explain the wealth gap. While there is some truth to the flaccid American competitiveness in some industries, there is also truth in the notion that many of our trading partners have taken advantage of hapless and feckless American leadership for decades, with devastating impacts on U.S. workers; the fact remains that America has not run an overall trade surplus since the mid-1970s, and has run a trade deficit with nearly all of our trading partners since the turn of the 21st century. To ignore the serious inconsistencies within free trade dogmatism, and the impact they have on millions of U.S. workers is a significant reason we stand on the cusp of a potential Bolshevik-like revolution in the country today.

The free-trade, free-market purists have essentially written off the bottom half of the workforce, making way for the Trump Presidency. If this chronic wealth imbalance is not remediated in the near term, the impulse of today's youth towards socialism will intensify. When nearly one third of American wage earners who have had to take on a second job just to meet basic expenses *and still struggle to cover basics*,[433] the political pressure for change is sure to mount. Getting back to a balance that America enjoyed in the middle part of the 20th Century must become one of our highest priorities.

What is so amusing with the billionaire class and their intellectual cheerleaders in the media in their attempts to justify wealth inequality, or attempt to explain it away with bland proposals concerning education and training, is what they leave out. They almost never – and I mean NEVER critique the policies of the U.S. Federal Reserve. This is an important digression for a moment because there is an argument to be made that the Federal Reserve's easy money policies since 2008 have massively contributed to wealth inequality.

Allow me to explain. After the 2008 financial crisis, the Federal Reserve went into panic mode and lowered the Federal Funds Rate to essentially 0 through the mechanics of their Federal Open Market activities. When zero interest rates were not enough to stimulate the economy in a timely fashion, the Fed resorted to what became known as "Quantitative Easing" (or "QE" in the industry lingo), a practice by the Fed whereby they purchased assets like mortgage backed securities and the like directly from market participants like banks and investment banks. This process provided the banking industry with liquidity and reserves to continue operations and also allowed them to structure their balance sheets with asset classes that allowed for the best performance. The Fed essentially acted as the buyer of last resort for various assets that had value but were not liquid in a financial crisis. The result was that the Fed's balance sheet ballooned from $750 Billion to $4.5 Trillion after four rounds of QE. This action taken by the Fed had never before been attempted.

The results of this experiment are very mixed. The American economy has not recorded even a single calendar year since QE began where GDP growth exceeded 3%. The GDP in the 10+ years of the current expansion expanded by less than half of the 90's boom.[434] And more ominously, there is an emerging line of thinking in the blogosphere that the Feds QE program is

---

[433] Brandon Gomez, *Nearly 1 in 3 American Workers With a Side Hustle Still Struggle to Make Ends Meet,* (CNBC.com, June 6, 2019), citing Bankrate.com's "Side Hustle" survey of 2,550 full-time and part-time working adults.
[434] Peter Coy, *U.S. Economy Celebrates 10 years of Growth, But No One is Partying*: (Bloomberg BusinessWeek, June 6, 2019).

at least partly responsible for exacerbating the issue of wealth inequality.[435] The reasons for this are commonly understood, as hyper-low interest rates and QE prop up the value of paper assets, which the bottom half of the population does not own. After all, how are you supposed to invest in stocks and bonds when you can't even come up with $400 for an emergency? As I have alluded to earlier, the average American is now starting to feel the American economy is rigged in favor of the well to do. When the Congress steps in, bails out Wall Street with taxpayer backed funds, then the Fed props up banks and investment banks with QE by buying assets they don't want and putting them on a federally supported balance sheet that is backed by the full faith and credit of the American taxpayer. Let's just say the optics are not very good on this front, and the Fed has to take a great deal of responsibility for aggravating the wealth gap in our country today. You can see why the Wall Street Tycoons like Ray Dalio do not mention reigning in the Fed when they attempt to explain the wealth gap. Actually doing anything about the failures of Fed policy over the past 10 years would kick the billionaire class right in the groin and they sure aren't going to let that happen. No, the system is starting to look rigged, and there will be no change coming from the current D.C. Cartel – None, zip. Change will have to come directly from the American people themselves.

   2) The Solution:

Towards that end, there are several poll-tested solutions the American people will accept in order to address this pernicious issue. Americans will tolerate some degree of increased taxes on the very wealthy but not the absurd levels espoused by Democrats.[436] Voters are telling pollsters that they are open to addition tax credits for the poor and middle class, and gradually rasing the minimum wage.[437] A more radical solution would be to proposed legislation that would regulate compensation of the highest paid corporate executives and formally cap their annual earnings to no more than 50 times the national median family income level. Corporations obviously will not self-govern themselves on this matter, so it may have to be done as part of Congress's role in regulating interstate commerce. Exemptions can and should be made for entrepreneurs who start their own businesses and for the employees who work for these start-ups. Exemptions would also be appropriate for the income earned on investments acquired using after tax dollars (i.e., no caps on such income). All other managers could be subject to a cap at a level that Congress can ultimately agree on. The cap could be administered via the U.S. Labor Department as the requirement should apply to both public and private companies. The SEC only has jurisdiction over publicly traded companies who issue "securities" on the public equity markets, so it will not be an adequate regulator. Finally, it is not unforeseeable that a very conservative Supreme Court would strike down such legislation as an unconstitutional infringement on the property rights for those facing a cap, the American People should be prepared to seek a Constitutional Amendment reinforcing Congress's power to execute such legislation. While there is no indication that the American people would accept such a solution – yet, it may ultimately wind up being a compromise as putting a cap on excessive incomes would not be socialism so long as the saved money is not re-distributed via taxes to other constituencies. If corporations find a way to invest the funds they are now lavishing on executives, perhaps that investment could be for better

---

[435] Sven Henrich, *It's Game Over for the Fed As the Central Bank's Credibility Crumbles,* (MarketWatch, June 7, 2019).

[436] Mort Kondracke, *Democrats Far-Left Lean Risks More Than the Presidency,* (RealClearPolitics July 20, 2019).

[437] Ibid.

compensation and benefits for the working class. At present this is purely theoretical, but what is not is the notion that if nothing is done regarding this festering problem, outright Marxism is a real possibility.

An additional notion regarding capping excessive income, if that is to be the route we ultimately take, is that it should not just be limited to the compensation of corporate executives. Entertainment personalities in cinema and music and other performing arts should join the fun as well; and so should professional athletes. Few are entrepreneurs, instead they start out their careers as grotesquely over paid employees. Why should movie stars get paid $25+ million per movie in some cases while vast numbers of support staff make minimum wage or a tad above? After all, aren't lefty Hollywood types always preaching "fairness" to the rest of us? Likewise, why should professional athletes who are not entrepreneurs earn what would once have been considered a vast estate for playing games that entertain us? A gifted teacher who provides your children with critical knowledge and learning skills that will alter the child's future for the better makes over a career what many of these professional athletes make in a single game. In many instances in major metropolitan areas, a teacher or other municipal, county or state employee cannot even afford housing in the areas where they teach or work. That says a lot about our value system as a people. It is not altogether flattering.

The degree of wealth concentration in the entertainment and sports industries is staggering. We'll begin with the entertainers. To illustrate just how lopsided it all is, consider that as of May 2019, the lowest paid salary for an "A" list movie star was Jessica Chastain for her role in IT/Chapter 2, and she was last on a list of 17.[438] You hear that right. She got $2 and-a-half million for *One Role!!!* Topping out the list was Actor Ryan Reynolds at a salary of $27 Million for his role in *Six Underground.* [439] In between were Leonardo DiCaprio, Brad Pitt, Margot Robbie and Gal Gadot all at $10 Million for a single project; Tom Cruise at $14 Million for his work in *Top Gun: Maverick*, and there was also $20 million apiece for Robert Downey Jr. for *The Voyage of Dr. Doolittle,* and Dwayne Johnson for his role in another *Fast and Furious.*[440]

Perhaps some of the best coverage of the facts on the ground regarding the compensation of entertainment celebrities versus top corporate executives comes from our friends at the Wall Street Journal, where a recent article illustrates in detail the exorbitant level of compensation for many big names in entertainment. The results are eye-popping. For example, half way through the current season of *American Idol,* the authors claim that Katy Perry's compensation for that show alone midway through the season surpassed what most S&P 500 CEOs made in all of 2018.[441] She was on track for $25 million annually as a talent judge.[442] Keep in mind that Perry's *American Idol* paycheck comes from the TV network ABC, which is owned by Disney. You decide whether or not you think it is fair and reasonable compensation for an entertainment "personality" to be

---

[438] Justin Kroll and Brent Lang, *Leonardo DiCaprio and Margo Robbie and More 2019 Star Salaries Revealed,* (Variety, May 2019). The full article can be viewed here: https://variety.com/2019/film/news/celebrity-salaries-leonardo-dicaprio-margot-robbie-dwayne-johnson-will-smith-1203200508/.

[439] Ibid.

[440] Ibid.

[441] Russell Adams and Hanna Sender, *How CEO Pay Compares with Hollywood Celebrities and Sports Stars,* (Wall Street Journal, May 17, 2019). For the full article, see, https://www.wsj.com/articles/think-ceos-are-overpaid-see-how-they-compare-with-hollywood-celebs-and-sports-stars-11558085402.

[442] Ibid.

paid that much for a single season on a TV show. The *WSJ* article noted other headline grabbers as follows: Howard Stern makes $90 million per year; Jennifer Aniston $22 million for new gig with Apple; and Celine Dion got $33 million ($500,000 per show) for her gig at Caesars Palace.[443] It is worth remembering that the average total annual compensation for an S&P 500 CEO is $12.4 million as of 2018.[444] In fact, you can take the 100 most highly paid actors and actresses and producers in Hollywood and they account for most of the compensation dollars and net worth from the industry. This has been going on for decade after decade and nothing is ever done.

Katy Perry's situation with Disney warrants some specific discussion in of itself. As noted, ABC is the one paying Ms. Perry such an astronomical amount. After all, $25 million in annual income could fund 403 American families for a year at the $62,000 annual median family income. And as ABC is owned by Disney, this kind of compensation for a celebrity is all-the-more befitting because Disney has a reputation for stingy compensation for their "worker bees" so to speak. Joel Kotkin, one of America's best known demographers recently observed the following about the Walt Disney Corporation, when he wrote: "The Walt Disney Corporation, for example, is known for paying pitiful wages to its blue-collar workers. As former Anaheim mayor Tom Tait observed, numerous full-time workers at Disney are homeless."[445] Think about that – ABC/Disney can come up with millions upon millions for Katy Perry to adjudicate talent on a TV show but many full-time Disney employees in Orange County California do not even make enough to afford basic shelter. The politics surrounding the travesty of this level of wealth disparity is now reaching hurricane levels; and it is a safe bet that the board of directors and executive suits at ABC and Disney will one day in the not too distant future be forced to take notice.

And then there is the professional sports industry. The numbers there are just as odious. A recent analysis by Forbes of the world's most highly paid athletes provides stomach churning numbers. The article starts off by noting that in spring of 2019, over a month long period, four of baseball's biggest names (Nolan Arendo, Bryce Harper, Manny Machado and Mike Trout) all signed contracts worth a collective $1.3 *billion*.[446] Apparently, each of these four rank as some of the biggest playing contracts in the history of sports.[447] The article survey's sports figures from around the world, evidencing that this is not necessarily just an American problem. For example, Barcelona soccer superstar Lionel Messi is thought to have total compensation for this year approaching $127 million when his contract is combined with hefty multimillion dollar corporate endorsements, making him the world's highest paid Athlete for 2019.[448] Some of the other big names came in with Roger Federer coming in at $93.4 million (and at 38, he's not even a title contender anymore); Lebron James at $89 million; Stephen Curry at $79.8 million; and Kevin Durant at $65.4 million.[449] Football's Russell Wilson tied Lebron at $89.5 million for 2019 including a $65 million sign on bonus.[450]

---

[443] Ibid.

[444] Ibid.

[445] Joel Kotkin, *California's Progressive Betrayal: The Golden State's Left-Wing Policies Hurt Working-class and Middle-class residents.* (City Journal, June 11,2019).

[446] Kurt Badenhausen, *World's Highest-Paid Athletes 2019: What Messi, LeBron And Tiger Make* (Forbes, June 11, 2019).

[447] Ibid.

[448] Ibid.

[449] Ibid.

[450] Ibid.

Let's digest that last one a bit. A "sign-on" bonus at $65 million would cover 1,050 American families' annual income at the median of $62,000 per year. As we have seen, there are only 80,000 households in America with a wealth corpus in excess of $50. A literal teeny tiny speck on the 328 million person U.S. population. Many of these athletes will wind up with net fortunes after all taxes, in the hundreds of millions – just like their CEO counterparts. In fairness, it is complete B.S. that the average American wails on about the injustice of what CEOs make but is much more accommodating where entertainers and athletes are concerned. Neither can be justified, and something must be done about it. The left is drifting towards Marxism, which will result in making all of us poor. The conservative ideologues continue to champion and ramble on supporting the rabid low taxes for the rich, free trade, globalist malarkey embedded in the status quo as the answer for all ills. And when the rising economic tide as Reagan so often used to say, fails to lift all boats as he so often promised, conservatives are left with the rancid dross of George Will telling us all that such absurd discrepancies in wealth between the top and everyone else are the natural order of things and that staggering inequities in wealth distribution are not unethical. If that is the best the conservative movement can come up with, then I would tell the reader brace yourself for the coming Marxist onslaught, because not enough voters will ever again accept, to borrow from John Maynard Keynes, such "turbid rubbish".

The foregoing discussion makes exceedingly clear and obvious our economic system in its present form is not capable of facilitating any kind of reasonable distribution of wealth. The center snapping the football makes 10% of the income the quarterback he is snapping the ball to. Both make far more than the average fan watching the game. The lifetime earnings of the average American will NEVER see anywhere close to what these celebrities bring home in pay for a single year. Winner take all baby! The tiny few get the lions' share of the spoils in almost any American industry or endeavor, while everybody else gets the finger. And the elites in America wonder why a new generation is losing faith in capitalism. Americans, particularly young Americans, are getting fed up with listening to conservative pundits and greybeards tell them how justifiable and "moral" all this is. The problem is not that young people are rejecting the economic obscenity they are living – they should; the problem is that they are looking to socialism rather than seeking solutions to reform the free market system – which would be a much better option.

In any case, the status quo is no longer acceptable to an entire generation, and when they comprise an electoral majority, there will be massive changes in the American economy. They have had enough with the decades long talk fest on the matter – and I agree. The best solution to this obnoxious level of income inequality is to statutorily cap income for wage earners who are not entrepreneurs, at 50 times the nationwide median family income level. Implementing regulations would need to come, as I note above, from the US Department of Labor. Ditch the Marxism, and go with some other reforms that have some bite. I am fearful that when the Millennials and Generation Z take over running things, they will do the reverse. Here's hoping we can avoid disaster and get them to abandon the Marxist urge and recognize the folly that it will bring, and embrace some other reforms instead. Any way you look at it, the era of baby steps and incrementalism is coming to an end, the change that will begin in earnest over the next decade will alter the nature and character of our civilization.

f)   <u>Terminating the Legal Principle of "At Will Employment:</u>

For those readers who have ever been employed by someone else, the notion of "At Will" Employment is something they would be intimately familiar with. It is a legal doctrine now unique to the United States among western democracies, as it has been terminated in nearly all other industrialized countries. The basic principle presumes the employer and employee enter an employment arrangement on an "at will" basis, allowing either party terminate the employment arrangement without notice and without cause. Generally speaking the employee can quit his job on the spot, without any regard for the impact on fellow co-workers or his employees; and the employer can terminate the relationship without notice and without cause (so long as there is no illegal reason behind the termination such as race or gender discrimination). Developments in the employment area of US law have put some guardrails around these basic principles, with the result being that large employers generally adhere to a "performance management" protocol before terminating employment for employees, but the basic premise is still the basis for employment for millions of other employers. For key positions requiring specialized talent, employment contracts can and do often superseded the "at will" employment doctrine, but these form a relatively small basis of the 155 million person US workforce.

The opportunity for mischief in this area is so profound one could write an entire book on that point alone. I have worked for large corporations for over 25 years, nearly all of it as a senior manager, and roughly 15 years as an executive level manager. I have seen the principle of at will employment used to enable unconscionable behavior over and over.

I can easily recall some examples. I have seen professional level employees recruited from distant cities only to have their employment terminated in the middle of a corporate relocation due to "corporate restructuring", and the only "remorse" shown by the offending company is for them to try and claw back sign-on bonuses awarded to the terminated employee as well as attempt to get reimbursement for corporate relocation expenses. The subject employees were mothers and fathers with families to support, and faced the prospect of near-term financial ruin due to the companies behavior – all perfectly legal under the rules of "at will" employment. I have seen many times employees, often in their late 60s, laid off due to cost cutting initiatives with literally no notice. They were called to a meeting early in the morning and told to clear out their desks by the afternoon. If they were laid off in groups of 50 or more, they got the benefit of the WARN Act where they got 60 days' notice, and usually a small severance. If they were isolated layoffs, then they got 0 days' notice and an even smaller severance. Their benefits were good only through the end of the month of termination and after that they could use the COBRA medical plans until they found something permanent. I have seen these cost reduction initiatives impact women in the very late stages of "at risk" pregnancies with enormous financial implications to their families. The corporate attitude in all these instances was that of "nothing personal – just business." Vito Corleone could not have said any better himself.

When I first got into American industry, fresh out of law school in 1994, this kind of behavior was often referred to as the Wild Wild West, or "cowboy capitalism." In fact, it is an abomination that has been tolerated by the American people for far too long and needs to be reined in – now. I believe that much of what is driving Millennial skepticism of capitalism is exactly this kind of obnoxiously impersonal treatment of fellow citizens for no other purpose than to generate profit for shareholders. Younger Americans, with an entire work career ahead of them are not wrong to view corporate behavior in this area as repugnant – as such behavior is in fact morally reprehensible. Our entire existence should not be made to revolve around the profit motive. Political candidates that see no other virtue in life outside of generating a revenue stream for an investor are candidates that must be resoundingly defeated in the years to come. Capitalism in its "state of nature", as Thomas Hobbs might have put it, is "a wild beast", as U2 rocker Bono once exclaimed. He's right. And capitalism needs to be house broken – again. It is the right system for America, always has been and always will be, but if we cannot smooth these nasty rough edges, we might risk a Marxist rebellion that could swamp any reform efforts. Political candidates who are nothing more than laissez-fair hard liners must be rejected. Their time has come and gone. The near-term future no longer belongs to them.

If we can elect a Congress and President that are not socialists, but more akin to populist reformers, we should be able to rid ourselves of the ridiculous doctrine of "at-will" employment that has destroyed millions of lives economically over the past half-century. To this end I caution the reader to beware of those who defend this employment practice, and warn us to exercise caution in repealing it. Specifically, I am referring to the apologists for the current system. There are those that will say "Wait! America is the fastest growing economy among the G7! We are the envy of the world! There has never been a better time to be an American!!! Why change what is working?" To which I will respond – working for whom? And who is getting the benefits of American economic growth? We know the billionaires and millionaires are; we know the corporate rich are; we know the entertainment and professional athletes are; but what about the other half of the work force?

In all my years as a corporate manger, in companies that were members of the S&P 500, I never saw the vulgarity of the present system play out any better than when it came to bonus time. Year in and year out I had to allocate a bonus pool to those who worked for me. There was a subset of employees who were bonus eligible and a far larger group who were not. The ones that were not had the lowest level jobs and received no bonus, and rarely ever got a raise or merit increase. I have had employees work for me and not get a raise in four years because there was no budget for merit increases except for only the "highest performers." Then when it came to dividing-up the bonus pool, the distribution was lop-sided, with a few employees getting the lion's share of the available pool. The company culture at all seven companies was universal – "this is how a meritocracy works", we were told. And if you believe that, I'll tell you I can sing as good as Pavarotti. Indeed, the many times I've had to interface with human resources on compensation matters, either for myself or on behalf of someone on my team, I would be told that the entire bonus pool company-wide basically goes to the top 10% of senior managers and executives. You heard that right, the top of the company very often got 80% of the entire bonus pool, and the remaining 90% would fight for the 10% left over scraps. This is common practice in corporate America. I have seen it first-hand, over and over and over again.

The doctrine of "at will" employment feeds this crap. Any employee who dared to stand up and challenge this kind of nonsense would be out of work in short order. His or her performance would be scrutinized for every move on every task. Each mistake, however minor, would be documented and when there ware enough grounds for dismissal that is exactly what would occur. Moreover, this aspect of American employment law has the perverse effect of enabling some of the most disgusting treatment of employees by management I have ever witnessed. I routinely saw co-workers and other managers bullied and berated with undignified scorn in front of peers. I have received this kind of treatment myself on occasion. The attitude of executive management is always to the effect that there is no law that says the abused employee "has to work here", suggesting that if the treatment is unacceptable, the employee is free to leave the company. Of course, when you have a family to support and debts like 95% of the workforce does, such comments are meant to be taken in the most sarcastic manner possible. It nearly goes without saying that the employee is not going to quit his job and risk the financial ruin that could result – at least not without enduring a fair amount of the mis-treatment. This legal doctrine assumes that the employer and employee are on equal bargaining footing, which is *per se* absurd. Obviously, the employee will have a much more difficult time when the relationship is severed than the company will. Any suggestion to the contrary is bogus. For these reasons at will employment must go. Congress and state legislatures will have to do it. There will be no assistance from the courts. I have my doubts on whether this will ever happen.

What I do know, is if the reforms I am suggesting are not taken seriously, or other alternatives found, and we remain on our present trajectory, there will come a point where the Marxists are given the keys to the American kingdom, with all the potential horror that might entail. As the older generations that were willing to tolerate this nonsense retire and die off, a younger crop of Americans will take their place and they are showing every indication of challenging this abominable behavior head on, even if it means taking risks with Marxism. They see the success that the European nations have had with ditching "at-will" employment for a more humane employment environment and want the same for us. And they will get it, one way or another. The business class, including the likes of the Business Round Table, The Chamber of Commerce, K Street Lobbyists, Wall Street and the Koch Industries will all be well advised to actively participate in reforming their employment practices or they will have it done for them. I am generally an optimist, but I will say that I am not at all optimistic that these entrenched interests will ever come to the table in good faith on this. They have had too much success at manipulating the political system over the past 40 years to compromise on this aspect of employment law now.

My guess is that we stay on the current trajectory, and these entrenched interests may score a victory with President Trump's reelection in the short run, but after Trump leaves office (I am guessing a 50/50 chance that it will be in January 2025) there is no telling what we will wind up with. We know for certain Trump won't be delivering any reform on the notion of ending "at will" employment because he has built his business fortune around the expendability of the employee, just like all the billionaires he surrounds himself. On this point, if the reforms are not made during the next decade, and corporations continue to be permitted to treat their average employee as disposable as personal property, over time, this will be a major contributor to the radicalization of our nation.

This will intensify if we face any economic stress in the near term. Remember that the current economic expansion is the longest in history. National Bureau of Economic Research statistics show that the average length of an expansion in the 11 measured business cycles since 1945 is 68.5 months.[451] That means the current expansion is nearly twice as long as the post WWII average

---

[451] National Bureau of Economic Research, *US Business Cycle Expansions and Contractions,* (As Posted on April 9, 2010). The NBER defines "Cycle" as "Peak from Previous Peak".

duration, and; therefore, is very much on borrowed time. If there is a recession in the intermediate term and incomes fall sharply, with a corresponding debt explosion, America could easily find itself with an extremist left government the likes of which it has never before seen. While this scenario is not necessarily "likely", it is plausible and most certainly not impossible.

g) Off-Shore Accounts and Tax Avoidance:

As an attorney myself, I have long been familiar with the notion of accounts in certain foreign countries like Bermuda, the Cayman Islands, Hong Kong and Singapore, where the only reason for the existence of the account is to avoid paying any taxes on the money. There are many ways in which these types of investment schemes are perfectly legal and where none too few tax attorneys make the focus area of their entire law practice. Now there is a developing area of the study of economics that seeks to understand in detail how and where the mega rich shield or hid their wealth from tax authorities in the U.S. and Europe.

In a recent article, Bloomberg's Ben Steverman describes the career of an up-and-coming whiz-kid buy the name of Gabriel Zucman, a thirty-two-year-old French economist teaching economics at UC-Berkeley, whose special area of expertise is tracking down exactly these kinds of schemes.[452] Professor Zucman's doctoral thesis exposed tax evasion via foreign accounts by the mega rich measuring in the trillions.[453] More recently, Dr. Zucman has teamed up with a UC Berkley colleague and fellow Frenchman, Emmanuel Saez for an academic paper published in 2016 entitled *Wealth Inequality In the United States Since 1913.*[454]

The results of their academic work in the area of wealth inequality is eye-opening to say the least. According to Steverman's interpretation of Zucman's work, the bottom 50% of American households have a *negative net worth,* [455] which is generally taken to mean they owe more than the sum-total of all their assets (the value of liabilities exceeds the value of household assets). The most unsettling aspect of what Zucman uncovered as a graduate student is the evidence he gathered depicting that the worlds mega rich have stashed at least $7.6 trillion in assets in overseas accounts, resulting in lost tax revenue to the tune of $200 billion per year.[456] When this fact is couple with the previously articulated statistic that half of American households have liabilities exceeding their assets, and the super-rich can get out of paying taxes to the tune of hundreds of billions per year, the reader should begin to see yet again where the socialist urge is coming from. Free market fundamentalist that attempt to justify this will no doubt find in the coming years that the tired arguments of the past 40 years will ring hallow for increasingly larger portions of the electorate who are pretty much done with raw Newt Gingrich economics. That train has left the station and will not be coming back.

The American people will not tolerate travesty of the type summarized above where the economy is starved of much needed tax revenue by virtue of purposely holding wealth overseas. If Conservatives and libertarians continue to attempt to justify such absurdity, they will find

---

[452] Ben Steverman, *The Wealth Detective Who Finds the Hidden Money of the Super Rich,* (Bloomberg, May 23, 2019).

[453] Ibid.

[454] Ibid.

[455] Ibid.

[456] Ibid.

themselves living in a Marxist civilization before the end of their lives. The bottom half of the population will not be told indefinitely that they are unworthy of participating in prosperity, that somehow their stagnant wages are their fault. They are beginning to reject in a massive way the long held and often extolled virtues of classical economics when they see nothing but economic misery in their own lives. And one thing conservatives and libertarians often forget – the fastest way to enrage someone is to actually get them employed, working 40 hours a week or more and have their earnings be insufficient to live on. Put someone on an economic tread-mill, work them good and hard only to see their wages are not enough to provide basic and decent housing for their families, get their kids through school and provide decent health care for their families, and you have the makings for a revolution. The current administrations constant eulogizing of the record low unemployment rate rings hollow for the bottom half of the population that is swimming in debt, has no savings and cannot afford the basics for their families. Trump may wind up victorious in 2020, but that is likely only because the Democrats are stupid enough to nominate an outright Marxist like Sanders or uber Progressive like Elizabeth Warren. For 2024 and beyond – look out!

3) <u>Conclusion</u>

With an increasing number of young Americans gravitating toward socialism in numerous public opinion polls over the past decade, and doing so at an accelerating rate, we can no longer categorically rule out the possibility that America one day may find itself governed by a radical leftist progressive regime, or an outright Marxist one. As outlandish as it seems, the day has come when the long-assumed notion of America as a land of democratic capitalism is no longer 100% certain. The risk of a Marxist takeover of the American system is perhaps greater now than ever. This risk is certainly the greatest it has been in the half century of my lifetime.

Should the unthinkable ever come to pass with Americans stooping to the dregs of Marxism, and American civilization finds itself run by a socialist or even communist strongman who sold himself as a moderate with enticing ideals of a wonderland for the common man; history gives us a pretty good idea of what to expect. The Venezuelan experience is but the most recent. There are a half dozen others referenced in this book, though many of those involved violent revolution where Venezuela did not. This book focused on the Soviet Kulak experience because it seems, with the benefit of a retrospective understanding of history (hindsight is 20/20 as the saying goes), that there are facets of the Kulak experience that would surely be repeated in a formal American Marxist regime as relates to affluent American professionals. While the super-rich will be able to withstand massive tax increases and have the financial means to buy influence and connections, for the middle and affluent class, not so much. For them, taxes will be raised to absurd levels, and just as with the Kulaks, and when they are unable to pay, the heavy hand of the state will be ready to exact retribution.

We have explored the already significant state of armament the federal law enforcement complex wields at present and the ease with which that militarization could be massively increased. Once a Marxist regime burs its totalitarian fangs into the American scalp, removing it will be about as easy as getting rid of a wood tick with your bare fingers and no fingernails. Once embedded, the risk of decades or even centuries of militaristic darkness should not be understated.

Voters who are repulsed by the intellectual, political and economic toxicity of Marxism need to be active, more politically active than they ever thought they'd be. We thought 2016 was a make or break election, but who would have thought that we'd see in the 2020 election cycle politicians openly argue in favor of massive federal takeovers of entire industries like healthcare, transportation and energy? Who would have thought the intensity of young people would swing in the direction of collectivism? As the 20th Century fades into a distant memory, it is up to those of use still around who lived it to ensure the stain of Marxism is properly understood for what it is – one of history's great blights on the human condition. Donald Trump, for all his faults and imperfections, just may well be all we've got standing between our glorious constitutional republic and raw Marxism. If the American people fail in their task to preserve for our children one of the greatest republics the world has seen in two millennia, then all I can say is – I'm guessing they'll want to ask Venezuelans whether they tried salt and pepper with their sewer water, and whether that made it go down any better because Americans may find themselves on a similar diet one day!

www.ingramcontent.com/pod-product-compliance
Lightning Source LLC
Chambersburg PA
CBHW081951260726
48657CB00009BA/2563